ROUTLEDGE LIBRARY EDITIONS: EVOLUTION

Volume 4

STUDIES IN HEREDITARY ABILITY

STUDIES IN HEREDITARY ABILITY

W.T.J. GUN

LONDON AND NEW YORK

First published in 1928 by George Allen & Unwin Ltd.

This edition first published in 2020
by Routledge
2 Park Square, Milton Park, Abingdon, Oxon OX14 4RN

and by Routledge
52 Vanderbilt Avenue, New York, NY 10017

Routledge is an imprint of the Taylor & Francis Group, an informa business

© 1928 George Allen & Unwin Ltd.

All rights reserved. No part of this book may be reprinted or reproduced or utilised in any form or by any electronic, mechanical, or other means, now known or hereafter invented, including photocopying and recording, or in any information storage or retrieval system, without permission in writing from the publishers.

Trademark notice: Product or corporate names may be trademarks or registered trademarks, and are used only for identification and explanation without intent to infringe.

British Library Cataloguing in Publication Data
A catalogue record for this book is available from the British Library

ISBN: 978-0-367-27938-7 (Set)
ISBN: 978-0-429-31628-9 (Set) (ebk)
ISBN: 978-0-367-27763-5 (Volume 4) (hbk)
ISBN: 978-0-367-27773-4 (Volume 4) (pbk)
ISBN: 978-0-429-29780-9 (Volume 4) (ebk)

Publisher's Note
The publisher has gone to great lengths to ensure the quality of this reprint but points out that some imperfections in the original copies may be apparent.

Disclaimer
The publisher has made every effort to trace copyright holders and would welcome correspondence from those they have been unable to trace.

STUDIES IN
HEREDITARY ABILITY

BY

W. T. J. GUN, F.R.Hist.S.

LONDON
GEORGE ALLEN & UNWIN LTD.
MUSEUM STREET

First published in 1928
(All rights reserved)

Printed in Great Britain by
Unwin Brothers, Ltd., Woking

INTRODUCTION

IN some biographies, particularly those of older date, it was quite customary for the writer, when introducing his subject, to assure his readers that they would not be troubled with anything so uninteresting as the ancestry of the hero. It does not matter what a man's ancestors were; it only matters what he was himself—such in effect was their motto. A very shallow and a very unscientific philosophy. It certainly does matter a great deal what a man is, but the root of the matter lies in his ancestors, for from them he derives those deeper qualities which make or mar a career. Environment unquestionably does count, but it chiefly affects the more superficial side. Out of grapes men do not gather thorns, nor out of figs do they gather thistles.

A great turning-point in the proper consideration of this most important subject was marked by the appearance in 1871 of Sir Francis Galton's well-known work, *Hereditary Genius*. This book was the first to show clearly how many of the eminent men of history had eminent ancestors or descendants or both, or how notable relatives could often be traced, even if distinction was lacking in both the direct ascending and descending lines. The influence of this book was profound, not least so perhaps on the treatment of biography. Very rarely now are ancestors wholly ignored in biographical works; generally the first chapter is devoted, and rightly devoted, to them and to their doings.

In some cases Galton did carry down the story for several generations, but on the whole he confined himself mainly to the immediate relatives of men of note, nor did he, as a rule, do more than make the very briefest reference to their characters and achievements. An attempt is made in these pages to carry the story further, and to ascertain for how long ability in various well-known connections really continued. A somewhat more extended delineation of character and achievements than that undertaken by Galton is also essayed. In this respect it seems sufficient merely to refer to those whose names are still household words and to concentrate more particularly on the many forgotten worthies who often missed enduring fame by the merest hair's breadth. A study of family histories shows, indeed, how little is often the difference between the best and the second best, and how frequently the latter might well, with a little more luck—often, no doubt, with a little more energy—have sat in the seats of the former. The proportion of men of note with relatives of note is, in any case, high, but for the rest, where actual distinction among the relatives is lacking, there is rarely, if ever, reason to suppose that they were commonplace. Almost invariably the more immediate, at any rate, were above the average in ability, but, after all, at any given period, only a few can succeed to any marked extent.

From the purely biological point of view, tracing the ancestry of a great man as far as may lie in every possible direction is a matter of great interest, but this is too complicated to attempt in any other than purely tabular form. Here, therefore, the story is begun in every instance in the past and carried down to later times. Every endeavour has been made to keep the genealogies clear, but for those to whom exact rela-

INTRODUCTION

tionships are a weariness of the flesh, I now take the opportunity to point out that in most of the chapters *all* those delineated are related to each other, while in certain chapters, " Six Modern Writers," " Five Great Gossips," " Two Philosophic Statesmen," " Four Great Artists," and " Giants of Old," all those in each section are related to the big character of the section, i.e. to the particular writer, gossip, statesman, artist, or " giant," as the case may be. It is by no means essential, therefore, for any one to trouble about the exact degrees of relationship who does not wish to do so.

The chapter, " Intellect and Athletics," is necessarily something of a pot-pourri, and it is hoped that jumps from one family to another in this case will be forgiven.

The work is entirely confined to British and American families, which assuredly furnish enough material for a first attempt. Even so, it is impossible, in one volume, to do more than touch the fringe of the subject, and a very large number of most eminent family connections are perforce omitted. Among those included, however, practically every form of distinction will be found.

Certain principles would seem to emerge from these genealogical researches. In the first place there can be no reasonable doubt that it is an absolutely equal chance whether ability descends through the paternal or maternal line. I am of opinion that there is no warrant for the popular belief that a son is likely to derive more from his mother and a daughter from her father. The mother has doubtless more effect on early environment, but this, though important, is, as I have indicated, of minor importance. At the same time the interest of working out the descent of ability through female lines is very great, the more so as male lines have hitherto received far more attention. While the influence of the mother herself has perhaps been over-estimated, that of her relatives has certainly been habitually underestimated. How often does one hear of resemblances, sometimes very fanciful, between distant relatives in the male line, while much nearer relationships through females are quite ignored, though the latter have obviously more biological significance. In the one case, however, the identity of surname strikes the imagination, in the other the absence of such identity often causes the relationship to be quite ignored.

And what of the women themselves? A perusal of family histories leads strongly to the conclusion that those women who acted as "connecting-links," those who were at once daughters or sisters and also mothers or grandmothers of men of note, were invariably themselves far above the average. Till comparatively recent times, however, their own opportunities of attaining actual personal fame were, of course, extremely limited.

A second principle that emerges is the comparative rarity of the descent of specialized ability. In highgrade stocks it is general ability which persists—ability which, in the different individuals, may, and generally does, turn into very varied channels. Many of the family connections here delineated have won distinction in almost every possible field, all without exception have won distinction in several, while none are completely specialized.

Thirdly, an interesting comparison may be drawn between powers of leadership and intellectual powers. While both are equally inherited, there seems some reason to suppose that the former are apt to persist in families longer than the latter. There certainly is no doubt that men engaged on public affairs have had more relatives of distinction than have writers, artists or scientists. Unquestionably, however, family influence, in the ordinary use of the word, has been more potent in the first case than in the others, and it can justly be urged that in many instances little note would have been achieved without such influence. For this reason, in treating of the history of families which have been mainly connected with public affairs, an endeavour has been made to select those which contain at least several names of outstanding distinction in order to dissipate any possible contention that their success was due to purely extrinsic circumstances.

With regard to writers, scientists and artists, the first named have had, as a rule, far more relatives of note than the other two. In this case, family influence would play a much smaller part, and the reason must lie in the longer heredity of culture usually essential for success in literature.

The longer persistence of powers of leadership is at least partly due to the greater physical virility of the "leadership" stocks. In the more purely intellectual families there is often a certain tendency to ill-health, not implying actual mental deterioration, but occasioning a loss of energy. Intellect without energy implies, in most cases, "a flower born to blush unseen."

The story of the "leadership families" is the more varied and interesting, but the study of the "intellectual" families is perhaps of greater value from the strictly scientific point of view. The former would make the most appeal to those chiefly interested in history, the latter to those chiefly interested in biology

I have endeavoured, as far as possible, to hold a balance between the two different types.

I have not thought it necessary to add a bibliography, but a very large number of biographies and family histories have been consulted. The foundations of such a work as this are, however, *The Dictionary of National Biography*, Appleton's *Encyclopædia of American Biography*, Burke's *Peerage, Extinct Peerage and Landed Gentry*, and G.E.C.'s *Complete Peerage*. Appleton, though in most respects an excellent compilation, fails grievously in rarely making any mention of the mother or of her relatives. In this respect *The Dictionary of National Biography* is immaculate, but the same failing as that observed in Appleton is noticeable in continental biographical dictionaries, and in addition the absence on the Continent of any works corresponding to those of Burke and G.E.C., would render the tracing of ability through continental family connections a matter of the greatest difficulty.

Genealogy has, it is to be feared, a certain reputation for dullness—a reputation hardly undeserved when it consists merely of long strings of names of individuals of whose character and achievements no knowledge now remains. Often enough these individuals would be intensely interesting if we knew enough about them. Where, at any rate, some facts are known; where character and achievements can be traced, if only in outline, generation by generation, then surely genealogy ceases to be dull, and becomes the handmaid, often the very romantic handmaid, of history, of sociology and of biology.

W. T. J. G.

CONTENTS

		PAGE
INTRODUCTION	. . . .	7

CHAPTER		
I.	WIT AND WICKEDNESS	15
II.	A DREAM OF FAIR WOMEN	33
III.	A GLANCE DOWN THE CENTURIES (ENGLAND) . .	59
IV.	A GLANCE DOWN THE CENTURIES (AMERICA) . .	76
V.	THE OLD DOMINION	88
VI.	TWO PHILOSOPHIC STATESMEN	99
VII.	FIVE GREAT GOSSIPS	111
VIII.	SIX MODERN WRITERS	139
IX.	SCOTLAND AND THE SOUTHERN STATES . . .	170
X.	THE CELTIC TOUCH	182
XI.	TWO RENEGADES	193
XII.	MOUNT EVEREST	209
XIII.	FOUR GREAT ARTISTS	223
XIV.	"GIANTS OF OLD" , ...	239
XV.	INTELLECT AND ATHLETICS	259
XVI.	THE ANTECEDENTS OF A CRIMINAL	275
	NOTES	282
	INDEX	285

Studies in Hereditary Ability

CHAPTER I

WIT AND WICKEDNESS

SIR JOHN ST. JOHN, Knight, of Lydiard Tregoze, in Wilts, and Lucy Hungerford, his wife, are quite unknown to history and practically no record of their life or character has been preserved. They transmitted, however, most striking characteristics, evidenced by the very considerable number of their descendants of note and the strong resemblance to be traced among many of these descendants. Of Sir John's immediate ancestors there is not much to be said, but his mother belonged to a family, the Blounts of Mapledurham, of which many members had particularly distinguished themselves in arms. A direct ancestor was the Sir Walter Blount mentioned in Shakespeare's *Henry IV*, who married a Spanish lady of the distinguished house of Ayala. A collateral relative was that Charles Blount, Lord Mountjoy, famed in history as the conqueror of Tyrone and scarcely less well known as the lover of the fascinating Penelope Rich. Strong passions seem indeed to have marked the Blount family, but were at least as marked in connection with the Hungerfords. The matrimonial histories of Lucy's immediate ancestors were singularly unfortunate. Sir Edward, her great-grandfather, married, with some indecent haste after her first husband's death, Agnes, the widow of one John Cotell. Sir Edward did not long survive, and Agnes, with two accomplices, was later indicted for the murder of Cotell, and all three were convicted and executed. Sir Edward was himself probably by no means guiltless, and his son, Sir Walter, Agnes's stepson, had a very unedifying career. His brutality to his third wife was notorious; he kept her incarcerated, and several times attempted to poison her. He was not, however, brought to book for these iniquities, but was executed for complicity in the "Pilgrimage of Grace"; before his death he "seemed so unquiet that many judged him rather in a frenzy than otherwise." He was probably more than half-mad. Sir Walter, his son, in his turn accused his second wife of trying to poison *him*; she was acquitted, and Hungerford, for failing to pay the costs of the proceedings, was committed to the Fleet Prison.

Greatly daring was John St. John when he married into such a family, but there can be little doubt that Lucy was possessed of great personal charm. We shall soon have abundant reason to see how the evil taint persisted. Of the immediate family of John and Lucy we learn something from Mrs. Hutchinson's Memoirs. The youngest daughter, Lucy, was the writer's mother, and she, at any rate, seems to have harked back to better stock. " Her father and mother died when she was not above five years old and she was brought up in Lord Grandison's house, he an excellent and honourable person, but his wife ill-natured and jealous and a most cruel 'stepmother.'" Eventually Lucy St. John and her elder sisters were brought to their brother's house on his marriage.

"There were not, in those days, so many beautiful women found in any family as those, but my mother was by most judgments preferred before all her elder sisters, who, something envious at it, used her unkindly, yet all the suitors that came to them still turned their addresses to her." Truly a Cinderella story in real life. Of the descendants of Barbara, one of those elder sisters, there will be more to be said. The brother, John St. John, eventually became jealous of his wife, who alone seems to have been kind to Lucy, and consequently vented his anger on his youngest sister, who took the wife's part. Still only sixteen, she escaped from this unquiet household by marriage with Sir Allan Apsley, Lieutenant of the Tower, aged forty-eight. Notwithstanding the disparity of years the marriage was a happy one. Apsley, according to his daughter, was a most worthy person : " If among his excellencies one outshined the rest it was the generous liberality of his mind, wherein goodness and greatness were so equally distributed that they mutually embellished each other." Described as a father to his prisoners in the Tower, his example was followed by his wife Lucy, who was particularly kind to Raleigh.

This branch of the St. John connection altogether escaped the evil taint, though Mrs. Hutchinson herself showed the literary tastes of many of her maternal relatives. As a child she translated Lucretius into English verse; later in life she became a strict Puritan, but in her youth she " thought it no sin to learn or hear witty songs and amorous sonnets or poems." She lived to see the rise to notoriety of her disreputable relatives, Rochester and Barbara Villiers, but we may be sure that she did not peruse the amorous poems of the former. She lives in literary history by the life of her husband, the stalwart Puritan, Colonel Hutchinson, whose "figure stands out from his wife's canvas with the grace and tenderness of a portrait by Van Dyck." Her brother, Sir Allan Apsley the younger, though without his sister's goodness, had none of the characteristic vices of so many of the St. John clan; his descendants married into the Bathursts, and that family, which achieved some prominence in the eighteenth century, hardly furnish material appropriate to the heading of this chapter.

For such we must turn to John St. John, the jealous brother, and to Barbara St. John, the jealous sister, of Mrs. Hutchinson's Memoirs.

Anne, the daughter of John St. John, was married twice, first to Sir Francis Lea and secondly to Henry Wilmot, first Earl of Rochester, by the latter of whom she became the mother of John Wilmot, the second Earl. It seems more than probable, from what we know of her ancestry, that she transmitted evil qualities to this scapegrace son, but such accounts as we have of Anne herself are favourable. St. Evremond remarks that she "was of the ancient family of the St. Johns of Wiltshire, a lady of equal parts and beauty, as I have been informed. Her prudent conduct in preserving such estate as the father left enabled the education of her son John to be preserved suitable to his quality." After John's death his mother, moreover, obtained possession of and burnt some of the worst of his manuscripts.

On the father's side Rochester had a by no means undistinguished descent. His grandfather Charles, first Viscount Wilmot, won fame in the Irish wars at the end of the reign of Elizabeth and the beginning of that of James I. The father, Henry, the first Earl, was a distinguished Cavalier, the victor of Roundway Down, a chief counsellor of Prince Charles during his exile; very popular on account of his good fellowship and companionable wit, says Clarendon, who, however, further states that he loved debauchery but never allowed it to interfere with business.

Some of his characteristics quite clearly descended to his famous, or infamous, son. Burnet, a somewhat partial witness, considers that the young Rochester was naturally modest till the Court corrupted him; environment, no doubt, came into play, but the combination of the Wilmot-St. John, not to speak of the Hungerford heredity, was probably mainly responsible for Rochester's amazing career. Possessed of considerable literary dexterity and no small share of wit, as evidenced by his famous lines on Charles II (1), he was withal one of the most shameless profligates of all history. Some of his pranks showed, at any rate, an original turn, as when he set up as a quack doctor under the name of Alexander Bendo, taking a stall on Tower Hill and hoaxing the credulous women who then, as now, abounded. How he would have enjoyed the character of a medium at the present day! A more disgraceful exploit was conducted with Buckingham, when they took an inn on the Newmarket Road, and, pretending to be innkeepers, seduced their female visitors. It was certainly in keeping with the spirit of his ancestry that Rochester should have abducted an heiress, Elizabeth Malet by name, but he does not seem to have actually ill-treated her, and some letters of his to her, which have been preserved, are, at any rate, respectful. On his death-bed, worn out at the age of thirty-three, Rochester summoned Burnet to his side and shed so many crocodile tears as to induce the latter to declare " that if he had recovered, he would have made good all his resolutions." The accomplished but exceedingly vain divine was no doubt greatly influenced by the interest Rochester had taken in his *History of the Reformation*, an interest that was probably quite genuine. In any case, edifying tracts concerning Rochester's " Death-Bed Repentance " were freely circulated in later years.

Mrs. Anne Wharton, the daughter of his half-brother, Sir Henry Lee, wrote an elegy on his death. This lady was assured by a very friendly critic that she was allied to Rochester in genius as well as in blood, but her writings in general are rather sorry stuff. The fact that, in addition to her elegy, she composed a paraphrase of the Lamentations of Jeremiah probably showed a lack of humour rather than versatility, though the prophet would no doubt have found plenty of material for his Lamentations in the Court of Charles II.

Rochester's only son died young. Of his three daughters it was Elizabeth, Countess of Sandwich, who most obviously inherited his characteristics. Her husband, though belonging to the very distinguished family of Montagu and grandson of Pepys's Lord Sandwich, was meek to the last degree and such a cypher that he was practically put in durance vile by his wife, who, says Macky, made him " very expensive." The rest of the world, or at any rate the male portion thereof, thought well of her. St. Evremond describes her as " aussi généreuse que spirituelle, aussi agréable que généreuse," while Lord Chesterfield says : " Old as she was when I saw her last, she had the strongest parts of any woman I know," and Mark Noble observes that she "partook of all the fire and vivacity of her father, the witty Earl of Rochester." Her son, Lord Hinchinbrooke, died in early life, leaving, however, a good impression behind him. Pope describes him as one of the few noblemen who possessed the "nobleman look," while the author of *Jimmy Twitcher* praises him. This last production, a violent attack on Hinchinbrooke's son, the famous Lord Sandwich, was probably, however, unduly biased in favour of the father in order to heighten the iniquities of the son. This son is the last that falls to be considered of this line. He had certain very obvious resemblances to John, Earl of Rochester, his great-grandfather, but perhaps Clarendon's description, above quoted, of the first Earl of Rochester, is most particularly applicable to Sandwich: "He loved debauchery but never allowed it to interfere with business." In early life a member of the famous Hell Fire Club, Sandwich was profligate throughout, but at the same time thoroughly industrious and in some respects an able politician. The author of *Jimmy Twitcher* was not far wrong when he stated: "With all his faults and what, perhaps, renders them greater, he is a man of uncommon sense and penetration. Suffice it therefore to say that he lives a monument of superior abilities prostituted to the worst of purposes." Wroxall speaks of "this distinguished votary of art, conviviality and pleasure who in all his official functions displayed perspicuity as well as dispatch." Like his forbears before him, Sandwich was charming and polished to the last degree in social intercourse; his musical parties were especially famous, presided over by his mistress, Martha Ray, whose murder under singularly dramatic circumstances led to his enforced resignation of the First Lordship of the Admiralty. By Martha, Sandwich had an illegitimate son, Basil Montagu. Such are the curious twists and turns of heredity that this son, so far from being a rake, developed into a most sober member of society and acquired note as a legal writer—a very similar case to one to which later reference will be made.

The eccentricity, however, which ran through many branches of the St. John connection, came out strongly in Sandwich's younger brother, William Montagu, a naval captain of considerable skill and daring, but more than half-mad. Two anecdotes of his peculiarities will suffice. In an affray at Lisbon he received a black eye in a scuffle. Next day, in order to keep him company, he made each of his boat's crew black their eyes with cork, the starboard rowers the right eye, the larboard the left, the coxswain both. On another occasion he asked leave of Sir Edward Hawke to go up from Portsmouth to London. The Admiral, unwilling to let him go, jokingly replied "that he could not give him leave to go from his ship farther than his barge would carry him." Montagu promptly had a carriage made on trucks, on which he placed his barge with his crew and then solemnly instructed these to go through the action of rowing. Hawke heard of this after the boat was landed for the purpose, and thereupon permitted Montagu to proceed to London in any way he thought fit.

Among the comparatively early descendants of John St. John and Lucy Hungerford, Bolingbroke was undoubtedly the most notable. This restless and versatile politician had in almost every direction a distinguished descent. Related on the side of his paternal grandmother to Cromwell, and on the side of his mother to Queen Elizabeth, he derived from John St. John in the direct male line. His grandfather Walter, son of the John of whom Mrs. Hutchinson complained, and uncle of Rochester, was an apparently respectable character, but the father Henry was a mere dissipated man about town. Of him, however, one witticism is recorded. On his son's elevation to the peerage, he remarked: " Ah, Harry, I ever said you would be hanged, but now I find you will be beheaded." The son, evidently not resentful, later procured a peerage for his father, one of the few instances in English history of a proceeding akin to that of the Chinese method of ennobling ancestors rather than descendants—a very sound method biologically, provided the right ancestor is selected, which was certainly not the case in this instance.

A much greater man than Rochester or Sandwich, Bolingbroke shared with both most profligate habits and with the latter great, if somewhat spasmodic, attention to business. During his famous administration, 1712–16, Swift, an intimate friend, said that he plodded whole days and nights like the lowest clerk in his office and that he partly broke off his habits of drinking, though he did not refrain from other liberties. His addiction to the fair sex was notorious. According to Voltaire, a woman said, on his assuming office: " Seven thousand guineas a year, my girls, and all for us." All authorities agree as to his charm, and the Chevalier Ramsay further instances his innate good breeding in this comment: " He outshines you, but then holds himself in and reflects some of his own light so as to make you appear the less inferior to him." Addison fully admitted the charm, adding, however: "If he had only as good a heart as he has a head." Pope mentions him as having the "nobleman look," a distinction which, as we have seen, he also attributed to Bolingbroke's little-known relative Hinchinbroke: "This strange product of a revolutionary age, so brilliant as a writer, so disappointing as a thinker, so famous as an orator, so shifty as a statesman, so profligate as a man." Thus his character has been summed up, and in one or another of his most interesting connections all these qualities may be found, but we have not to go far to discover the charm and the profligacy, which runs like a thread through the St. John connection.

Two later statesmen resemble Bolingbroke to a very marked extent, Charles Fox and Brougham, and both, it is to be noted, had most distinguished connections.

From Barbara St. John, daughter of John and Lucy Hungerford, and one of the jealous sisters mentioned by Mrs. Hutchinson, sprang a race in which this charm and profligacy were present to the fullest extent. This is, however, matter for little wonder. Barbara married Sir Edward Villiers, half-brother of Buckingham, favourite of James I, and the Villiers strain bore the closest resemblance to the St. John, giving a double dose of original sin to the more immediate descendants of Sir Edward Villiers and Barbara, his wife. The complete Villiers connection, deriving from Sir Edward's father, Sir George, produced, by the eighteenth century, personalities of the most outstanding distinction: the first Duke of Marlborough, the Duke of Berwick,

Lady Mary Wortley Montagu, Henry Fielding, the Pitts, Charles Fox, Sir Charles and Sir William Napier, the Herveys, Charles Townshend, Lord Castlereagh. Those descended from Sir Edward alone fall to be considered in this chapter.

From the hints we have of her ambitious disposition, we may feel sure that Barbara St. John expressed great satisfaction at the rapid rise of her husband's family, occasioned by the success at Court of his half-brother, Buckingham. One result of this Court favour appears in the diversion to her heirs of the viscounty of Grandison, which had been created in favour of her uncle, in virtue of which her son William succeeded. This Lord Grandison fell early in the civil wars, but to judge from Clarendon's account he had none of the family failings. "He was," says the historian, "a young man of so virtuous a habit of mind that no provocation or temptation could corrupt him, and of the most rare piety and devotion, his personal valour and courage of all kinds very eminent." His virtues, however, were far from descending on his daughter Barbara, successively Countess of Castlemaine and Duchess of Cleveland, the notorious mistress of Charles II. Quite clearly this lady harked back to one or more of the disreputable ancestors with whom she was cursed, and of all the descendants of John St. John and Lucy Hungerford she was perhaps the most fundamentally worthless, "at once the fairest and lewdest of the royal concubines, with black eyes and a plump baby face." All authorities indeed agree as to the beauty which she shared with so many of her relatives, all equally agree as to her utter heartlessness and shameless rapacity. Technically married to Roger Palmer, created through her influence Earl of Castlemaine, Charles readily accepted the paternity of all her numerous children, although in some cases this was almost as doubtful as that of Lord Castlemaine. In one instance there was hardly any doubt at all. The father of her youngest child was quite unquestionably her cousin, John Churchill, the future Duke of Marlborough largely owing his early rise to her favour. This child, yet another Barbara, inherited the Villiers strain on both sides; a propensity to sexual intrigue was almost inevitable and did, in fact, occur. In 1690 Barbara Fitzroy, who was allowed to use a surname to which she was not entitled, bore an illegitimate son to the Earl of Arran, then a prisoner in the Tower. Times had changed, however, and the daughter shared none of the good fortunes of the mother. The virtuous Queen Mary was then on the throne, and promptly arranged for the dispatch of the unfortunate girl to a French convent, from which she never emerged. Her son, Charles Hamilton, might well have turned out an utter rake, but, as in the very similar case of Basil Montagu, quite a different result occurred; heredity played one of its curious pranks: Hamilton became a most respectable member of society, and mildly distinguished himself by the publication of certain historical works.

Barbara Villiers' characteristics came out more strongly in others of her descendants, notably in the third Duke of Grafton, a Premier of the time of George III, a most profligate individual, who, however, possessed much of the ability characteristic of both the St. John and Villiers strains. More remote descendants were the Seymours, Marquises of Hertford, and distant as is the descent, we can discern the influence of these connections in the third Marquis, the original of Thackeray's Lord Steyne, a most abandoned man, but to whose exquisite taste in art we owe the Wallace collection.

The Duchess of Cleveland was not alone among her relatives in finding favour in the eyes of a monarch. Arabella Churchill, Marlborough's sister, bore to James II the famous Duke of Berwick, but Arabella, though she had Villiers, had, however, no St. John descent. On the other hand, Elizabeth Villiers, mistress of William III, was a granddaughter of Barbara St. John. Her mother, a scion of the great house of Howard, was governess to the Princesses Mary and Anne, with whom Elizabeth was brought up, and the latter accompanied Princess Mary to Holland on her marriage to the Prince of Orange. The qualities which would appeal to Charles were not likely to attract the chilly-natured William, but Elizabeth, who possessed little beauty, was gifted with great ability. Swift later called her " the wisest woman he had ever known." Her relationship with William was probably purely platonic, but none the less distasteful to Mary, who, when dying, besought her husband to sever the connection. With this request he complied, marrying Elizabeth to Lord George Hamilton, whom he created Earl of Orkney, granting her, at the same time, large forfeited estates in Ireland. The success achieved with two monarchs so essentially different as Charles and William sufficiently illustrates the versatility of the family.

Elizabeth, during the days of her influence, took occasion to secure the advancement of her relatives, particularly of her eldest brother, who was created Earl of Jersey. This nobleman possessed the good looks denied to his sister, but, from all accounts, none of her ability. His daughter, who married George Granville, Lord Lansdowne, does not in any way cross the stage of history, but she lives in the vivacious pages of her husband's niece, Mrs. Delaney, and from those we can discern some of the characteristics clearly traced in her ancestors. At first the writer likes this aunt: " Very handsome and behaved herself very well; I soon grew fond of her." But later she says: " I told you that she was very handsome and gay; she loved admiration—a most dangerous disposition in an agreeable woman, and proved a most ruinous one to Lady Lansdowne. The libertine manners of France accomplished what her nature was too prone to. No woman could less justify herself than she could. Alexander (Lord Lansdowne), whom she had married, had every agreeable quality that could make a husband amiable and worthy of the most tender and constant affection. Had she married a man of a resolute arbitrary disposition, she might have made a decent wife, but she was extravagant and given to dissipation, and my uncle's open unsuspecting temper gave her full liberty to indulge the unbounded vanity of her heart."

Mention may finally be made of three famous eighteenth-century families who shared the St. John and Villiers blood: the Herveys, the Townshends and the Pitts. The Herveys derived from still another Barbara, daughter of Barbara St. John; she married the third Earl of Suffolk, and her daughter, Elizabeth Felton, was mother of Elizabeth, wife of John Hervey, first Earl of Bristol. Little is known of either Lady Suffolk or of Lady Elizabeth Felton; the latter died very young, but Lady Bristol figures prominently in the memoirs of her time. Some of her letters have been published in *John Hervey's Letter Book*, without actual literary merit they are easy, natural, light, pointed and graphic. She was full of wit and vivacity, adored town life, and was a confirmed gambler; her temper was anything but equable, and her tears flowed in great abundance at the least provocation; in all respects she was a great contrast to her excellent but somewhat phlegmatic husband, to whom, however, she was entirely devoted, as her letters quite clearly show. The best of her not very brilliant attempts at literary composition is probably the following stanza:

> Could I like Cowley think or Dryden write,
> In Otway's tender words my soul indite,
> I then in verse might hope to soar above
> All other mortals, as I do in love.

The qualities of this vivacious lady were most evidently transmitted to her family, that family whose abilities and eccentricities were summed up by Lady Mary Wortley Montagu when she wrote, " God created men, women and Herveys." Her son John, Lord Hervey, the famous memoir writer, was the special favourite of women from his wit and charm of manner; the keenness of his observation of character equals that of the still better known Horace Walpole, who was not improbably a relative. (2)

Several of Lord Hervey's family were of note in their day, more especially the eccentric Bishop of Derry, who played so leading a part in the Irish Volunteer movement of 1777. In the next generation we find the second of the two brilliant Duchesses of Devonshire, who flourished early in the nineteenth century; and George Robert Fitzgerald, in whom the eccentricities of the family culminated in a mad career which ultimately led him to the gallows.

The Townshends of St. John descent derive from Audrey, a sister of Elizabeth, the mistress of William III, who married one Richard Harrison. Her granddaughter, Audrey Harrison, became the wife of Charles, Viscount Townshend, the son of Walpole's great opponent. Lady Townshend, in her turn, is described as celebrated for her gallantries, her eccentricity, and her wit, and is supposed to be the original of Lady Bellaston in *Tom Jones*. The best known of her *bons mots* related to Whitefield, the Methodist. When asked if he had recanted, she replied : " No, sir, he has only canted."

Her son, Charles Townshend, showed all the talents and all the instability so conspicuous in the St. John descent. As an orator and a talker he was quite unrivalled ; the Select Society of Edinburgh, contrary to its rules, made him a member for one night only, in order to hear him hold forth. Burke says that " he was the delight and ornament of the House and the charm of every private society that he honoured with his presence." Horace Walpole describes him as having every great talent and every little quality, and Smollett remarks : " He would be a really great man if he had any stability or consistency of character." His statesmanship was unfortunately hopelessly at fault, and though he did not live to see the result, he, more than any other man, is responsible for the loss of the American colonies. His less brilliant brother George, Lord Townshend, shared some of his qualities ; frank, social and popular in manners, he threw away a great chance as Lord-Lieutenant of Ireland in critical times by his utter lack of tact and judgment.

The great Earl of Chatham's mother was Harriet Villiers, and he shared the St. John descent. Of all the connection he was the greatest, and the oratorical power, so notable in Bolingbroke and Charles Townshend, was most conspicuous in the "Great Commoner." But in his later years, at all events, the eccentricity also characteristic of the connection was strongly exhibited in his case, and though from this his even more brilliant son was free, it comes out strongly in his grand-daughter, Lady Hester Stanhope. With Lady Hester, the Villiers, and still more the St. John strain, had become very remote, but her domineering disposition, her supreme self-reliance, the charm of which she was capable when she pleased, her whole character as an Arab chieftainess, so brilliantly depicted in Kinglake's *Eothen*, must indubitably owe something to this particular line of descent.

It has often been remarked that some nations present, on the whole, masculine, and others, on the whole, feminine characteristics. This would seem applicable also to family stocks, and there can be little doubt that among the descendants of John St. John and Lucy Hungerford feminine characteristics predominated. Women themselves, as we have seen, figure to no small extent, but the men exhibit with great frequency characteristics which may be considered more particularly feminine, to wit, brilliance and instability. A marked predilection for the opposite sex runs through the whole connection, and its members, male and female, were for two centuries at least exceedingly prominent members of the smart society of their day. Good looks were certainly hereditary in the strictest sense of the term. With the single marked exception of Mrs. Hutchinson, Puritanism, and all that it connotes, was conspicuous by its absence, and during the whole of the two centuries referred to hardly a member of the connection entered the Church, certainly not one achieved prominence therein. (3) It is not indeed one of those on which the greatness of England was built, with the exception, the important exception, however, of the Pitts, brilliant talents led to little or nothing. But its history illustrates one side of life, not only in this country, but in others, and there are few connections wherein the continuance of certain qualities can be more clearly marked and defined.

CHAPTER II

A DREAM OF FAIR WOMEN

IN comparison with descents in the direct male line, comparatively little attention is given, even by genealogists, to descents in the direct female line, from mother to daughter and daughter's daughter. This line of descent is sometimes termed matrilineal, and in an early period of history had great practical importance. By the Middle Ages, however, a strongly patrilineal theory had developed, aided, no doubt, by the introduction of surnames, and descents from mother to daughter ceased to receive any special consideration. They remain, however, of great interest, especially from the biological point of view, having regard to the greater certainty of such descents, which, if traceable at all, must invariably be exactly what they seem.

Of all such matrilineal lines the most interesting is that of which Queen Elizabeth may be regarded as the central figure. The earliest ancestress traceable is Elizabeth, daughter of John Cockayne, of Bury Hatley, in Bedforshire, who lived in the early part of the fifteenth century. From her descended in the direct female line not only Anne Boleyn, but the latter's supplanter, Jane Seymour.

The following table will make the connection clear :

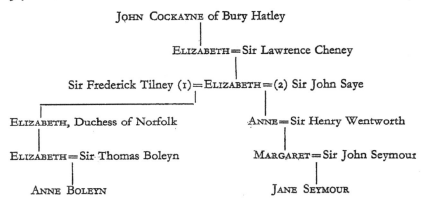

Anne and Jane were therefore half-second cousins, their maternal grandmothers having been half-sisters. It can hardly be fanciful to suppose that they alike inherited personal fascination from their joint descent. Such fascination may well be attributed in particular to Anne's grandmother, Elizabeth Tilney, who won the affections of Thomas Howard, second Duke of Norfolk, the victor of Flodden and the greatest noble of his time.

Jane Seymour had several sisters, but their descendants appear to have been of little interest; in this line the distinction died out.

Very different was the case of the descendants of Anne Boleyn's only sister Mary. Her posterity in general, and the matrilineal line in particular, played very notable parts in their day. Rising, no doubt, in the first place to eminence through the favour of their great kinswoman, the ladies of the connection at any rate owed nothing, and less than nothing, to such favour in the latter part of Queen Elizabeth's reign.

Of Mary Boleyn herself remarkably little is known. She was undoubtedly older than Anne and was married to William Carey before her sister won royal favour. It has, however, been stated that Mary herself was Henry's mistress and that the king was the father of her son, Henry Carey. This son, afterwards Lord Hunsdon, certainly bore some resemblance in character to King Henry, and if the surmise is true, he would have been Elizabeth's half-brother as well as first cousin. Certainly she was always attached to Hunsdon, though he, practically alone among her courtiers, never flattered her. Catherine, Hunsdon's only sister, was far less probably the daughter of the king. If she had been of marriageable age during her aunt Queen Anne's glory, Catherine Carey would indubitably have made a very brilliant match, but scarcely a happier one than that with Francis Knollys. The latter's strong Protestantism stood the young couple well during Edward's reign, but during Mary's they had to seek refuge in Germany. The Princess Elizabeth had already a great devotion to her cousin Catherine, who was some three years her senior, and during her exile wrote hoping for her speedy return, which was not brought about till her own accession. Thenceforward all went well with the Knollys: Francis became vice-chamberlain of the household and Catherine a woman of the bedchamber. In the midst of her prosperity Catherine died in 1568, aged only thirty-nine. The Queen's regret was bitter; probably Catherine Knollys was the only woman to whom, during her long life, Elizabeth was genuinely attached, and her husband, though he survived till 1596, never married again.

Gentle and amiable, Catherine had perhaps no great force of character, but very different qualities were to appear in her eldest daughter, much the most distinguished of her numerous family, the daughter called by Fuller the great pillar of her house.

When very young, Lettice Knollys, whose personal attractions must have been great, was married to Walter Devereux, Viscount Hereford, whom the Queen later created Earl of Essex. The marriage was a brilliant one. Walter Devereux was one of the greatest nobles of the time, and for some years life went smoothly for the young couple. Hereford assisted in the suppression of the Northern Rebellion in 1569, and in 1572 received from the Queen the great honour of promotion to an earldom—an honour the distinction of which can be measured by the fact that during her long reign Elizabeth created four earls only. This was the culminating moment of Essex's glory; thereafter his misfortunes began. The effort which he made to colonize Ulster in the following year proved a terrible failure in every respect, and not least so in the effect it had on his private finances; by 1575 his debts amounted to over £35,000, an enormous sum for those days. And as his public prosperity decreased so did his domestic happiness. During Essex's absence in Ireland, Lettice commenced an intrigue with Leicester, the Queen's favourite—an intrigue which was probably at its height at the time of Elizabeth's famous visit to Leicester at Kenilworth in 1575, when Lettice was present but Essex absent. It has frequently been thought that the well-known lines in Oberon's Vision in *A Midsummer Night's Dream* refer to this visit. The Vestal is, of course, the Queen and Cupid may well be Leicester, and Lettice the little western flower, the " western " perhaps referring to her husband's estates in Wales. The Queen was, at any rate, quite unsuspecting at that time of the state of affairs or she would certainly never have allowed Lettice to come near the pageant. The following year Essex died, worn out by his exertions in Ireland, and to those alone his death may fairly be attributed, but rumour freely stated that he was poisoned by his wife and her paramour. In any case, Lettice and Leicester were married two years after, in 1578.

The Queen was furious—more furious, perhaps, than at any other incident of her reign. She wished to throw Lettice at least into prison, but was dissuaded therefrom by Sussex, one of the few who would stand up to his royal mistress. Elizabeth never, however, forgave her cousin and never actually saw her again. Nor if contemporary accounts may be trusted was Lady Leicester's subsequent conduct in any way likely to assuage the Queen's wrath. A vivid account of Lettice, from an extremely hostile point of view, is given by one R. F., in a letter to a friend in 1584: " He (Leicester) next procured the murder by poison of the Earl of Essex, pretending he was ill of an incurable disease. The news of his death caused such regret that had the truth been known, the Earl had been torn to pieces, but he shed crocodile tears. Dame Lettice put on black, to veil her conduct, and though there was much whispering, no man dare speak, he was so grown in Her Majesty's favour. Then being a widower he proposed to the Countess of Essex, giving presents to blind the world to what had passed between them, and they had a sumptuous wedding. She now demeaned herself like a princess, vied in dress with the Queen, till Her Majesty, after sundry admonitions, told her as but one sun lightened the earth, she would have but one queen in England, boxed her ears and forbade her the Court. Yet she is still proud as ever, rides through Cheapside drawn by four milk-white steeds, with four footmen in black velvet jackets, and silver bears on their backs and hearts, two knights and thirty gentlemen before her and coaches of gentlemen, pages and servants behind, so that it might be supposed to be the Queen or some foreign prince or ambassador."

R. F. is not a very trustworthy witness, and not only the poisoning, but also the boxing of Lady Leicester's ears by the Queen is probably apocryphal; indeed, it does not seem that Lettice was really ever at Court after her second marriage. There is little doubt, however, that her love of display was very great, and this is also referred to in a letter from Thomas Dudley to Leicester of February 11, 1586. The Earl was then in the Low Countries, and Dudley reports that "it was told Her Majesty that my lady was prepared presently to come over to your Excellency with such a train of ladies and gentlemen and such rich coaches, litters and side saddles as Her Majesty has none such, and that there should be such a court of ladies, as should fair pass Her Majesty's court here. This information, though false, did not a little stir Her Majesty to extreme dislike of all your doings there, saying with great oaths she would have none other court but her own." The Queen was on this occasion ultimately pacified by assurances that report lied, but there is little doubt that all through the period of her marriage to Leicester, Lettice acted as if she were the second lady in the land. But little is known of her actual relations with her second husband, a man who could not possibly have continued absolutely faithful, but it is probable that husband and wife, each in their own way the smartest of the smart, suited each other well enough. Lettice was to be accused, with even less probability, of poisoning Leicester as well as Essex; certainly she took to herself a third husband, Sir Christopher Blount, a man much younger than herself and obviously her inferior in position. The days of her grandeur were over, but her position was still remarkable, for having been the wife of one favourite of the Queen, she was now to be the mother of another. To Essex, her only son by her first husband, she was undoubtedly devoted. In February 1596 she writes to him: " Your lordship is grown, I will not say slothful, but somewhat sparing of your pen . . . wherefore do not think to excuse yourself by much business, which I know you want not, for I must have you, notwithstanding, bestow sometimes a few idle lines on your mother, to whom they are most welcome, and who otherwise may grow jealous that you love her not so well as she deserves. And as she hath made you chief comfort of her life, so I doubt not of your noble nature that you will be careful to maintain it with all childlike kindness."

When this rather charming letter was written Essex was at the height of the royal favour. In the days of his disgrace Lettice once again approached the Queen, bringing a gown worth no less than a hundred pounds as a present; but though the gown pleased Her Majesty, she still refused to admit Lady Leicester into her presence, and indeed no suppliant for Essex could have had less chance of success than his mother.

The period of the execution of her beloved son marked the culminating point of Lettice's misfortunes, for her third husband, Christopher Blount, who had joined in Essex's mad rebellion, was likewise condemned and executed. In addition, the matrimonial affairs of her daughters were at this time at their worst. Lettice was made, however, of tough fibre, and though she lived henceforth retired, she survived for more than thirty years, dying at the age of about ninety, an extraordinary longevity for the time. Till within a year or two of her death she was active and could walk more than a mile. She, the reigning beauty of the early years of Elizabeth's reign, lived to see her grand-daughter, Lucy, Countess of Carlisle, the reigning beauty of the Court of Charles I. Some lines in her praise of no great poetic merit were written on her tomb by a great-grandson, Gervase Clifton, the grandson of her lovely daughter, Penelope Rich. (4)

Lettice, Countess of Leicester, was not an exemplary character, but she was undoubtedly a brilliant and attractive woman, and many of her qualities were destined to continue in her descendants for more than one generation to come.

Her two daughters, Penelope and Dorothy Devereux, were but children at the time of their father's death. That father, on his death-bed, "lamented the time, so foul and ungodly, considering the frailty of women. God defend them, bless them, and make them to fear His name and give them grace to lead a virtuous life." His pathetic prayer was certainly not answered in the case of Penelope, hardly in that of Dorothy. Penelope was a most lovely child, and when only about fourteen attracted the attention of Philip Sidney, who then began the long series of sonnets, *Astrophel to Stella*. There can be little doubt that Penelope returned his love; in birth he was all but her equal, but there were fatal money difficulties in the way. Philip's means were slender, and the impoverished condition of the Essex estates rendered a rich marriage desirable for Penelope, in the eyes, at any rate, of her stepfather Leicester and her guardian Huntingdon. So she was forced into marriage with Robert, Lord Rich, a young man wealthy in fact as well as in name. Her disconsolate lover thereupon indited a famous sonnet:

> Toward Aurora's court a nymph doth dwell
> Rich in all beauties which man's eye can see,
> Beauties so far from reach of words, that we
> Abase the praise, saying she doth excel.
> Rich in the treasures of deserved renown
> Rich in the riches of a royal heart,
> Rich in those gifts which give the eternal crown.
> Who the most rich in these and every part
> Which makes the patents of true worldly bliss
> Hath no misfortune but that Rich she is.

Till his death Sidney wrote sonnets to Stella, but in his case the relationship was undoubtedly platonic. After his death it was immortalized by his friend Edmund Spenser's lines:

> To her he vowed the service of his days;
> On her he spent the riches of his wit;
> For her he made hymns of immortal praise;
> Of only her he sang, he thought, he writ.

What children might have sprung from a union between Philip Sidney and Penelope Devereux! We can well conjecture the frustration of the marriage to have been England's loss.

Robert Rich was a dull, plodding, but apparently worthy man, utterly unsuited to his brilliant wife. She bore him, however, many children, and while Sidney lived her conduct seems to have been irreproachable. After his death, however, there appeared on the scene Charles Blount, probably, but not certainly, the brother of Penelope's stepfather, Christopher Blount. With Blount Lady Rich soon carried on a *liaison*, and of her twelve children she fathered five on him; he only, however, accepted three. An interesting account of Penelope at this time is given by Robert Whyte, the secretary and correspondent of her first lover's brother, Robert Sidney, who had invited her to be the godmother of his eldest boy. Lady Rich agreed to attend the christening when she heard that Lord Mountjoy was to be a godfather, and when Whyte approached the latter, he, in his turn, " was much pleased at it, assuring me, whenever the day was appointed, he would not fail to be there." The christening was nevertheless put off, Penelope declaring that she could not come because of urgent business, but Whyte assumed the reason to be a " tetter which suddenly broke out on her fair white forehead." In the end, the tetter having presumably healed, the godparents duly attended the christening, giving " fair standing bowls, that may be worth £20 apiece."

Penelope was devotedly attached to her brother Essex. During the critical period of his fortunes she wrote many letters and sent many jewels to the Queen. Whyte drily remarks that the letters were read and the jewels received, but no leave was granted even to see Essex, and eventually the Queen, angered at Lady Rich's importunity, commanded her to keep to her own house. After Essex's execution, Penelope's lover, Mountjoy, was sent to conduct the Irish wars which Essex had so sadly mismanaged, and the lover was as successful as the brother had been unfortunate.

Her relations with Mountjoy must have been well enough known at James's accession, but at the beginning of his reign she was in great favour, and was given a special precedence at the Coronation. The new king knew something of her; as far back as 1589 she had corresponded with Robert Douglas, in Scotland, on her brother's behalf, in matters of statecraft. James, who saw the letters, "commended much the fineness of her wit, her invention and good writing." Thinking herself no doubt secure of royal countenance, Penelope arranged a divorce with Rich and married Mountjoy, now Earl of Devonshire. The ceremony was performed by the Earl's chaplain, William Laud, afterwards the famous Archbishop. The king's attitude must have deeply disappointed Penelope, conniving, as he had done, at the *liaison*, he was furious at the marriage, and refused to receive the pair at Court. Neither survived long, Devonshire, indeed, only a few months, his wife not much more than a year. Laud, whose conduct of the ceremony nearly ruined his career, expressed the deepest contrition. Nevertheless it is probable that it was he who, when installed at Lambeth Palace, placed there the portrait, still extant, and inscribed at the back, "Countess of Devon." It is the only portrait that survives of the brilliant and beautiful Penelope, one of the most charming and seductive personalities of social history. (5) Three of her sons, two by Rich and one by Mountjoy, achieved some note. The Earls of Holland and Newport had many of her characteristics; the Earl of Warwick, an able and rather stolid man of business, little or none. Not one of her numerous daughters, however, played any prominent part, and it was from her sister that further distinction in the direct matriarchal line was to continue.

That sister, Dorothy Devereux, though lacking Penelope's brilliance, was far indeed from being a nonentity. Her first marriage to Sir Thomas Perrott, son of the Sir John Perrott who played a conspicuous part in the Irish wars and who was reputed to be an illegitimate son of King Henry VIII, took place under sufficiently romantic circumstances. The lovers, having obtained a licence from the Bishop's Faculty Office, went with " a strange minister " to the parish church of Broxburn, in Herts, near where Dorothy was staying. Green, the incumbent of the parish, tried to stop the ceremony, alleging that the licence was insufficient, but Perrott insisted on carrying on with the aid of the strange parson, one Lewis by name, who, as the account states, performed the ceremony without any " surplice, dressed in his cloak with riding-boots and spurs," two men meantime guarding the door. There was a great commotion later about the granting of the licence; probably the Bishop was bribed, but he succeeded in exonerating himself, and, in any case, the validity of the marriage was not called in question.

The Queen, however, did not approve of these irregular proceedings, and was furious with her pretty young cousin. Four years later, in 1587, she showed her displeasure in significant fashion. She came to stay with Lady Warwick, and the latter had invited Dorothy also, no doubt hoping that she would now be forgiven. When the Queen arrived, however, and heard of Dorothy's presence, she ordered the latter to keep her chamber. Essex was of the party, and, though only a youth of twenty, was already a great favourite of Elizabeth's, and was bold enough to upbraid her after supper. Words ran high; the Queen added fuel to the fire by slighting references to Lettice, and Essex, flinging himself out in a fury, left early next morning with his sister. Lady Warwick's house-party was not a success, but the incident certainly reflected great credit on Essex.

We know little of Dorothy's life with Perrott, who was dead by 1592, and not long after his widow made an outwardly brilliant marriage with Henry Percy, ninth Earl of Northumberland, a marriage which, however, brought little happiness. Northumberland, a man of some learning, was a great pedant and his wife was more than a little of a shrew. The gossip Robert Whyte refers in 1599 to their domestic quarrels: " A muttering there is that there is unkindness grown between her and her husband, but I do not write you this as a truth, but mistrusted." The birth of a son and heir in 1602 brought about a certain reconciliation, and husband and wife, who were, at any rate, alike in pride of birth, were probably at one in agreeing to call this son Algernon, " after," says John Chamberlain, the letter-writer, " one of his first ancestors that came of the house of Brabant, it is thought somewhat a strange and disused name." The name has nevertheless continued in the Percy family and has occasionally been used elsewhere.

The reconciliation did not last long, Chamberlain soon after tells us : " I find the Earl of Northumberland lives apart from his lady now she hath brought him an heir. She lives at Sion with the child, being otherwise of a very melancholy spirit."

Public as well as domestic misfortune was now to

affect the Northumberlands. The Earl accused, quite unjustly, of complicity in the Gunpowder Plot, was imprisoned for many years in the Tower. This kind of misfortune was one to bring out the best traits in Dorothy's character; she became the most untiring advocate of her husband, and with the pertinacity shown before by her mother and sister, bothered Salisbury to such an extent that he refused to see her, writing to Northumberland to complain of the contumacious language which the Countess used. The Earl may have been grateful for his wife's efforts, but he never ceased to grumble at her mismanagement of his affairs while he was in prison. He left behind him some quaint rules for the guidance of his son, the second of which ran: "That you never suffer your wife to have power in the management of your affairs."

In 1612 she wrote in the most outspoken manner to the King with regard to the enormous fine levied on her husband. "For though this is likely to prove the undoing of me and my children, yet it will be so small a supply to Your Majesty's pretended wants, that it will be scarcely seen, much less felt, and God forbid that one or two poor creatures should suffer because Your Majesty's coffers are empty."

A long further dissertation on the part of Northumberland in the instructions he left for his son gives, at any rate, his side of the case. Speaking of women, he admits that in some respects they are almost the equals of men, for "their wits are tempered as ours be, but they are apt to lose the sense of right and wrong and act only upon example and custom, not what is fit for them and their children to wear out of the abilities of their callings, but because such and such wears this and that, and so in general their affections are founded upon what others do." As for women's conversation, " it is," says Northumberland, " for the most part but of nursery company, or if extraordinary, they do converse with men, what will be their entertainment but to tell them they are fair, proper, witty and pretty passages of flattery to gain their good wishes. In fact, women are incapable of making progress in any learning, saving in love, a little craft and a little thriftiness if they are so addicted out of disposition, handsomeness and trimness being the idol of their hearts."

Furthermore, the Earl informs his son what should be done if a woman begins to scold. " The remedy I have found best is to let them talk and you to keep the power in your own hands, that you may do as you list. If a woman should threaten to do herself a mischief give them a knife or open the casements. I can never hear of any that have finished by these mournful deaths."

In thus treating of women, Northumberland can hardly fail to have had his wife in mind. Admittedly she must have been hot-tempered, probably vain and extravagant, but it is extremely doubtful that she was silly. She probably had a sense of humour denied to her lord, and it is a thousand pities that we have no views on men from her. But notwithstanding all their quarrels, Northumberland was undoubtedly wretched when Dorothy died in 1619. " His friends found it necessary to remind the Earl of his former disputes with his wife, in order to lessen his grief at her loss."

Taking her for all in all, Dorothy, Countess of Northumberland, was unquestionably less brilliant than her sister Penelope or than her younger daughter Lucy.

Northumberland was still a prisoner in the Tower when, in 1617, Lucy Percy attracted the attention of James Hay, a favourite of the king. The Earl, who regarded Hay as the merest upstart, was furious at the idea of the match. He made Lucy live with him for a time in the Tower, but allowed her to visit a fellow-prisoner, the notorious Frances, Countess of Somerset, who encouraged the match in every way, probably with the idea that Hay might ultimately obtain her release, and so, says Chamberlain, " the Earl has sent his daughter away from the Tower." Her mother was by no means so averse to the marriage; with Lucy she feasted twice a week at Hay's expense, but at such cost that Lady Northumberland never dared to ask him back, though " he be commonly in the house from morning till dinner, from after dinner till supper, from after supper, till late at night." James Hay was indeed extravagant even in an extravagant age, but, unlike the King's other favourites, Somerset and Buckingham, he never presumed on his position, never lost his temper, and showed distinct ability in the diplomatic services which he was from time to time called upon to perform. From the first his wife Lucy took a striking position at Court, but in the reign of Charles the power of herself and her husband was distinctly increased, more particularly by the fact that the Countess of Carlisle, as she had now become, stood first in the confidence of the new Queen, Henrietta Maria. Poets praised her beauty and statesmen admired her brains. Among the former were Carew, Cartwright and Herrick, among the latter Stratford and Pym. Her portrait, by Vandyck, now in the Egremont Collection, has been published in Lodge's Portraits. Her face shows decided will-power, and that she might be difficult to manage her determined mouth seems to testify. Of the pictures of sixteenth- and seventeenth-century women published by Lodge, that of Lucy Hay stands out as the most striking.

She lost her husband in 1636, and as he died enormously in debt, her affairs at this time must have been very embarrassed. She had already begun her friendship with Strafford, a friendship which was probably wholly platonic. Sir Tobie Matthew, whom she evidently greatly interested, says that " she cannot love in earnest, so contents herself to play with love as with a child." In this respect she was certainly a great contrast to her aunt Penelope, and on the whole she seems to have inherited more of the cold blood of the Percys than the hot blood of the Devereuxs.

Strafford, in writing to Laud, said of Lady Carlisle : " I judge her ladyship very considerable, for she is often in place and is extremely well skilled how to speak with advantage and spirit for those friends she professeth unto. There is this further in her disposition : she will not seem to be the person she is not, an ingenuity I have always observed and honoured her for." Shortly before his death Strafford referred to her noble and intelligent friendship. But whether or not during Strafford's lifetime, not long after his death she had transferred her allegiance to John Pym, and, says Philip Warwick, " has become such a she-saint that she frequented their (the Puritans) sermons and took notes."

It was certainly strange that the Queen's chief favourite should adopt the parliamentary side at the beginning of the civil wars, but this she did, giving notice to the five members that the King intended to arrest them. Later she veered round again to the royal side. The death of Pym may have wearied her of the other, but she was, of course, not singular in this respect. She was deeply involved in the rising of 1648, and on its suppression suffered imprisonment in the Tower for about eighteen months. "This busy stateswoman," as Philip Warwick calls her, continued to intrigue during the Commonwealth, but her influence was waning and she died very shortly after the Restoration.

Tobie Matthew's character of her probably approaches the nearest to the truth: "Her wit being most eminent among the rest of her great abilities, she affects the conversation of the persons who are most formed for it." And again: "She more willingly allows of the conversation of men than of women, yet when she is among her own sex, her discourse is of fashions and dressings, which she hath ever so perfect upon herself." Decidedly the ablest, if not perhaps the most fascinating, of the female descendants of Queen Elizabeth's aunt, Mary Boleyn, Lady Carlisle in many respects resembled that Queen herself, and with the same opportunities would probably have made quite as great a name for herself in history.

Lucy Hay had no children, and the direct female line was carried on by her elder sister Dorothy, who married Robert Sidney, second Earl of Leicester, the nephew of her aunt Penelope's first admirer. The connection brought about in this generation between the brilliant Sidney and Devereux relationships bore fruit in a family of great distinction. Dorothy, Countess of Leicester, though described as of excellent understanding and the most refined politeness, was far from showing her sister's political ambitions. Her portrait in Lodge's Collections indicates great sweetness and gentleness of character, and her hands are singularly beautiful, with long tapering fingers. She was absolutely devoted to her husband, and few more charming letters can ever have been written than that which she penned in 1636, eighteen years after their marriage. Lord Leicester was then in Paris on a diplomatic mission. "Mr. Saladine came in with your letter, whom I am engaged to entertain a little, besides it is supper time, or else I should bestow one side of this paper in making love to you, and since I may with modesty express it, I will say that if it be love to think on you sleeping and waking, to discourse of nothing with pleasure, but what concerns you, to wish myself every hour with you, and to pray for you with as much devotion as for my own soul, then certainly it must be said that I am in love."

Lord and Lady Leicester were well described as the chief ornaments of the Court of Charles I, but she had also something of her mother's impulsiveness and was undoubtedly of a somewhat over-anxious disposition. As a wife and mother, however, she was beyond all praise and her husband and children were alike devoted to her; the latter, one may well imagine, had more awe than love for their aunt Lucy.

Lady Leicester's position in the civil wars was peculiarly painful; her husband stood by the King, as did his son-in-law Sunderland, but her brother Northumberland and her elder sons took the Parliament side. It was, perhaps, however, the connection with both parties which led the Parliament in 1649 to place the younger royal children, the Duke of Gloucester and Princess Elizabeth, in her charge after the King's execution, allowing the considerable sum of £3,000 a year for their maintenance. Lord Leicester accordingly took occasion to cut down his wife's allowance from £700 to £300 a year, evidently considering that she could save considerably out of the £3,000. He also quaintly gives as a reason that he would have less liberty in his house. "This," he writes, "caused a huge storm, but I persisted in it."

Lady Leicester was strictly enjoined to treat the children with no special respect; outwardly she complied, but not in private. It must, however, have been a most difficult position, but that the heart of the young Princess Elizabeth was won there can be no doubt, as on her early death soon after she left her hostess a valuable diamond. The Commonwealth was mean enough to claim this as Crown property, and though the Sidney family strongly contested that claim, they eventually lost the case.

Dorothy, Countess of Leicester, died just before the Restoration; of her daughters, Dorothy, the eldest, alone maintained the brilliance so conspicuous on the side of both her father and her mother.

Dorothy Sidney has been immortalized by Edmund Waller under the name of Sacharissa, and as a girl she was as favourite a subject for Vandyck's pencil as for Waller's pen. The portrait reproduced by Lodge is not, one thinks, as attractive as that of her mother, shows less intellectual power than that of her aunt, but most distinctly indicates the possession of wit and humour.

Waller can at no time have been regarded seriously

as a suitor, and probably himself only thought of Dorothy as a fit subject for the display of his poetic powers. A younger and perhaps more fervent admirer was William Temple, whose uncle, Henry Hammond, was rector of Penshurst. Temple, at any rate, became possessed of a portrait of the fair lady, playfully referred to by a later Dorothy, who, when on her betrothal she sent Temple her portrait, begged him not to presume to disturb that of my Lady Sunderland.

Lord and Lady Leicester would have probably most preferred Lord Cavendish as a husband for their much-prized daughter, but that young man, after hesitating, eventually paid his attentions elsewhere. Lord Lovelace was next passed in review, but Lady Leicester found him "so uncertain and so idle, so much addicted to mean company and so much addicted to debauchery, it is now my study how to break off with him, in such a manner, as it may be said we refused him." Against this his good estate, his pretty person and his more than ordinary wit, were rightly considered as of no weight whatever. But Dorothy's eventual husband, Henry, Lord Spencer, was everything that her fond parents could desire. Sprung from a family which had but recently come to the fore, but which has since carved its name deep in English history, Henry Spencer, though perhaps a little too serious-minded, was justly regarded as a pattern of every excellence. He was maternal grandson of the Lord Southampton, Shakespeare's patron, who was a close and faithful friend of his bride's unfortunate great-uncle Essex.

Dorothy's married life was supremely happy but of very short duration. Her husband, created Earl of Sunderland in 1642, followed the King in the civil wars, but, like many other young men of his stamp, with but little enthusiasm. "If," he writes from camp to his wife, "an expedient could be found to solve the punctilio of honour, I would not continue here an hour." A year later he was killed at Newbury by the side of Falkland, a man of like pattern to himself.

During the years immediately succeeding her husband's death, Lady Sunderland, living in retirement in Northamptonshire, occupied herself largely in befriending distressed Royalists, to whom, says Lloyd, "her house was a sanctuary, her interest a protection, her estate a maintenance, and the livings in her gift a preferment."

In 1652 she married again, choosing as her second husband Sir Robert Smythe. Dorothy Osborne, then in the middle of her correspondence with Lady Sunderland's old admirer, William Temple, was much incensed by her ladyship's attitude. "I think I shall never forgive her for one thing she said of him, which was that she married him out of pity." And again: "She has lost by it much of the repute she had gained by keeping herself a widow." And again: "We do abound with stories of Lady Sunderland and Mr. Smythe, with what reserve he approached her and how like a gracious princess she receives him, that they say 'tis worth going twenty miles to see it." But if Dorothy Osborne disapproved on this occasion of her namesake, she was to her, as a rule, the perfect type of a great lady. The second marriage, too, seems to have turned out happily, though one suspects that Smythe was always the under dog.

During the latter period of her life Lady Sunderland's interests were largely bound up in her brilliant son by her first marriage. Brilliant as he was, Robert, second Earl of Sunderland, was hopelessly unstable and untrustworthy, and it was probably as well that his mother did not live to see his astounding tergiversations during the reign of James II. Heredity seems indeed to have played some strange pranks in Robert's case. It is easy to see why he was able, but not so easy to see why he was so morally worthless. His ancestry in every direction was remarkably the reverse, and even when we get back to the faulty Devereux, their faults were not his. It is remarkable, however, that the writer of his memoir in the *Dictionary of National Biography* compares him to John Dudley, Duke of Northumberland, from whom he was in effect actually descended. Some bad strain may have been handed down through the excellent Sidneys—who can tell?

Dorothy, Countess of Sunderland, in any case occupied shortly before the end of her life a very remarkable position, related as she was to an extraordinary number of leading politicians of the time. In addition to her son, there were her brothers, Algernon and Henry Sidney, and her son-in-law Halifax; Lord Shaftesbury had married her sister-in-law, Margaret Spencer, and Lord William Russell, her husband's first cousin, Rachel Wriothesley. William Temple and Edmund Waller were still among her friends, but her friendship with the latter can hardly perhaps have survived his well-known answer to her query as to when he would write more verses on her: "When you are as young again, madam, and as handsome as you were then."

An interesting glimpse of Sacharissa in her old age is afforded by her correspondence with her brother, Henry Sidney, on the subject of the marriage of her niece, Lucy Pelham, the daughter of her sister Lucy, and a member therefore of the direct female line which we have been considering. The proposed bridegroom was Gervase Pierrepont. Lady Sunderland, who was evidently extremely active in making the match, approved highly of his personal resources and projects, but after going into these, continues: "Now I have told the good show, I must come to the ill one. His person is ugly, but he is well enough drest and behaved, but of very few words. I desired her to tell me if she had any distaste to him and I would order it so that it should not go on, and her father should not be angry with her, but she is wiser than to refuse it. He is not more ill-favoured than Montagu, and his wife kisses him all day and calls him her pretty dear." The marriage duly came off, but in the next letter we find Lady Sunderland doubtful about the bride, " for she loves more compliments and mirths than she will ever find. I prepared her as well as I could not to expect it. He is not a pleasant man—very few are, neither is he the very next sort for entertainment." Later Lady Sunderland finds fault with her niece's management, " which we suspect; for she is giddy and delighted with liberty and money . . . her great rich relatives will not think well of her if she is too expensive." Pierrepont, for his part, seems to have been a great nuisance in the house: " He calls the women all the ill-names there are and meddles in the kitchen much."

Here the curtain falls on the Pierrepont marriage. Lucy had an admiration for her aunt, but was doubtless also afraid of her. Lady Sunderland, though essentially kind-hearted, was quite clearly *très grande dame*. She is the last of note of the great matriarchal line to which Queen Elizabeth belonged. Her only daughter Dorothy married George Savile, afterwards famous as

Marquis of Halifax, but died quite young. Halifax remained on the closest terms of intimacy with his mother-in-law, and each relied much on the judgment of the other. His and Dorothy Spencer's only daughter Anne married John Vaughan, Earl of Carbery, famed for his good looks but not apparently for anything else. Their only child, Anne, had a singularly sad life. A great heiress, she was married in 1713 to Lord Winchester, afterwards Duke of Bolton, and as soon as 1715 Lady Mary Wortley Montagu writes: " My lord made her an early confession of his aversion." They separated not long after, the Duke consoling himself with Lavinia Fenton, the " Polly Peachum " of the first performance of *The Beggar's Opera*, whom, however, he was not able to marry till 1754, in which year the Duchess died. Lady Mary then wrote of her: " Educated in solitude with some choice books by a saint-like governess, crammed with virtue and good qualities, she thought it impossible not to find gratitude though she failed to give passion, and upon this threw away her estate, was despised by her husband and laughed at by the public." It would not appear that Anne, Duchess of Bolton, inherited any of the charm of her ancestresses in the direct female line, but she might well have pleased some of her ancestors, notably the Earl of Northumberland. She had no children, and with her this branch of the great matriarchal line of Queen Elizabeth came to an end. Other branches continued till later, notably one descended from Penelope, Lady Rich, of which, however, a venerable lady, Alice, Countess of Strafford, is the sole survivor, and, so far as the present writer is aware, the only surviving representative of the great Queen's direct female line. The brilliancy of the line culminated with the generations from Lettice, Countess of Leicester, to Dorothy, Countess of Sunderland; then, as we have seen, it faded out in sadness, but among other descendants of Lady Sunderland the brilliancy was again to be revived. Mention has already been made of her son Robert. The latter's son Charles, third Earl of Sunderland, who married the daughter of the great Marlborough, was, like his father, an able politician, who played no small part in the affairs of the nation. The two next generations of the Spencers of Althorp were of lesser note, but with the children of John, first Earl Spencer, a revival of distinction takes place. The descendants, indeed, of this Earl Spencer have played many and various parts and have achieved distinction in statesmanship, in diplomacy, in the Church, and to a remarkable degree on the cricket field. Without any one man of absolutely outstanding ability, they have represented English aristocracy at its very best, but relatively the women have played a more prominent part than the men. The first Lord Spencer's daughters, Georgiana, Duchess of Devonshire, and Henrietta, Countess of Bessborough, Countess Granville, daughter of the former, and Lady Caroline Lamb of the latter, (6) Lucy, Lady Lyttelton, the niece of both, and finally Harriet, Duchess of Sutherland, grand-daughter of the Duchess of Devonshire, these ladies were all distinguished for their social charm and in some cases also for their literary ability.

The relative degrees of kinship of this group bear a striking resemblance to those of their ancestresses, direct and collateral, who have been treated of in this chapter, and the parallels between the earlier and later groups are in most respects strikingly complete.

CHAPTER III

A GLANCE DOWN THE CENTURIES

ENGLAND

FEW English statesmen have been more unfortunate than Henry VII's Minister, Edmund Dudley. Unlucky in his life, Dudley, like Banquo in *Macbeth*, was, at any rate, fortunate in his descendants, who, with the break of scarcely a generation, have continued prominent in public affairs right down to the present day.

Dudley's own origin has been the subject of much discussion. Sixteenth-century writers asserted that he was of humble parentage, but there can be little doubt that he was the son of John Dudley, of Atherington, in Sussex, himself the younger son of John Sutton, Lord Dudley, of an old baronial family, who, however, had not in earlier times produced men of any marked distinction. An uncle, William Dudley, was indeed Bishop of Durham, but Edmund was the first of this line to achieve any real note. Aged about twenty-three when Henry came to the throne, Edmund early attracted that monarch's attention, and, after filling diplomatic appointments, became principal financial adviser to the Crown, and in that capacity, together with Richard Empson, the chief instrument of the King's financial policy. Empson and Dudley gathered taxes with a heavy hand, and became the special objects of hatred on the part of the nobility. Undoubtedly a hard, undoubtedly also an efficient man, Dudley seems, however, to have worked for the State rather than for his own personal profit, though he did incidentally acquire a considerable fortune. At Henry VII's death there was a sum of no less than four and a half million pounds in the Treasury, a sum which his successor was careful enough to enjoy, and of all the maleficent deeds of the Eighth Henry none was actually baser than his treatment of Empson and Dudley, who, in deference to aristocratic clamour, were brought to the block under the most ridiculously trumped-up charges. Henry seems, however, in effect to have repented of this action, as Edmund's only son John was not long after restored in blood and allowed to inherit his father's fortune.

If the nobility of John Dudley's paternal descent was somewhat dubious, there is no sort of doubt as to the nobility of his descent on the maternal side. Edmund Dudley's wife was Elizabeth Grey, great-granddaughter on her mother's side of the famous warrior, John Talbot, first Earl of Shrewsbury, and the direct representative of the Beauchamps, Earls of Warwick, one of the greatest of the Norman families. John Dudley, in addition to this distinguished descent, clearly inherited much of his father's ability, but whether from natural disposition or from policy, his rôle in his early days was mainly that of the courtier. The Dudley son knew as well how to please the Tudor son as did the Dudley father the Tudor father. Showing also considerable military talents, John Dudley, first as Earl of Warwick and later as Duke of Northumberland, played a leading part in English history, till his overweening ambition finally brought about his ruin. The marriage of his son Guildford to Lady Jane Grey, to whom through his mother he was related, brought about the

A GLANCE DOWN THE CENTURIES 61

attempt on the part of Northumberland to place Lady Jane on the throne, the failure of which led the Duke himself to the scaffold, together with his unfortunate son and daughter-in-law. Suffering the same fate as his father, Northumberland far more emphatically brought that fate upon himself.

His wife was Jane, daughter of Sir Edward Guildford, Marshal of Calais and Lord Warden of the Cinque Ports, and grand-daughter of Sir Richard Guildford, a distinguished soldier who died on a pilgrimage to Palestine, an interesting account of which has been printed in the Camden Society's 1851 volume. The Guildfords showed considerable ability for some generations, and the Duchess herself is described as a lady of great piety, virtue and prudence. She experienced a miserable time after her husband's fall, but succeeded in obtaining the pardon of her remaining sons, all of whom had been under sentence of execution. Two of those sons became men of mark, but while Robert, afterwards Queen Elizabeth's famous favourite Leicester, inherited the less amiable qualities of the Dudleys, Ambrose, subsequently Earl of Warwick, took more from the maternal side. Roger Ascham praised his high intellectual attainments, but though an active promoter of maritime enterprise, Warwick preferred to pass his life on the whole in scholarly pursuits, and, unlike his brother, attained no note in history.

It is the line of his sister Mary with which we are now, however, concerned. This sister married Henry Sidney during the days of her father's greatness. It must have been a brilliant match at the time for Henry, whose own descent was, however, scarcely less distinguished, tracing back as he did through the Brandons to the Fitzalans, Earls of Arundel. His father, Sir William, (7) had been Chamberlain to Prince Edward, and during the latter's short reign Henry was in high favour, a fact which no doubt made him acceptable as a son-in-law to the ambitious Northumberland. He was wise enough to take no part in the episode of Lady Jane Grey, and successfully made his peace with Queen Mary, whose husband, Philip of Spain, was godfather to Henry and Mary Sidney's own brilliant son—ironical enough in the light of subsequent events. Thrice Lord Deputy of Ireland under Elizabeth, Henry Sidney was perhaps the most faithful of all the servants of that Queen; his character was indeed as nearly as possible irreproachable, but his fame has suffered in comparison with that of his elder son. His wife, Mary Dudley, was in every respect worthy of him. Holinshed's Chronicle is enthusiastic in her praises: "She exceeded most of her sex in singularity of virtue and quality, as good speech, apt and ready concept, excellency of wit and notable elegant delivery, where none could match her and few come near her." She, like her brother Ambrose, quite clearly resembled more nearly her mother's side, but though the hardness of the Dudleys disappears from that most fortunate family, the Sidneys, much of their ability undoubtedly remained.

From such a father and mother as Henry and Mary Sidney exceptional children might well have been expected, and expectation was not disappointed, though Philip completely outshone the remainder of the family, who were themselves, however, far from being obscure. The only daughter, Mary, was married to Henry Herbert, Earl of Pembroke, a man much older than herself and of loose morals, whom she may have tolerated but whom she can hardly have loved. Whilst he lived, her brother Philip stood first in her affections; he often stayed with her at Wilton, where he assisted her in the beginnings of a fine library, which contained the nucleus in particular of a noteworthy collection of Italian literature. After Philip's death Lady Pembroke became *par excellence* the great patroness of literary men, and was probably, on the whole, the most highly-cultured woman of her time. Her own verse showed, however, few poetic qualities, but much evidence of wide reading, coupled with a certain literary sensibility. For most of us, however, she lives as the subject of Ben Jonson's famous epitaph, probably, taking it for all in all, the finest ever composed in any language. (8)

Of her two sons who succeeded successively to the Earldom of Pembroke, William the elder was much the most worthy of her, a highly intelligent and cultivated man delighting in literary society, but with no great force of character. The great stain on his memory is his seduction of Mary Fitton, generally identified as " The Dark Lady " of Shakespeare's Sonnets, which seduction was followed by a base abandonment. Philip, the younger brother, was by no means unintelligent, but cared comparatively little for literature, and his moral character was detestable. The brothers received the supreme honour of the dedication of the First Folio of Shakespeare's Plays, deserved slightly by William, not at all by Philip. In later years the Herberts, Earls of Pembroke, continued on the whole worthy of their Sidney descent, especially that remote descendant who bore the name of his maternal ancestors, the Sidney Herbert who almost alone among politicians came well out of the ordeal of the Crimean War.

Robert Sidney, Philip's younger brother, was in early life much overshadowed by the latter. Few men owed more to matrimony than did Robert, his marriage with Barbara Gamage, a great Welsh heiress, bringing him not only great wealth, but almost unclouded happiness. Barbara was related to two distinguished men, Lord Howard of Effingham, who commanded against the Armada, and Walter Raleigh. Both concerned themselves in her marriage, and an interesting letter is extant from Raleigh to Sir Edward Stradling, Barbara's guardian. In it he says: " Her Majesty hath now thrice caused letters to be written to you, that you suffer not my kinswoman to be bought and sold in Wales, without Her Majesty's privity and the consent and advice of my Lord Chamberlain (Lord Howard) and myself, her father's cousins germane, considering she hath not any nearer her, nor better." But while Lord Howard and Raleigh seem to have approved of her marriage with Robert Sidney, the Queen, as was her wont, did not, and two hours after the wedding a royal message arrived to stop it. Elizabeth seems, however, to have been ultimately pacified.

The lives of Robert and Barbara read almost like a fairy story. Successful enough in the days of Elizabeth, where he won fame as a soldier in the Low Countries in the days of James, Robert rose step by step to the Earldom of Leicester, adding by inheritance the wealth of his Dudley uncles to that of his wife. Barbara seems to have been an altogether excellent woman. Ben Jonson, the protégé of Robert's sister, was equally at home at Penshurst, and was especially struck by Lady Leicester's excellence as a housewife, as evidenced by his lines on a visit from the King:

> Her linen, plate and all things right
> Though she was fair, and every room was drest
> As if she had expected such a guest.

Devotion to the Leicesters was shared with Ben Jonson by the Earl's secretary, Robert Whyte, whose letters to his chief give so many interesting glimpses of the times.

It will be seen that the children of Robert Sidney and Barbara Gamage possessed a relationship to perhaps the two most romantic figures of Elizabethan times, Philip Sidney and Walter Raleigh. One of these children, Lady Mary Wroth, achieved, in her turn, some reputation as a patroness of literary men, and herself attempted a poem called *Urania*, which, however, except for one or two lyrics, is a tedious work. Lady Mary by no means inherited her mother's capacity for management and was constantly in debt. In the Sidney Correspondence is to be found a letter anent her marriage. Sir William Brown, then second in command to her father at Flushing, writes to the latter that, " having understood that you are busy with the marriage of your eldest daughter, I, with the rest of my captains, have given order to Mr. Meredith to present £200 in our names, to buy her a chain of pearl, or otherwise to employ as she pleases." Two hundred pounds was an enormous sum in those days, and speaks well for the popularity of the father; but it is to be feared that the chain of pearl, if ultimately purchased, probably went in satisfaction of the daughter's debts.

With the incidents relating to the christening of

the only son of the Earl and Countess of Leicester, another Robert, we have become acquainted in the preceding chapter. Twenty-three years later the younger Robert married his godmother's niece, Dorothy Percy, and thus the Sidneys became linked to the almost equally brilliant Devereux connection. The second Countess of Leicester, of the Sidney family, a worthy successor to Mary Dudley and Barbara Gamage, has already been described. Her husband, the second Earl, was, says Clarendon, "a man of great parts, very conversant in books, and much addicted to the mathematics." A fine linguist, he could speak Latin, French, Italian and Spanish, and purchased many curious books in these languages, " but," adds Clarendon, " he was of a truth rather a speculative than a practical man." Still, his embassy to Paris from 1636 to 1639 was highly successful. On his departure the King gave him a jewel worth £1,200 and the Queen gave his wife a jewel worth £600. His wife, as we have seen, was devoted to him; she was jealous only of his books. "If," she writes, "either business or ceremony to such persons as may be useful to you, be the occasion of your seldom writing, I do dispense with the omission, but if your old inclination to reading be the cause, I do not forgive it."

Lord Leicester's character was not specially suited to prominence in the civil wars. Though a Royalist, he was by no means an active one; but the reproach of inactivity could not, at any rate, be levelled against his two elder sons. His children, possessing one of the most brilliant and varied of heredities, were a singularly interesting family, but, taken as a whole, their abilities, though sufficiently diversified, were perhaps less than might have been expected. The best known daughter, Dorothy, Countess of Sunderland, has been previously delineated. The sons were four. They fall naturally into two groups, Philip and Algernon the elder, Robert and Henry the younger. None of these four sons inherited alike the high morality and social charm of their parents; the two elder lacked the charm, the two younger the morality. Philip and Algernon both took the Commonwealth side in the civil wars. Philip was high in Cromwell's favour, but never really came to the front. After the Restoration he gave up politics altogether; he had inherited, however, the family taste for literature, and entertained the wits of the age at his house at Sheen, setting aside one day for literary men in particular. With Sir William Temple he was in frequent correspondence.

Algernon was a much more remarkable character. When a boy, his mother writes that he was commended for a " huge deal of wit and much sweetness of nature." The sweetness he certainly seems to have lost; wit, or at any rate intelligence, he always possessed. Burnet describes him as " a man of most extraordinary courage, steady even to obstinacy, severe, but of a rough and boisterous temper that could not bear contradiction." (9) All through his life he held advanced republican views—views which ultimately brought him to the block after the Rye House Plot. Though very unlike his mother herself, Algernon's characteristics seem most evidently to be a compound of those of his maternal grandparents, the Earl and Countess of Northumberland.

The two younger Sidney brothers were cast in an entirely different mould. Both were remarkably handsome men. Robert, who died comparatively young, was said to be the real father of the Duke of Monmouth. This parentage would fully account for the good looks of that unfortunate Duke, but certainly not for his cowardice, which may have arisen from the maternal side.

Henry Sidney, much the youngest of the family, is described by Collins as " graceful in his person and of a sweet and affectionate disposition, of great humanity and benevolent to all in distress." There is no doubt as to the first of these characteristics, and Henry Sidney was, moreover, a great rake, described in his younger days as a " terror to husbands," and later in life pestered by numerous letters on behalf of the illegitimate children for whom he refused to provide, in this respect, at any rate, showing no benevolence at all. His abilities were far from contemptible, and he played no small part in the bringing over of William of Orange. His character had obvious resemblances to that of Charles II, and among his own kin to his mother's aunt, Penelope, Lady Rich.

Of these Sidney brothers, only Philip left legitimate descendants; those of Henry are quite untraceable. Among Philip's posterity ability died out and the surname of Sidney disappears from history. The Sidney ability was, however, to reappear among the descendants of two of the daughters of this generation, Dorothy, Countess of Sunderland, and Lady Lucy Pelham. Reference has already been made to Lady Sunderland's descendants; it now remains to consider those of Lady Lucy.

The Pelham family, into which she married, had long been settled in Sussex, but except for her husband's great-grand-uncle, a Sir William Pelham, who was a Lord Justice in Ireland in the time of Queen Elizabeth, there had been no great note in the family. The matrimonial affairs of her daughter Lucy have already been discussed. Lady Sunderland, who took such an interest in this case, was troubled also with regard to the marriage of her nephew, Thomas Pelham, to a daughter of Sir William Jones, Attorney-General, who was termed by Temple "a very wise, able man and the greatest lawyer in England." Lady Sunderland dubs him "Father Jones," and evidently much disliked him; the daughter she terms, "a pert, ill-bred creature." She clearly regarded the marriage with Miss Jones as a great *mésalliance*. To Elizabeth, the only child of this marriage, we shall again have occasion to refer. Lady Sunderland would have thoroughly approved of Thomas Pelham's second marriage to Lady Grace Holles, but this she did not live to see. It was, nevertheless, the Jones rather than the Holles descendants who ultimately kept up the distinction of this branch of the Sidney descent.

Thomas Pelham filled certain offices with credit; according to Collins, he was distinguished for his knowledge of men and business, and was ultimately raised to the peerage, but he was in no way a remarkable man. Vast wealth came into his family through his second marriage, the greater part of which was inherited by his elder son by that marriage, Thomas, so well known as Duke of Newcastle. With this Duke and his brother, Henry Pelham, the family connection entered again into history, but it would be idle to assert that the Pelhams possessed much ability. Henry has, however, been rather unjustly treated on the whole; he showed considerable skill in finance and, though no orator, had merits as a plain and direct speaker, was very tolerant and full of common sense. His Premiership was, perhaps, the most uneventful that there has ever been in England, but this, in so far as it carries any weight, is distinctly to his credit.

Newcastle is, of course, the butt of all who write on eighteenth-century history; his foolish bustling qualities can certainly not have been derived from his stately Sidney ancestors. The caustic remark of Lord Wilmington, "He loses half an hour every morning and runs after it during the rest of the day without being able to overtake it," might lead one to think that Newcastle was merely born before his time and would have been perfectly at home at the present day. Energetic he certainly was; with his wealth he might easily have merely sat down and amused himself, and the Pelhams at any rate exemplify a persistence of inherited energy, with distinct traces of something more in the case of Henry.

Newcastle left no descendants, and those of Henry were quite undistinguished; it is from their half-sister Elizabeth, the grand-daughter of Sir William Jones, that further descent of interest can be traced. This Elizabeth was the first wife of Charles, Viscount Townshend, sometime Prime Minister and Walpole's great antagonist, who, though the first of note of the name of Townshend, was great-grandson of Horace, Lord Vere, a notable soldier of the Elizabethan period.

The Townshend family came more than once to the fore in the eighteenth century, notably in the case of the brilliant if very unreliable Charles Townshend, grandson of the first Viscount and Elizabeth Pelham, whose character has already been sketched in the first chapter. Charles Townshend's characteristics were perhaps derived more particularly from the side of his mother, but there seems also in him to have been at least a touch of certain Sidney characteristics. His uncle Thomas, Elizabeth Pelham's son, was a man of scholarly accomplishments and great social charm, who never brought himself forward in politics. He was the father of another Thomas, who, on being raised to the peerage, took the title of Viscount Sydney in memory of his ancestors. In 1788 this Lord Sydney was Home Secretary, an office which then included colonial affairs, and in that year the first settlement was formed in New South Wales. This settlement was named Sydney, after the Secretary of State, and so the most beautifully situated city of the southern hemisphere derives its name from the most graceful of English families.

Elizabeth, daughter of the first Viscount Townshend and Elizabeth Pelham, married into the Cornwallis family, and became the mother of three sons who attained some distinction. Of these, James became Bishop of Lichfield, but there is nothing in his career to indicate that he could have attained any such position without family influence. Another brother, Sir William, who rose to the rank of admiral, had more opportunity to prove his worth, and at the outset of the French revolutionary wars acted with decision and promptitude while commanding off the coast of India. He seems to have been a typical sea-dog of the old school, distinctly popular, with a wealth of nicknames, of which " Billy go tight " was the one most used. (10)

Much the most distinguished, however, of the family was the eldest brother, Charles, eventually first Marquis

Cornwallis. Lord Cornwallis was not a startling genius, but was alike an able general, a clear-sighted statesman, and, above all, a highly honourable English gentleman. For thirty eventful years, 1776-1806, Cornwallis was an eminent figure in public life. Although he opposed the measures which led up to the American War, he was too loyal to refuse the command offered to him. In this command he showed much ability, and it was almost entirely the force of circumstances which led to his final defeat and surrender at Yorktown. So little did this reflect to his discredit that he was actually offered the Governor-Generalship of India while a prisoner on parole, and eventually accepted this position in 1786. In India he was able to show alike his statesmanship and his generalship in the war with Tippoo, and the whole period of his rule was eminently successful. Contrary to his inclination, but in accordance with his sense of duty, he next became Lord-Lieutenant of Ireland, where he suppressed the rebellion of 1798 and carried the Union. The former was effected with as little severity as the Lord-Lieutenant could help; the latter he regarded as indispensable, though deeply regretting the means needed to bring it about. Finally Cornwallis died in India in 1806, a victim in this case to a feeling of duty that was almost quixotic, the acceptance of a second term being, at his age and in those days, almost equivalent to a sentence of death.

In Cornwallis we may safely say that we see the English aristocracy at its very best; his descent in every direction was from the soundest of stocks, but we are inclined perhaps to derive his qualities either from the Sidney strain or from an ancestor on his father's side, James Butler, Duke of Ormonde, the *preux chevalier* of the seventeenth century, to whose character that of Cornwallis bore a very marked resemblance.

The sister of this great administrator, Mary Cornwallis, was married in 1769 to a successful brewer, Samuel Whitbread, whose son of the same name by a first marriage was subsequently a well-known politician. Lady Mary Whitbread died in childbirth a year after her marriage; the child, a daughter, survived and in due time married Sir George Grey, a younger brother of the well-known Prime Minister.

The Greys are the last of the families in this long line from Edmund Dudley, and assuredly not one of the least. Charles, first Earl Grey, general; Charles, second Earl, Prime Minister; Henry, third Earl, Secretary of State; and Albert, fourth Earl, Governor-General of Canada, form a most distinguished line. Sir George, who married Mary Whitbread, was an efficient naval officer, who never, however, attained any great distinction. Lady Grey, a great friend of Wilberforce, was a woman of very strong religious character. Her son, another Sir George Grey, bore many marked resemblances to his maternal great-uncle, Lord Cornwallis. He was Home Secretary almost continuously for twenty years, 1864–66, and would no doubt have made a greater figure in history if he had been more ambitious. He was, however, content to shine almost entirely as an administrator, but was an ideal member of a Cabinet, very skilful in composing differences, a man on whose word all relied— in short, like his great-uncle, a great gentleman.

His character, and especially his domestic character, has been well portrayed in the first chapter of his grandson's autobiography. With that grandson, the present Viscount Grey of Fallodon, the long line closes. Of his career it is not necessary to speak here; it is obvious enough that some of his characteristics have already appeared among those ancestors, both direct and collateral, who have formed the subject of this chapter. From Edmund Dudley to Lord Grey of Fallodon there have been thirteen generations. With one exception only, that of Lord Grey's father, who, himself an only child, died comparatively young, every generation has produced at least one man or woman commemorated in the *Dictionary of National Biography* and in some cases several. Almost all the way through, the intermarriages of the line have been into families of some distinction, and herein no doubt lies the secret of the continuance of note. Beginning with Edmund Dudley, the families of intermarriage were, to quote them in order, Grey, Guildford, Sidney, Gamage, Percy, Pelham, Jones, Townshend, Cornwallis, Whitbread, Grey, Ryder, Pearson. In all but two cases members of these families have figured in the *Dictionary of National Biography*, in most cases frequently. The first exception is the family of Gamage, but though there was no Gamage of note, Barbara, Countess of Leicester, was, as we have seen, related to two men of the utmost distinction, Lord Howard of Effingham and Walter Raleigh. The other exception appears to be that of Lord Grey's mother, a Pearson.

An endeavour has been made to portray the characters of all the striking individuals of the line, and from such a study it comes out remarkably well. John Dudley and his son Robert, Earl of Leicester; Henry Sidney, Earl of Romney, and his nephew Sunderland, were certainly anything but estimable individuals, but an actual majority were men and women of the highest character, and there is a practically complete absence of weaklings. On the other hand, there is certainly no genius, nor even perhaps any real outstanding intellectual talent.

It is for the qualities of leadership, rather than for the qualities of intellect pure and simple, that this line is mainly distinguished, but it is this very quality of leadership which, more than aught else, has made England what she is.

CHAPTER IV

A GLANCE DOWN THE CENTURIES

AMERICA

IN the year 1515, when the reign of Henry VIII was yet young, a Suffolk lad of the name of Adam Winthrop was bound apprentice in London to one Edward Altham, a clothier. Adam's father was probably a yeoman, but of his actual status nothing is known; the clothing business, however, stood at the head of the industrial pursuits of the time, and an apprenticeship thereto was no doubt much sought after.

Adam prospered. In 1526 we find him admitted to the liberty of London citizenship, and by 1551 he had attained the dignity of Master of the Clothworkers' Company, and had purchased an estate at Groton in his native county, which estate descended to his son Adam. The second Adam was called to the bar and filled the important post of Auditor of Trinity College, Cambridge. It was probably through his influence that a Latin tragedy, called *Roxana*, and written by his nephew, William Alabaster, son of his sister Bridget, was produced in the College Hall in 1592. This tragedy seems to have made some stir at the time, and Fuller terms Alabaster "a most rare poet as any age or nation hath produced." On the occasion of the production, Fuller further informs us that "a gentlewoman, hearing a Latin word hideously pronounced, fell into distraction and never fully recovered her senses." So singular an occurrence may have contributed to the notoriety of

A GLANCE DOWN THE CENTURIES

the play, which is quite unreadable now, but, in any case, William Alabaster was the first, though very far from the last, of the descendants of the Suffolk clothier to achieve general note.

His uncle Adam, the auditor, left a diary which shows that he took part in every kind of county business, and was evidently considered one of the landed gentry. He married, however, the daughter of an Edmonton clothier, one Henry Browne. Two of their children, John and Lucy, were destined to become founders of highly distinguished connections.

John, like his father, both a Londoner and a lawyer, adopted Puritanism with fervour, and his decision in 1629 to sail for New England was the turning-point in the family history. With him on the *Arabella* sailed Richard Saltonstall, Thomas Dudley and Simon Brasdtreet, all three of whom also became founders of notable connections, but that Winthrop ranked as the most considerable man is shown by the fact that the Massachusetts Company appointed him the first Governor of the Colony. For twelve eventful years he filled that position, and if George Washington is Father of the United States, John Winthrop may certainly be claimed as the Father of New England. For many generations his descendants in the male line showed high intellectual distinction, and in any list of notable American families the Winthrops would be among the first to be included.

It is proposed here, however, to follow the careers of some of the descendants of John Winthrop's sister Lucy, the descendants of the sister showing a continuance of intellectual powers to an even greater extent than those of the brother.

Lucy Winthrop had married in 1622 Emanuel Downing, the son of the Master of Ipswich Grammar School. Downing shared the Puritan views of his brother-in-law, though to a less marked extent, and would probably have accompanied him to the New World in 1629 but for the objections of his wife, who has recorded that to her " changes were ever irksome and the sea still more." A voyage in those days was indeed apt to be extremely irksome, but in 1638 Lucy finally braved its terrors, she with her husband and family crossing in that year and settling at Salem. Their only son George was sent to the newly established University at Harvard. But he was not destined to pass his career overseas. By 1646 he was back in England, whither his parents eventually followed him, leaving, however, at least one daughter in Massachusetts.

The ability of the Winthrops descended on George Downing, but not their moral worth. Taking service under the Commonwealth, he proved a successful diplomatist, a career which he was dexterous enough to continue after the Restoration, laying the blame for his previous activities on " his training in New England, where he was brought up and sucked in principles that since his reason had made him see were erroneous." Sir George Downing (Charles rewarded him with a baronetcy) was largely responsible for one act of statesmanship of immense historical importance, the annexation of New York. But his career, as a whole, was utterly selfish; though he acquired a large fortune, his habits were penurious and were complained of by his mother in her old age. He purchased land in the City of Westminster on which was built the famous street called after his name, and it is curious that the very centre of the British Empire should be thus designated from one whose collateral descendants were, almost without exception, to sever their connection with that Empire.

George Downing's direct descendants remained in England, but his male line failed with his grandson, another Sir George, a man who shared his grandfather's miserliness without his abilities, but who, by his posthumous bequest for the foundation of a college at Cambridge, in a second way immortalized the family name.

The first Sir George Downing was singularly unlike his mother's family, and very unlike him in their turn were the descendants of his sister, who clearly harked back to the earlier strain. This sister, Mary Downing, was married not long after her parents' arrival in New England to Anthony Stoddard, who had come over with John Winthrop. A man of note in the colony, Anthony was a member of its General Court from 1665–84.

Solomon Stoddard, son of Anthony and Mary, was the first of a long clerical line. Graduating, like his uncle, George Downing, at Harvard, he subsequently pursued a singularly different career. After a short interlude as chaplain to the Governor of Barbados, Solomon settled down as a Congregational pastor at Northampton, in Massachusetts, occupying the charge there for no fewer than fifty-seven years, 1672–1729, through the reign of no less than seven sovereigns. He was indeed an exact contemporary of the " Vicar of Bray," but a Congregational pastor in New England would have had little inducement to change his opinions. Solomon Stoddard was known, however, in his day as a man of intellectual power, and in 1700 he entered the lists in controversy with Increase Mather, then the foremost divine in the colony.

Born six years before the death of his great-uncle, John Winthrop, whom he could therefore just have remembered, Solomon Stoddard lived to associate his grandson, Jonathan Edwardes, with himself in his pastorate. He is therefore an interesting link between these two notable men, and on the younger he no doubt exercised a considerable influence.

Two of Solomon's sons, Anthony and John, were very prominent citizens of the colony. Anthony, though, like his father, primarily a pastor, was in addition a farmer and unofficial lawyer and physician, while John, a member of the Council of the colony, was Chief Justice of the Court of Common Pleas and colonel of militia. Life in Massachusetts in the early part of the eighteenth century was, no doubt, in some ways very narrow, but a remarkable opportunity of varied occupation was afforded to those possessing intellectual power, and the interest in life for men like the Stoddards compares in many ways favourably with that of the specialists of the present day.

In the male line the Stoddard family has continued to hold a high position, its most notable member at the present day being the well-known sociologist, Mr. T. Lothrop Stoddard, who is a direct descendant of Solomon.

Again, however, in order to find the line of most sustained interest, we must turn to the distaff side. Esther, daughter of Solomon Stoddard, married Timothy Edwardes, son of a prosperous merchant of Welsh origin. Educated, like his future wife's relatives, at

Harvard, Timothy received the degrees of B.A. and M.A. on the same day, " an uncommon mark of respect paid to his extraordinary proficiency in learning." Ordained a pastor at East Windsor in 1694, the same year in which he married Esther Stoddard, Timothy Edwardes surpassed the record of his father-in-law, holding his charge for no less than sixty-four years. When he was eighty-six years of age he thought it time to ask for an assistant. He died only a few months before his famous son, whom he was generally considered to have surpassed in learning, while he himself was surpassed by his wife " in native vigour of understanding." Tall, dignified and commanding in appearance, but affable and gentle in manner, Esther Edwardes forms a remarkable link between great men. She was great-grandniece of John Winthrop, great-niece of George Downing, mother of Jonathan Edwardes, grandmother of Aaron Burr and Timothy Dwight.

Jonathan, the son of Timothy Edwardes and Esther Stoddard, was perhaps the only American other than Benjamin Franklin who won a European reputation in colonial days. This reputation is now, however, not easy to understand, for Jonathan Edwardes' theological views would seem to us altogether intolerable; alike as a preacher and a writer, however, he made a deep impression on his contemporaries. It is curious that so extreme a Puritan should have married into a family which claimed connection with the intensely worldy English Pierreponts. The American Pierponts were, however, in all respects unlike their English namesakes. James Pierpont, the father-in-law of Jonathan Edwardes, was an earnest divine who was one of the founders of Yale, a University with which many of his descendants were to be most closely associated. Jonathan Edwardes and Sarah Pierpont had a large family, three of the sons attained note, three of the daughters had notable sons. The family were subjected in childhood to a terribly stern discipline, " thoroughly subdued " by their father on showing any tendency to self-will. Jonathan Edwardes was in the habit of referring to children as malignant young vipers, an expression to be taken, no doubt, in a strictly theological sense, for though a stern he does not appear to have been an actually tyrannical parent. In any case, his young vipers turned out uncommonly well. Timothy became a considerable merchant, Pierrepoint a judge, and Jonathan, like his father, a divine. Though the younger Jonathan never achieved the reputation of his father, by whom he was no doubt overshadowed, he was probably quite as able a man. The careers of the two Jonathans were singularly alike. Each, after serving as a pastor for twenty-six and twenty-four years respectively, quarrelled with his parishioners and spent the next few years in out-of-the-way places, from which each was called to the presidency of a college, only to die, the father within a few months, the son within two years. Most curious of all, the father, on the first Sabbath of the year in which he deceased, preached from the text, " This year shalt thou die," and the son, again on the first Sabbath, choosing the same text, met with the same fate. One would certainly have thought that the younger Jonathan would have avoided this text at all hazards, an avoidance, however, which the stern Calvinist would doubtless have regarded as an act of deplorable weakness.

In the next generation of the Edwardes family we

A GLANCE DOWN THE CENTURIES

find four lawyers of distinction, a college president, and a successful manufacturer, who gave a new turn to the family ability by his success as an inventor. To this William Edwardes the discovery of a new process in tanning leather is due.

More notable, however, were the descendants of the first Jonathan Edwardes through his daughters. One of these daughters, Lucy, married Jahleel Woodbridge, a judge of the Probate Court. Their son, Timothy Woodbridge, lost his eyesight at the age of fourteen, but triumphed in a remarkable manner over this disability, making a considerable name as a Congregationalist minister. He acquired by heart all that he would otherwise have read in Church services, and was never known to make a mistake. In the vigour of his intellect he was said to greatly resemble his maternal grandfather.

Timothy Woodbridge's first cousin, Aaron Burr, the son of Esther Edwardes, was totally unlike his immediate relatives, all steady and religious men. Nor apparently were his qualities derived from his father's side, not at least from that father himself, a college president of the same general type as that of the Edwardes family. It is perhaps not fanciful to suppose that Aaron Burr may have harked back to his great-great-granduncle, George Downing, whom he certainly resembled much more than he did his nearer relatives. Aaron had every possible charm of manner and appearance, together with much ability, coupled, however, with a fatal instability of character and great moral obliquity. His early life was singularly prosperous. Distinguishing himself successively as a soldier, a lawyer and a politician, he became Vice-President of the United States in 1801, with an excellent prospect before him of the Presidency. His career was, however, ruined by a quarrel with the famous Alexander Hamilton—a quarrel in which Burr was from first to last in the wrong, and which ended in his killing Hamilton in a duel. Although he had to hide for a time, he was ultimately allowed to complete his term as Vice-President, but his career in politics was over. A mad attenpt to make himself President of a Western Republic led to his arrest for treason; though acquitted, he found it necessary to resort to Europe, where he spent some time in great poverty, but, eventually returning to America, he actually, in his old age, acquired a considerable practice as a lawyer. During this period his only child, Theodora Alston, was lost at sea. She was a singularly brilliant woman, who stood by her father in all his troubles and who was largely instrumental in obtaining his acquittal on the charge of treason. Aaron himself survived to the age of seventy-eight, having not long before his death married a well-to-do widow and spent all her money. His career was one which would have well fitted into the St. John connection, where one would expect to find him, just as one would have expected to find Mrs. Hutchinson in the Edwardes connection. The exceptions are there to prove the rule.

Mary, the remaining daughter of Jonathan Edwardes, married into the Dwight family, many branches of which were distinguished in the annals of New England. Mary Dwight herself is described as a woman of great mental ability and force of character, qualities which descended to the full on her eldest son Timothy. After a brilliant scholastic career at Yale, Timothy Dwight was for a time a chaplain in the revolutionary wars, during which period he wrote several patriotic songs, notably *Columbia*. He then for a time conducted a highly successful private school, which included girls as well as boys, the former sharing alike in the most advanced portions of the curriculum. As a pioneer of the higher education of women, Timothy Dwight repaid the gifts he owed to brilliant ancestresses, his mother, his Edwardes grandmother, his Edwardes great-great-grandmother and his Stoddard great-great-grandmother. He owes his fame mainly, however, to his admirable rule at Yale, of which University he was President from 1795–1817.

He inherited his grandfather's extreme interest in theology, and his works on the subject went through innumerable editions, but nothing that he wrote really represented his undoubted genius; it was the energy, variety and charm of his personality that most thoroughly impressed his contemporaries. He possessed a noble presence, a voice of extraordinary strength and richness, and the most varied all-round knowledge, embracing even mechanical crafts. He was familiarly known as "Old Pope Dwight." He was one of those truly remarkable men who have achieved much though hampered by constant ill-health. Seldom free from pain, his indifferent eyesight prevented him from reading to any great extent and from writing himself at all, but his dictation was such that he hardly ever had occasion to alter a syllable.

Timothy Dwight is a fine, in many respects an heroic, figure; possibly his fame somewhat suffered from his rather unromantic name, a disability he shared with his cousin, Aaron Burr. Theodore Dwight, a younger brother of the President of Yale, was at one time a law partner with Burr, with whom, however, he found it impossible to get on. Theodore was later well known as a journalist and won a considerable reputation as a wit. His capacity in this direction was most certainly not inherited from his grandfather, Jonathan Edwardes, perhaps the least humorous man that ever lived. Nathaniel, younger brother of Timothy and Theodore, was a distinguished physician, the first to publicly advocate reasonable treatment of the insane.

Ability in the Dwight family was far from dying out with President Timothy Dwight and his brothers. Four sons of the President achieved some note in various directions, Benjamin as a physician, William as a divine, and Sereno and Henry as writers; but while inheriting much of their father's mental ability, they also inherited his ill-health, against which they hardly made so successful a fight. In a third generation appeared Benjamin, a writer on philology; Theodore, a professor of law, of the very highest rank of his time; and Timothy, who, like his grandfather of the same name, was sometime President of Yale and was a member of the American Committee for the revision of the Bible. He had been preceded both as President of Yale and as member of the Revision Committee by a cousin, Theodore Dwight Woolsey, whose mother Elizabeth was a daughter of the great Timothy Dwight. It will be noted that the Presidency of Yale had become for a time almost hereditary in this family. Theodore Dwight Woolsey was a man of the greatest erudition, a notable Greek scholar and a leading authority on International Law. To his distinction in this last subject his son, Theodore Salisbury Woolsey, has succeeded, holding for thirty-three years the professional

A GLANCE DOWN THE CENTURIES 87

chair in International Law, naturally at Yale. The Professor's son, a younger Theodore Salisbury Woolsey, has won distinction in an entirely fresh subject, that of forestry, on which he is a recognized authority. He was a member of various important commissions on forestry during the late war.

Eleven generations have elapsed from John Winthrop to the younger Theodore Woolsey, and every one of these generations contains at least one individual figuring in Appleton's *Encyclopædia of American Biography*, the standard work on the subject, or, in the last two generations, in the American *Who's Who*. The parallel with the English line treated of in the last chapter is in many ways very close, and, as in that case, the intermarriages were in almost every instance into families of marked distinction.

Whereas, however, the English line was almost exclusively connected with public affairs, the American line, after its early days, was concerned mainly with intellectual pursuits. Leadership is especially characteristic of the one, intellect of the other, and for long continuance of intellectual power, a parallel to this American line can hardly be found elsewhere.

CHAPTER V

THE OLD DOMINION

IN the latter part of the reign of Queen Elizabeth one William Randolph was steward to Edward, Lord Zouche, a man of no little note in his day, who was, among other activities, a member of the Council of the Virginia Company. While thus interesting himself in colonial expansion, little could the peer have foreseen the distinction to be afterwards attained by the descendants of his steward in the colony on whose Council he sat. Randolph may at the time have been more concerned with the horticultural experiments for which his principal had a taste, and probably also with the care of the latter's wine-cellar, a cellar which met, it would appear, with the approbation of Ben Jonson, who wrote:

> Wherever I die, oh here may I lie
>   Along with my good Lord Zouche,
> That when I am dry, to the tap I may hie,
>   And so back again to my couch.

The Zouche family vault adjourned the wine-cellar.

Ben Jonson proved a good friend to Randolph's gifted son Thomas, who successively won scholarships at Westminster and Trinity College, Cambridge. At the University Thomas Randolph became well known as a writer of both Latin and English verse and in addition as an organizer of dramatic entertainments. At Cambridge he wrote his best known work, *The Jealous Lovers*, but in the same year, 1632, he, unfortunately for himself, repaired to London and there ruined his health completely by dissipation, dying three years after at the age of only thirty. His poems were edited after his death by his brother, who himself dabbled in poetry.

Thomas and Robert were the sons of William Randolph by a first wife. By a second he had two more sons, Richard and Henry, sons who, it would seem, inherited more than their half-brothers the business ability probably possessed by their father. First of the family, Henry went to Virginia in 1643, and there left descendants, who never, however, attained any special note. Henry's departure may have been occasioned by Royalist proclivities in the days of failing Royalist fortunes; his brother Richard was undoubtedly a staunch adherent of the King. To all such, Virginia would at this time have been the colony of their choice, and to Virginia in 1674 went Richard's son William, then a young man of twenty-four.

Many descendants of this, the second William Randolph, have played a greater part in history, but none exceeded their ancestor in business acumen; a greater contrast to his scatter-brained uncle, the poet, it would be impossible to imagine. Highly successful alike as a planter and as a shipowner, William was possessed at his death in 1711 of no fewer than seven separate estates, and was without doubt the richest and most influential man in the colony. His interests were by no means exclusively in business; he was one of the founders of William and Mary College, an institution which was to produce many notable alumni, not least among William's own descendants, and he took a special part in efforts to civilize the Indians of the province. All contemporary mention indeed unites in his praise, and his character was quite evidently of the highest.

William Randolph married Mary Isham, the daughter of another Virginian planter, Henry Isham. This Henry may have belonged to a branch of the old Northants family of Isham, and it is at any rate interesting that Thomas Randolph, the poet, was born at Barby in that county, and at Barby some of the Ishams were seated.

The relationships and interconnections of the descendants of William Randolph are so complex that it is not proposed to set them out in detail. Suffice it here to say that all these hereinafter mentioned were descended from William Randolph, and that reference to many of his descendants who achieved no inconsiderable note must perforce be omitted.

The first generation from William, the emigrant, lived in quiet and comparatively uneventful times, and while filling between them almost every leading office in the colony itself, had little chance of extending their fame beyond its bounds. One member of the family in this period, John Randolph, a man of great culture, who collected the finest private library in Virginia, should, however, be mentioned, inasmuch as he received the honour of knighthood, a distinction then hardly ever conferred on a colonial.

With the advent of the Revolutionary War, conditions changed. All the members of the connection took an active part, two only on the side of the mother country; but by far the most eminent at this time were Thomas Jefferson and Harry Lee, the one as a statesman, the other as a soldier.

Jefferson's mother was a Randolph. Her marriage

with Peter Jefferson, a small planter with few pretensions to gentility, must at the time have been regarded by her family as a great *mésalliance*; but, as in the case of many another *mésalliance*, the result was good. It seems probable that Thomas Jefferson derived his abilities from his mother's and his democratic sympathies from his father's side. The Declaration of Independence, of which he was, of course, the author, contained many phrases which cannot have appealed overmuch to his maternal relatives, and they themselves in general, and Jefferson himself in particular, were living refutations of the most famous of these phrases, " All men are born equal."

While Jefferson's fame was far indeed from being limited to the war period, that of Harry Lee was confined to it almost entirely. Deriving his Randolph descent from his paternal grandmother, his relatives on the Lee side were equally distinguished. When only twenty-one he was put in command of three troops of horse, which became known as " Lee's Legion," and he himself as " Light Horse Harry." He and his legion were actively engaged throughout the rest of the war, and his skill and dash were almost equally remarkable. Whether he would, under other circumstances, have proved so great a general as his famous son can never be known; he was only twenty-six when the war came to an end, and he never had an opportunity of showing capacity in the highest forms of leadership. Though later distinguished also by his eloquence in the Virginian Assembly, he never attained any position in the political world, and he remains an interesting example of a man whose fame was wholly confined to a very early period of life.

When the first United States Administration was formed in 1789, Washington selected two members of the Randolph connection for his Cabinet, Jefferson as Secretary of State and Edmund Randolph as Attorney-General. While the former was destined to proceed from strength to strength, and to become one of the five or six greatest Presidents, Edmund Randolph's career was chequered. He had led the Virginia delegation in the famous Convention of 1788 which drew up the United States Constitution, and had been specially complimented for his brilliance on that occasion by Franklin himself. (11) A tolerable success as Attorney-General, Edmund Randolph was later a failure as Secretary of State, in which office he succeeded his cousin. At this period distinct political parties were first being formed in American politics, and Randolph was unable to decide to which to attach himself, and ultimately fell completely between two stools. His undoubtedly brilliant intellectual gifts, though unsuited for politics, were, however, admirably adapted for the Bar, and during his later life he led that of Virginia with pronounced success.

By far the greatest of the connection as a lawyer was, however, John Marshall, whose maternal grandmother was a Randolph. While serving as a young man in the Revolutionary War, Marshall gave early proof of the qualities which were to bring him fame, being frequently chosen by his brother-officers to act as umpire in disputes. He then served under Edmund Randolph in the Convention which drew up the Constitution, and of that Constitution, of which he was to become the great interpreter, he was one of the most conspicuous advocates. A brilliant career at the Bar was interrupted by an appointment as one of the envoys to France at a critical period in 1797, and four years later John Adams appointed him Chief Justice of the United States Supreme Court. This appointment he obtained only just in time, as Jefferson, who succeeded immediately afterwards to the Presidency, would most certainly not have given it, the two relatives being on anything but good terms.

The Chief Justiceship, Marshall filled for no less than thirty-five years, and to his tenure of the office, alike in length and in distinction, that of Mansfield in Great Britain can alone be compared. With the Constitution in its infancy, and with difficult points constantly arising, Marshall had a wonderful opportunity, of which he took the fullest advantage. His decisions show a complete mastery of judicial analysis, and his interpretations of the Constitution, the most important of the multifarious work of the Chief Justice of the Supreme Court, have emphatically stood the test of time.

On one memorable occasion in 1806 the three then greatest members of the Randolph connection were brought into close contact. The occasion was the trial of Aaron Burr, himself, as we have seen, a man of most notable ancestry. Jefferson (then President) was active in the prosecution, Edmund Randolph defended, and Marshall was the presiding judge.

The abilities of the Marshall family were by no means limited to those of John, though none of his numerous younger brothers attained anything like his prominence. One of those brothers, Louis, is said to have been in every way the intellectual equal of the Chief Justice, but his character, like that of more than one of his relatives, was unstable. This Louis had a very exciting experience in early life, being in Paris during the Reign of Terror; his activities led to his condemnation to the guillotine, from which fate he was, however, rescued by his brother James, who was at that time acting as American commercial agent in France.

During the later years of Jefferson and John Marshall a younger relative was winning a less permanent prominence. John Randolph of Roanake belonged to the connection on the side of both his father and his mother; in another direction he was descended from the famous Indian "princess" Pocahontas. Losing his father in early life, John Randolph became heir to a considerable estate. His own personal advantages were very great; strikingly good-looking, he combined keen intelligence with great gifts of eloquence, and when he entered Congress in 1800, the ball seemed to be at his feet. In those days he criticized his cousin Edmund as "a chameleon in the aspen, always trembling, always changing," and the criticism, however true of Edmund, was to prove fatally true of the speaker himself. In politics he was everything by turn and nothing long; his genius proved essentially destructive rather than constructive, and high as he ranked as a critic, he was rightly never given a chance in an administration. Alike in his character and his career, he greatly resembled Bolingbroke, as his relative Jefferson resembled Bolingbroke's relative Cromwell.

John Randolph's mother, Frances Bland, herself of Randolph descent, was described as "a woman of rare intelligence, with an altogether captivating charm of manner and grace of person." After her first husband's death she married St. George Tucker, of a Bermuda family, which has had the rare distinction of producing men of eminence both in England and the United States. During the troubled political period preceding the Civil War the members of the Randolph connection were, on the whole, ardent Southerners, but none was more ardent than Beverley Tucker, son of St. George Tucker and Frances Bland. A professor of law at Virginia University, Beverley Tucker's best claim to remembrance is his novel, *The Partisan Leader*, perhaps the most remarkable piece of prophecy which has ever occurred in literature. Written in 1836, the scene was laid in 1848, in which year the Civil War is supposed to have broken out. If the actual occurrence is antedated by thirteen years, the general course of events is predicted in the most remarkable manner, particularly the difference of opinion which actually arose in Virginia. With his keen Southern sympathies Beverley Tucker concludes on a note of hope for the cause of his State. "Let this fragment go forth," he says, "as the first bulletin of that gallant contest in which Virginia achieved her independence." Dying in 1851, Beverley Tucker lived only to see his original date unfulfilled, but the book was republished by a Virginian firm during the course of the war. In an introduction thereto the author himself is described as "slim and straight, bright hair and eyes, looked as keen as a night-hawk," the actual words of a mountaineer who knew him well.

If any man could have fulfilled Beverley Tucker's wishes, that man was his distant relative, Robert Edward Lee, son of "Light Horse Harry." He, Thomas Jefferson and John Marshall constitute the "Big Three" of the Randolph connection. One of the greatest generals of all history, by some considered the greatest of all, Robert Lee's supreme gifts for leadership can be well accounted for by his ancestry. All his sixteen quarterings are known; nearly all are Virginian, all were families in which leadership qualities were constantly displayed. In this respect he can well be compared with Wellington, a man whose abilities greatly resembled his own, though Lee's was by far the more lovable character. Wellington, whose ancestry can also be traced in great detail, descended in almost every direction from Anglo-Irish families. The position of the Anglo-Irish squirearchy and that of the Virginian planters was remarkably similar; oligarchy occasioned many and grievous faults, but such classes were likely to produce great generals, and they did produce two of the greatest.

Robert Lee is the bright particular star of the Randolph connection in its later days. His two sons, George and William Lee, and his nephew, Fitzhugh Lee, also, however, showed much ability during the war, and none of the three can be said to have owed his position to family influence, as no man that ever lived was less likely to show nepotism than Robert Lee. Fitzhugh Lee lived to serve the United States as a whole in the Spanish American War, his career greatly resembling those in later years of Generals Botha and Smuts.

In recent times no descendant of William Randolph has rivalled the achievements of the giants of the past, but distinction is far from having died out. Up to the middle of the nineteenth century no woman in the connection had achieved any actual note, though many clearly possessed ability, but in the sixties and seventies the Womersley sisters, descended from Sir John Randolph, the only knight of the family, made their mark in literature, Mary, the eldest, as a novelist, Katherine, the second, as a translator, and Ariana, the youngest, as a playwright. Their family was settled in the North, and largely also of Northern descent are some of the most distinguished of the Randolph connection at the present day. Martha Randolph, granddaughter of Thomas Jefferson and doubly descended from the original William Randolph, married into the Coolidge family, to which the present President belongs. Her eldest son, Thomas Coolidge, was for some years American Minister in Paris; his brother Joseph was father of four sons, who appear in the present American *Who's Who*, Randolph as an architect, John as a diplomatist, Archibald as a historian, and Julian as a mathematician. The last two named both hold professorships at Harvard. Some twenty-five years ago Joseph Coolidge and his sons purchased the estate of Tuckatoe, in Virginia, which had belonged to their Randolph ancestors but which had been alienated. On this occasion some five hundred invitations to a housewarming were sent out, and it is believed that an actual majority of the five hundred belonged to the Randolph connection!

Closely associated with the Great War were Surgeon-General Jefferson Kean, who was second in command of the American Army Medical Department therein, and Thomas Nelson Page, who was American Ambassador in Rome during that period. (12) The fame of the latter was somewhat dimmed by that of his namesake, Walter Hines Page, but he was himself a man of considerable ability and great culture, who, before entering diplomacy, had made a name as a writer of novels and stories dealing with the South.

Present-day relatives of Beverley Tucker have been distinguished in the Church; his namesake, another Beverley Tucker, has been for many years Bishop of Southern Virginia; his own son is a missionary Bishop in Japan, while a nephew is a well-known neurologist.

The last named and Surgeon-General Kean alone represent medical note in the great Randolph connection, and since the days of its founder commercial activities have been almost altogether lacking. It is in administration, in military affairs and in the law, in a lesser degree in literature, that the greatest brilliance has been shown. The special gifts have been quite clearly those of leadership, and the characteristics are strongly reminiscent of those of the great English governing families. They exemplify the striking resemblance which conditions in the South long bore to those in the mother country. But of all the many brilliant connections of the mother country in her oligarchical days, none exceeded the brilliance of the Randolphs in " The Old Dominion," the most romantic of all the mother country's daughters.

CHAPTER VI

TWO PHILOSOPHIC STATESMEN

DURING the seventeenth century a family of the name of Lombe was settled in Norwich, where they held a comparatively humble position. Towards the end of that century Henry Lombe followed the calling of a worsted weaver. He begat, among others, two sons, Thomas and John, but died in 1695 when the elder boy, Thomas, was but ten years old. A youth of great energy, Thomas, in the early part of the next century, found his way to London, where he was apprenticed to a silk-weaver and in due course established himself as a merchant. By the year 1715 he had attained to a position of some prosperity and took the resolution to penetrate the secret of silk-throwing, an art then known only in Italy. To that country Thomas accordingly dispatched his brother John, who was distinguished as a good draughtsman and an excellent mechanic. John succeeded in discovering the secret, it is said, by bribing workmen, but this was probably too dangerous, and it is more likely that he acquired the knowledge by working as an employee himself. Be this as it may, it is certain that John returned to England with two expert Italians whom he had persuaded to come with him. Thomas took out a patent, and the brothers established a mill in Derby. This was from the first successful, but John did not live to enjoy its fruits. He died in 1722, poisoned, it is said, by a woman sent over for this purpose by the Italian manufacturers, whose trade he was displacing. No arrest appears, however, to have been made, and a mystery hangs over John's death, but the tradition that he met with foul play long lingered in Derby.

Thomas survived and greatly flourished. His patent expired in 1732 and he was unable to obtain its renewal, but was granted by Parliament a compensation of £14,000, and after serving the office of Sheriff of London, died in 1739, leaving £120,000, a very large fortune for those days. His two daughters were, of course, great heiresses, and ten years later the younger, Mary, granddaughter of the worsted weaver, was married to James Maitland, seventh Earl of Lauderdale, in the Scottish peerage. This Earl was not himself a man of any mark, but the Maitland family had in earlier days played a great part in Scottish history, notably Sir William Maitland of Lethington, in the time of Queen Mary, and James, Duke of Lauderdale, in the time of Charles II.

The Lombe marriage brought fresh vigour into the stock, notably in the case of one of Mary Lombe's younger sons, Thomas Maitland, who quite obviously inherited the determined character of his maternal grandfather, though he was destined to exercise it in a very different sphere. Entering the army, he as a young officer greatly distinguished himself in the Mysore campaign in India in 1783, and in later years showed vigour in the Governorships of Ceylon and Malta. His chief title to fame, however, rests on his High Commissionership of the Ionian Islands, to which he was appointed immediately after the British occupation in 1814. To him was assigned the duty of drawing up the form of government, and he succeeded in making his office practically despotic, well suited to the temperament of one who had already acquired the nickname of "King Tom." Charles Napier, who served under him, and whose character in some respects resembled his own, described him as "a rough old despot with talent but not of a first-rate order." He had sufficient talent at any rate to keep the volatile Greeks in order. Faced at first with great opposition, in the end, as he himself told the Colonial Secretary, "it was a race among his foremost opponents as to who should run fastest into his arms." It was well said of him that, "if he sometimes handled the inhabitants roughly himself, he took care that no one else should presume to treat them ill." "King Tom" was, in fact, a type of those who make Britons respected, if not loved, and the lack in his case of sixteen aristocratic quarterings most certainly did not make his own views the less aristocratic.

Those views were not, in the first instance at any rate, shared by his elder brother, the eighth Earl of Lauderdale, who might perhaps under other circumstances have been, like his grandfather, a successful man of business. The Earl, at least, showed a distinct aptitude for political economy, but in effect he passed his life as a rather impracticable politician. During the period of the French Revolution he adopted in an extreme degree the Radical side, appearing on one occasion in the House of Lords "in the rough costume of Jacobitism." This was too much for his brother Scottish peers, who removed him from his position as one of their representatives. Later in life, however, Lauderdale, like so many of his contemporaries, veered completely round to Toryism, and at one time nearly obtained the Viceroyalty of India, but the Directors, with his earlier career in mind, successfully vetoed his appointment. His daughter Eleanor married James Balfour, the younger son of an old but hitherto undistinguished Scottish family, the Balfours of Balbirnie. James Balfour made a fortune and purchased the estate of Whittingehame, and his son James married into a family even more historic than the Maitlands.

The immediate descent of his wife, Lady Blanche Cecil, daughter of the second Marquis of Salisbury, bore a curious resemblance to that of her husband's Maitland grandfather, for her mother, Frances Gascoigne, came of a family as strictly commercial as the Lombes. The founder of its fortunes, Crisp Gascoigne, started in business as a brewer, improved his position by marriage with the daughter of a successful physician, John Bamber, and rose to be Lord Mayor of London in 1752, being the first to occupy the present Mansion House. A singularly worthy first occupant he seems to have been, for, making due allowance for the flattery of such addresses, the terms in which he was thanked by the Court of Common Council at the end of his year of office mark him out as an excellent magistrate. Special reference was made to "his generous protection of the distressed and his remarkable humanity," qualities none too common among eighteenth-century officials. This benevolence of character was inherited by his grandson, Isaac Gascoigne, who distinguished himself in Parliament by his efforts to obtain higher pay for captains and subalterns and by his determined opposition to attempts to cut down compassionate allowances to the families of deceased officers. This Isaac was uncle of Lady Salisbury, who was thus great-grand-daughter of Sir Crisp.

Her immediate predecessor at Hatfield, the first Marchioness of Salisbury, came of stock widely different from the Gascoignes, but also presenting features of considerable interest.

One John Jeffreys, a small Welsh landed proprietor in the middle of the seventeenth century, was the grandfather of two lawyers, who achieved considerable celebrity and more infamy at the end of that century. John, Lord Jeffreys, was the most detestable character who ever achieved the Lord Chancellorship, but his abilities were, without doubt, considerable. His cousin, Sir John Trevor, was neither so detestable nor so able, but while an excellent lawyer, whose decrees in private cases were sagacious and equitable, as a politician he was venal and corrupt and was eventually expelled from the Speakership for the taking of bribes. (13) Very penurious, he was likewise addicted to his bottle, both traits being illustrated by the following anecdote. On one occasion he was enjoying his wine quietly by himself, when his cousin, Roderic Lloyd, was announced by a side door. "You rascal!" said Trevor to his servant, "you have brought my cousin, the Protonothary of North Wales, to see me by a side door. Take him down instantly and bring him up by the front stairs." While this was being done, the wine disappeared and none was offered to the Protonothary.

It is singular that from such a man as Trevor descended not only the later Cecils, but also the great Wellesley family; but while the moral obliquity of the Trevor-Jeffreys connection fortunately faded away, the best part of their ability survived.

Trevor's only child married Michael Hill; the daughter of one of her sons was mother of the great

Duke of Wellington and his hardly less distinguished brother, Lord Wellesley; the grand-daughter of another was the first Marchioness of Salisbury. The latter lady's father, Wills Hill, successively Earl of Hillsborough and Marquis of Downshire, played some part as a politician in the early part of the eighteenth century. At the outset of his career he made a favourable impression on so critical an observer as Horace Walpole, who, in respect of his moving the address in the House of Commons, described him "as a young man of great honour and merit, scrupulous in weighing his reasons and excellent in setting them off by solemnity of voice and manner." Though he rose to high office, Hillsborough did not, however, bear out this early promise. As President of the Board of Trade at the time of the American troubles, he showed little judgment, being one of those who most actively supported the obnoxious taxation, and all through the subsequent war his opinions were reactionary to the last degree. A man of fine presence, he was more of a courtier than a statesman, and from him his daughter, Lady Salisbury, inherited charm and grace to a striking degree, but the sound judgment of her grandson, the great Lord Salisbury, was quite evidently derived from his Gascoigne ancestry.

So strikingly varied were the qualities of the ancestors of Lord Balfour, the first of our philosophic statesmen. Let us now turn to the ancestors of the second.

Among the many versatile characters of the seventeenth century, Gilbert Burnet, bishop, politician and historian, stands in the first rank. Playing himself a leading part in the stormy politics of the reigns of Charles II, James II and William III, the Bishop of Salisbury has left us in his *History of his Own Times* a work of the utmost value, which, with little merit of literary style, is distinguished by philosophic insight and, on the whole, by impartiality. A Scotchman by descent on both sides, Burnet came of notable legal stock on that of his mother. Her grandfather, Sir Thomas Craig, was the most learned lawyer of his time; her brother, Archibald Johnston, Lord Warriston, immortalized by Scott in *The Tales of a Grandfather*, played a very prominent part under the Commonwealth. Others of Mrs. Burnet's relatives achieved note, nor was Gilbert her only distinguished son. His younger brother, Sir Thomas Burnet, was a physician of European eminence, and it was through him that the distinction of this great Scottish connection was destined to be kept up, though for some generations, however, it remained in abeyance. Thomas Burnet's daughter Helen married Ralph Dundas of Manour, and her grand-daughter, Mary Dundas, married George Abercromby. The marked ability shown by her sons was in all probability derived from their ancestors on the Burnet side.

Of these sons, the greatest was Sir Ralph Abercromby, the most notable general of the earlier period of the French Revolutionary Wars, but his brother James, also a military man, was Commander-in-Chief in India, and another brother, Alexander, was a Scotch Lord of Session. Nor did distinction die out in the next generation of the Abercrombys. John, son of Sir Ralph, who acted as his father's military secretary, ranks as one of our Empire builders in virtue of his conquest of Mauritius, and James, another son of Sir Ralph, became Speaker of the House of Commons and ultimately Lord Dunfermline. High moral worth, combined with great sweetness of disposition and charm of manner, were distinguishing characteristics of the Abercromby family, and these qualities descended to Mary Joass, whose mother was a daughter of George Abercromby and Mary Dundas of Manour. This Mary Joass in 1796, at a time when her uncles were at the zeniths of their careers, became the wife of a man of singularly striking characteristics, James Haldane.

Although the wife was the niece of a great general and the husband was the nephew of a great admiral (his mother being sister of the celebrated Admiral Duncan, the victor of Camperdown), Mr. and Mrs. James Haldane were destined to lead a career singularly removed from either naval or military activities. Sprung from an old Scotch family, which, however, like the Balfours of Balbirnie, had hitherto achieved but little note, James Haldane and his elder brother, Robert, were early left orphans and were brought up by their Duncan grandmother. Under the auspices of their uncle, both brothers entered the navy, but neither stayed long in the service. Robert first, and under his influence James, adopted extreme religious views; the elder brother organized, the younger preached. The former ultimately sold his estate at Airthrie, and with the purchase-money set up a Congregational church in Edinburgh, of which James became pastor, in which position he continued for the remainder of his life, pouring forth innumerable controversial writings. The political as well as the religious views of both brothers were very democratic, and they were far from popular with their own class, but the strength of their characters and their high moral courage is sufficiently evident.

James, son of James Haldane and Mary Joass, again,

in his turn, married into a family of distinguished antecedents.

One William Scott, a coal-factor in Newcastle, in the middle of the eighteenth century, was a successful man of business, who, however, owes his niche in history entirely to the fact that he was father of two great lawyers, Lord Eldon and Lord Stowell. Eldon was the more successful of the brothers, but Stowell was probably the greater, certainly he was the more intellectual man. As Admiralty Judge during the Napoleonic wars, his decisions practically remade maritime law and were the admiration of the legal world. A wit and a scholar, Stowell's manners were courteous and his conviviality great; he was, however, very penurious, and in some respects his character resembled that of Sir John Trevor. His personal appearance was less striking than that of Eldon, whose dignity was unsurpassed and whose manners, like those of his brother, were full of charm. The mantle of these great lawyers might well have fallen on their nephew, Richard Burdon, the son of their sister Jane and Sir Thomas Burdon. Richard's scholastic career was extraordinarily distinguished. At Oxford he in 1811 won the Newdigate, in 1812 took a first class, and in 1814 carried off the English Essay Prize. His achievements were commemorated in the following doggerel lines:

> In eighteen hundred and eleven
>   I gained the Newdigate.
> In eighteen twelve a first class man
>   As chroniclers relate.
> In thirteen next at Oriel's prime
>   A fellow I was found,
> And in fourteen for English prose
>   My brow was laurel bound.

Called to the Bar, Richard Burdon was appointed by his uncle Eldon, Secretary of Presentations, but so disgusted was he by the manner in which clerical appointments were made that he abandoned alike the law and the Church of England and, retiring into the country, adopted a life of isolation. He was assisted, no doubt, in this course by the fortune acquired with his wife, daughter of a certain Sir James Sanderson. Sir James, the son of a grocer at York, made this fortune in the hop trade in London, later became a banker, and was Lord Mayor in 1792. Afterwards entering Parliament, the success of his political was by no means equal to that of his commercial career; an ally of Pitt's, the latter allowed him to second the Address, but his speech was " so full of bad grammar and bold assertions that it created general laughter." His second wife, the mother of Mrs. Burdon, was herself the daughter of a Lord Mayor, Sir Thomas Skinner, who, curiously enough, filled the civic chair at a later date than his son-in-law. Lady Sanderson, after Sir James's death, came under the influence of and ultimately married a popular preacher of the name of Samuel Huntington, who was probably the original of Thackeray's Charles Honeyman in *The Newcomes.*

Mr. and Mrs. Richard Burdon adopted the additional surname of Sanderson. Their son John was intended for the Bar, but, like his father, did not persevere in that course. Unlike his father he, however, by no means adopted a life of seclusion, but became one of the best-known scientists of his day, being specially distinguished in physiology. He inherited the fine presence of his great-uncle, Lord Eldon, and the charm of manner possessed by both Lord Eldon and Lord Stowell.

It was Sir John Burdon-Sanderson's sister Mary who became the wife of the second James Haldane, and whose recent death as a centenarian attracted universal attention. She was the mother of the second of our philosophic statesmen, Lord Haldane.

Lord Balfour and Lord Haldane are the two of our elder statesmen who pre-eminently show powers of intellect combined with striking versatility and catholicity of tastes. Though the most notable members of their respective family groups, they are far from being alone in distinction, and the Balfour and Haldane families of the present day exhibit striking and, on the whole, remarkably similar attainments. As will have been seen by the foregoing pages, there is also a remarkable similarity in their ancestries, distinguished as these were in almost every direction. In some one or other of their groups of relatives almost every field of human endeavour has been represented. The Prime Minister, Lord Balfour's uncle, the Prime Minister, Lord Salisbury, is balanced by the Lord Chancellor, Lord Haldane's great-grand-uncle, the Lord Chancellor, Lord Eldon. Remote legal connections on the one side are the Jeffreys-Trevor, on the other the Craig-Johnston. Rather less remote are the military connections, the Wellesleys and Sir Thomas Maitland in the one case, the Abercrombys in the other. The Balfours have indeed no naval relative as distinguished as Admiral Duncan, though more than one of the Maitlands attained flag rank.

Religious interests figure in both connections, but the strong High Church views of the Cecils are in contrast with the strong Low Church views of the bygone Haldanes.

It is interesting to note the descents from successful commercial men, the Haldanes numbering among their ancestors two Lord Mayors, Sanderson and Skinner, the Balfours one Lord Mayor, Crisp Gascoigne, and one Sheriff of London, Thomas Lombe.

The strong scientific bent shown at the present time by both families does not directly appear to any extent among their ancestry, direct or collateral, with the important exception of Sir John Burdon-Sanderson, but it should be remembered that the late Lord Salisbury showed considerable aptitude in the natural sciences. The opportunities, however, for the pursuit of pure science were till recently very limited, and men of the type of Sir Thomas Lombe might well, under other circumstances, have made a reputation in this field. The truth of the matter would appear to be that a scientist is most likely to be produced by a good general heredity with varied ability among connections, and such heredity with such varied ability most clearly exists in the families, the leading representatives of which are the two philosophic statesmen, Lord Balfour and Lord Haldane.

CHAPTER VII

FIVE GREAT GOSSIPS

IN the year 1621 Paulina Pepys, daughter of John Pepys, yeoman of Cottenham, in Cambridge, married Sidney Montagu. It was a remarkably brilliant marriage for Paulina, as the Montagu family, though their greatest distinction was yet to come, already held a very good position. Sidney Montagu's grandfather, Sir Edward Montagu, had been Chief Justice of the Common Pleas, and the grandson no doubt derived his first name from the connection of his mother, Elizabeth Harrington, with the great Sidney family.

The son of Sidney Montagu and Paulina Pepys was that Edward Montagu, first Earl of Sandwich, so well known to all readers of his cousin's diary. Sandwich played a great part in naval affairs both under the Commonwealth and in the reign of Charles II, but his fame in history is perhaps rather greater than his abilities warranted. He was ancestor of two celebrated statesmen, John, fourth Earl of Sandwich, and John Carteret, Earl Granville. Two of his grandsons, not themselves men of any mark, married two notable women, Lady Mary Pierrepont and Elizabeth Robinson, the former so well known as Lady Mary Wortley Montagu, and the latter as Mrs. Montagu, the first " blue stocking."

There was thus a connection, though not a relationship, between two eminent gossips, Lady Mary and Samuel Pepys. The latter, of whose connections we now treat, was great-grandson of the yeoman of Cottenham. His immediate ancestry was not only undistinguished, but would appear to have been falling rather than rising in the social scale, till Samuel was taken up by his cousin, Lord Sandwich, who most emphatically made his career. It is difficult, however, to discern in Pepys's actual ancestry the source of his undoubted abilities alike as an administrator and as a writer, and in his case the interest lies chiefly in tracing a continuance of ability in his collateral descendants. It may be surmised, however, that Paulina Pepys must have possessed qualities above the average to have attracted the well-connected Sidney Montagu, and the Pepys distinction may perhaps be considered to have commenced with her.

Her great-niece, Samuel's sister, was also named Paulina, no doubt after the great lady of the family. The younger Paulina appears several times under the name of "Pall" in her brother's *Diary*, but he does not seem to have had much opinion of her. At one time she lived with Samuel and his wife, but ultimately, "troubled at how proud and idle Pall is grown, I am resolved not to keep her," Pepys remarks. Just previously "Pall" was "left to do all the work till another mayde comes," so probably the fault was by no means all on one side. Paulina then resided with her parents, and we find Samuel on his visits presenting her first with ten shillings and then with twenty shillings, but all the time complaining of her being "so cruel a hypocrite that she can cry when she pleases." Her brother was much exercised as to her marriage; he is at last almost in despair, "she grows so old and ugly." Finally, however, a suitable *parti* appeared in the person of one John Jackson, who had inherited an estate at Brampton, in Hunts, from Louis Philipps, a friend of Samuel's. The latter recounts his first meeting with Jackson, "a plain young man, handsome enough for Pall, one of no education or discourse, but of few words." Later he says: "My mind pretty well satisfied with this plain young fellow for my sister, though I shall have no pleasing content in him, as if he had been a man of reading or parts. He have few words, but I like him none the worse for it."

Jackson was probably not allowed much leeway while the voluble Pepys was holding forth, and very possibly neither he nor his wife were such fools as we are led to suppose. But Samuel would certainly have been immensely astonished if he could have foreseen the ultimate distinction of the descendants of the pair whom he rated so lightly. Such distinction certainly did not speedily arise. Pepys, childless himself, thought of making a Jackson his heir. He fixed first on Samuel, Paulina's elder son and no doubt his own godson. He was, however, disinherited, his uncle remarking: "Samuel Jackson has thought fit to dispose of himself in marriage against my positive advice and injunction, and to his own irreparable prejudice and dishonour. I do think myself obliged to express the resentment due to such an act of disrespect and imprudence."

John, the younger brother of the erring Samuel, stepped into his place, and was his uncle's companion in his later life. This John Jackson, though he made no particular mark, was a man of some parts; letters from him to his uncle, which are extant, show a certain descriptive power. He inherited Pepys's papers, including the cipher diary, and it was on his death that these passed, under Pepys's will, to Magdalene College, Cambridge, where the *Diary* was ultimately deciphered.

John Jackson's daughter and heiress, Frances, married John Cockerell, of Bishop's Hall, in Somerset, and in the Cockerell family distinction was again to arise. Their eldest son, Sir Charles, was maternal grandfather of that veteran sportsman, the present Lord Coventry, whose tastes and career would undoubtedly have appealed greatly to Samuel Pepys.

Another son of John Cockerell and Frances Jackson was christened Samuel Pepys, to the pious memory merely of a benefactor, it may be presumed, for in the eighteenth century the *Diary* was still unknown, and its author was remembered, if remembered at all, only as a painstaking Admiralty official. This Samuel Pepys Cockerell achieved some note as an architect towards the end of the eighteenth century, and was the first descendant of Paulina Jackson to attain biographical mention. He was, however, altogether surpassed by his son, Charles Robert Cockerell, who followed the same profession. Starting his career as assistant to Smirke in the rebuilding of Covent Garden Theatre after the great fire in 1809, Charles, during the following years, travelled in Greece, was instrumental in obtaining certain important bas-reliefs for the British Museum, and made a great effort to obtain also the famous Ægina marbles, which, however, went to Germany. Quite undeterred by hardship, his zeal and his curiosity were boundless, and in the latter quality he much resembled the great Samuel. After his return to England, Cockerell was made surveyor to St. Paul's, and rose to the undoubted headship of his profession. Though primarily an architect, he was, in addition, an artist, possessing a wide knowledge of art in all its branches, while his own drawings of the human figure were quite unrivalled. Charles Robert Cockerell married Anna, daughter of John Rennie, the engineer of Waterloo Bridge; their son, Frederick Pepys Cockerell, was the third architect in succession in the family. Less brilliant than his father, though probably surpassing his grandfather, he had a considerable practice, but died at a comparatively early age. He built the present Freemasons' Hall, and his design for the Albert Memorial was accepted by the judges of the competition. Queen Victoria, however, preferred that of Sir Gilbert Scott, so the Memorial as it now stands cannot be laid to the charge of Frederick Cockerell.

On the distaff side other descendants of Samuel Pepys Cockerell have achieved note. His second son, Richard Howe Cockerell, was father of Theresa, Countess of Shrewsbury, and grandmother of Theresa, Marchioness of Londonderry, ladies of determined character very well known in the social world of their day, who also would have greatly appealed to Samuel Pepys. Frances, a daughter of Samuel Pepys Cockerell, married Edward Goodenough, Dean of Wells and previously Headmaster of Westminster, son of Samuel Goodenough, Bishop of Carlisle, scholar and botanist, a founder of and first treasurer of the Linnean Society.

James Graham Goodenough, son of Edward Goodenough and Frances Cockerell, had therefore a most brilliant heredity on both sides. First of the descendants of Paulina Jackson to enter the service with which her brother the diarist was so intimately connected, his comparatively short career in the navy was eventful and brilliant. After serving with distinction in the Baltic during the Crimean War and in the attack on the Taku forts in China, James Goodenough was specially selected to observe the naval operations in the American Civil War, and as a volunteer, while on leave, served in France in 1870 on the French Peasants' Relief Fund. Finally appointed Commodore on the Australian station, he in 1875 was treacherously wounded by natives on one of the Pacific islands, and died soon after. A man of the most varied accomplishments, a brilliant linguist and an excellent swordsman, the name of James Graham Goodenough, had opportunity been given, would have ranked among the very highest in naval annals.

His son, the present Admiral Sir William Goodenough, served with distinction in the Great War, while his nephew, Mr. Frederick Goodenough, has adopted an entirely fresh line. Chairman of Barclay's Bank, Mr. Goodenough is one of the greatest financial authorities of the present day.

One other family remains for mention. Anne, another daughter of Samuel Pepys Cockerell, married Richard Pollen. Their son, John Hungerford Pollen, had a career of great versatility. After taking orders in the Established Church, he resigned and became a Roman Catholic, devoting himself partly to literature but more to art in many forms, particularly stained-glass windows and fresco decoration. A most trenchant critic, John Hungerford Pollen was a pioneer of reform, in especial in domestic furniture. He was for many years Professor of Art in the Catholic University, Dublin, and also art critic to the *Tablet*. In addition he was an ardent sportsman and volunteer. Two of his sons are well known as writers, Mr. Arthur Pollen on naval matters, the Rev. John Pollen, S.J., on English Catholic history.

It will be seen that great ability and great versatility have been characteristics of the descendants of Charles Cockerell and Frances Jackson, great-niece of the diarist. While it is impossible to say how far this ability and versatility is traceable back to the Pepys stock, the fact remains that Samuel himself was eminently able and versatile, and no man that has ever lived would have taken more interest in all the varied activities of the descendants of that sister whom he apparently esteemed so little.

IN a previous chapter an account has been given of a remarkable line of descendants emanating from Henry VII's unfortunate Minister, Edmund Dudley. The latter's equally unfortunate colleague, Richard Empson, was also the progenitor of descendants of note. The son of a sieve-maker at Towcester, a man, however, of means and local influence, Empson rose to distinction at the Bar, was closely associated with Dudley as financial agent for King Henry, and with equal injustice met the same fate on the same day. Empson's daughter Jane married a Sir William Pierrepont, who obtained at the Reformation a considerable estate in Nottinghamshire. Their son, Sir George Pierrepont, was father of Anne, who became the wife of Francis Beaumont, a Judge of the Common Pleas, and the mother of Sir John Beaumont, who achieved some reputation as a minor poet, and of the much better known Francis Beaumont, the famous collaborator with John Fletcher, Beaumont and Fletcher in their time ranking as dramatists second only to Shakespeare, of the two, Beaumont being perhaps the greater. One the son of a judge, the other of a bishop, hereditary ability comes out clearly in both, though neither was in any way fitted for administrative work. Both had several other near relatives of distinction on the paternal side, but in the case of Fletcher, unlike that of Beaumont, no special note is traceable on the side of the mother.

Sir Henry Pierrepont, Francis Beaumont's maternal uncle, married Anne Cavendish, the daughter of that very remarkable woman known as "Bess of Hardwick." Elizabeth Hardwick was first married, when only fourteen, to Robert Barlow, who died shortly after, leaving her his estates. She next married William Cavendish, also a man of wealth, who at her instigation sold his southern estates to purchase others in her own county of Derbyshire, thereby laying the foundation of the leading position in that county which the Cavendish family have held to the present day. William also died comparatively early. His widow next wedded Sir William St. Loe, who, dying in his turn, devised to her his great Gloucester property, to the intense and justifiable indignation of his kinsfolk. Finally she became Countess of Shrewsbury. Over her earlier husbands she had domineered; she did not find it so easy, perhaps, to manage the Earl. Dissensions soon sprang up between them, and in 1586 Shrewsbury wrote to her as follows: " There is no creature more happy or more fortunate than you have been, for where you were defamed and to the world a bye-word when you were St. Loe's widow, I covered these imperfections by my marriage to you." The allusion, no doubt, is to her retention of the St. Loe estates. She survived this marriage also and continued to go her own way, ruling her children and her stepchildren with a rod of iron, and engrossed in building, for which she had a passion. This passion is said to have been occasioned by a prophecy that she should not die "while building," and she did actually meet her death in a hard frost, when work could not be carried out. To her is due the erection of Chatsworth and Hardwick Hall. Continually flattered, but seldom deceived, she is described by Lodge as "proud, furious, selfish and unfeeling." The marriage of her daughter Anne to so considerable a neighbouring landowner as Sir Henry Pierrepont no doubt met with her approval; it certainly would not have taken place without it.

Her love of acquisition descended on her grandson, Robert Pierrepont, created Earl of Kingston, who for many years spent annually a thousand pounds in the purchase of land. On the advent of the Civil War, Kingston, however, showed none of the determination which would most certainly have been exhibited by his grandmother. He endeavoured to remain neutral, "divided his sons between both parties and concealed himself," but eventually joining the side of the King, he was taken prisoner and accidentally killed by his own side, who fired upon the convoy that was taking him to Hull. (14) Like that of his grandmother, his death apparently fulfilled a prophecy. When the war broke out he is said to have remarked: "When I take arms for the King against the Parliament or the Parliament against the King, let a common bullet divide me between them." And so it actually fell out.

His Royalist elder son was a studious person who "took all knowledge for his province," but who seems in character to have been rather absurd. The younger son William, who joined the Parliament side, was of a very different type, and was generally known as "Wise William." An influential statesman under the Commonwealth, he was always on the side of moderation, and so escaped penal effects after the Restoration.

"Wise William," the great grandson of Bess of Hardwick, and the first cousin once removed of Francis Beaumont, was destined to be the great-grandfather of two of the most celebrated writers of the eighteenth century, Lord Chesterfield and Lady Mary Wortley Montagu. The latter derived her descent in the direct male, the former in the direct female line. His mother was the daughter of George Savile, Marquis of Halifax, the statesman immortalized by Macaulay, by his second wife, Gertrude Pierrepont, daughter of "Wise William." The latter's son, Robert Pierrepont, Lady Mary's grandfather, married Elizabeth Evelyn. This lady was a cousin of the famous diarist, John Evelyn, their common ancestor being a George Evelyn, who in 1565 obtained a monopoly for the manufacture of gunpowder. His mills were the first to make this compound in England; all powder had previously been imported from Flanders. George Evelyn made a large fortune, and most of his Evelyn descendants were during the seventeenth century men of substance and influence. In John Evelyn's *Diary* there are one or two references to his cousin, Mrs. Robert Pierrepont. In 1649, before her marriage, he visited her father's house, and notes: "*Mem.* the prodigious memory of Sir John of Wilts' daughter."

And nearly fifty years later, in 1693, he relates: "My cousin Pierrepont died, a most prudent and excellent lady." In the judgment of John Evelyn, and there could have been no better judge, Lady Mary's grandmother was a woman far above the ordinary.

Her son, Evelyn Pierrepont, was perhaps hardly worthy of her, though in some ways a man of note. Very fortunate, he succeeded through many unexpected deaths to the Earldom of Kingston, and was ultimately created a Duke. Described by Macky as "a very fine gentleman, of good sense, well bred, and a lover of the ladies," the first Duke of Kingston was without doubt the most prominent leader in the social world of his day, but farther than that he did not go. He married Lady Mary Fielding, whose great-grandmother, Susan, Countess of Denbigh, was sister of George Villiers, Duke of Buckingham, and who belonged therefore to the great Villiers connection. One of the daughters of Evelyn, Duke of Kingston, and Lady Mary Fielding was Lady Mary Pierrepont, universally known under her married name of Lady Mary Wortley Montagu, and the second of the *Five Great Gossips*. Lady Mary's literary connections are perhaps unique. As we have seen, she was related on her father's side to Francis Beaumont, the dramatist, to Lord Chesterfield, the letter-writer, and to John Evelyn, the diarist; and on her mother's side she was related to Henry Fielding, the prince of eighteenth-century novelists, who was her second cousin, and more distantly to her almost exact contemporary, John, Lord Hervey, the memoir-writer, who, like herself, was descended from Sir George Villiers, the father of James I's favourite. In later years Charles Greville, the nineteenth-century diarist, could also claim relationship with Lady Mary. Of this more anon.

Lady Mary's own descendants, through her daughter, Lady Bute, were by no means wholly undistinguished, notably Lady Louisa Stuart, Lady Bute's daughter, whose letters show much of her grandmother's sprightliness. But while the distinction in the case of Samuel Pepys lay mainly in the future, in the case of Lady Mary Wortley Montagu it lay mainly in the past.

WILLIAM COPE, of Hanwell, in Oxfordshire, cofferer to King Henry VII, married for his second wife Joan, daughter of John Spencer, of a family destined in later days to play a great part in English history. William and Joan Cope had two sons, Anthony and John. Anthony, after education at Oxford, travelled extensively on the Continent, visiting the leading universities and becoming acquainted with most of the learned men of his time, including the great Erasmus. A true son, alike of the Renaissance and of the Reformation, Anthony Cope dabbled in various forms of literature, translated portions of Livy, and wrote *Godly Meditations on twenty select Psalms, necessary for them that desire to have the dark side of the prophet declared. Also for those that delight in the contemplation of the spiritual meaning of them.*

In later life Chamberlain to Queen Catherine Parr, Anthony, shortly before his death in 1551, continued his essays in religious literature by a commentary on the first two Gospels, which he dedicated to King Edward VI. His grandson, Sir Walter Cope, a member of the Elizabethan Society of Antiquaries, was a successful courtier who acquired property in Kensington, where he built Kensington House, re-christened Holland House by his son-in-law, Henry Rich, Earl of Holland, to whom it was devised, and destined in much later times to be so great a centre for men of letters. Also descended from Sir Anthony Cope, through a daughter, was the Sir Kenelm Digby of the time of Charles I, author, philosopher, scientific investigator, diplomatist, naval commander and husband of the greatest beauty of the time, a man of the utmost versatility, who might have left a greater name had his energies been more concentrated, like those of some of his kinsfolk to be hereafter referred to.

To return now to Sir John Cope, younger brother of Sir Anthony, he took to wife Bridget, daughter of Edward Raleigh (15) by Margaret, daughter of Sir Ralph Verney, Lord Mayor of London in the time of King Edward IV. Sir John Cope, like his brother, appears to have been a friend of Erasmus, who was godfather to his son, Erasmus Cope, who died young. The name was not, however, allowed to die out, as it was later bestowed on Erasmus Cope's nephew, Erasmus Dryden, son of his sister, Elizabeth Cope, and John Dryden, of Canons Ashby, in Northamptonshire, and later on a second Erasmus Dryden, son of the first. This second Erasmus Dryden was the father of the famous poet.

In addition to his descent from the Copes, John Dryden may have derived ability from the side of his mother, Maria Pickering. Her first cousin, Sir Gilbert Pickering, was a man of note under the Commonwealth, successively a Presbyterian, an Independent, a

Brownist and an Anabaptist, but always a zealous Puritan. He was one of the King's judges, but did not sign his death-warrant, and was himself saved from death at the Restoration by the good offices of his brother-in-law, Edward Montagu, Earl of Sandwich, whose sister was Gilbert Pickering's second wife, and it is interesting to note that his first wife was also a relative of Samuel Pepys. Pickering was for a time Chamberlain to Cromwell, and in that capacity employed his cousin, young John Dryden, as his secretary.

Many years later, in 1691, Dryden, then at the height of his fame, cast a glance at some poetical efforts of a young kinsman which appeared in the *Athenian Mercury*. "Cousin Swift, you will never make a poet," was the verdict of the Laureate, and it was not untrue, but little could the great John have then foreseen that the fame of his obscure relative was ultimately even to exceed his own. Jonathan Swift's poverty and dependent position in early life have tended to obscure the distinction of his descent in, at any rate, one direction. Nicholas Dryden, a younger son of the first John Dryden and Elizabeth Cope, was the father of a large family, one of whom, Elizabeth, married Thomas Swift, rector of Goodrich, near Ross, an ardent Royalist in the Civil Wars, in which he lost nearly all his means, thus having little or nothing to leave to his younger son, Jonathan, the father of the great satirist. Neither on the side of his mother nor on that of his paternal grandfather can any notable relatives of Swift be traced, and there can be little doubt that it was the Dryden, or more probably still the Cope, descent which was mainly responsible for his intellectual gifts.

John Dryden and Jonathan Swift alone conferred

distinction on their surnames, though some slight achievements lie to the credit of the poet's son, a younger John Dryden, who wrote a play and published some translations. Some little note also was attained by the satirist's cousin, Deane Swift, who published a life of his relative, of, however, but slight merit. This Deane Swift's son, Theophilus Swift, was the last of the family to receive biographical mention, and he was chiefly distinguished for his wild eccentricities.

For real distinction in the connection in the later eighteenth century we must search elsewhere. Elizabeth, daughter of the first Sir Erasmus Dryden, and aunt therefore of the poet, married Sir Richard Philipps, of Picton, in Pembroke, who was probably descended from King Henry VIII, as his mother was a daughter of Sir John Perrott, generally considered to have been an illegitimate son of that monarch. Richard Philipps and Elizabeth Dryden called their son Erasmus, after his mother's kinsfolk. This Erasmus Philipps married Catherine Darcy, maternal grand-daughter of the first Earl of Chesterfield, by which a relationship was brought about between her descendants and the fourth Earl, the author of the *Letters*. Elizabeth, daughter of Erasmus Philipps and Catherine Darcy, married John Shorter, son of a Lord Mayor of London, who met his death in a very singular manner while holding that office. He was riding to open Bartholomew Fair, a duty then performed by Lord Mayors, and on his way, at Newgate, according to custom, he was offered a drink from a large and glittering tankard, which caused his horse to shy, throwing the unfortunate Lord Mayor, who died of his injuries. His business of a Baltic timber-merchant was continued by his son, John

Shorter, the husband of Elizabeth Philipps, who was able to give his daughter Catherine a dowry of £20,000 on the occasion of her marriage to a young Norfolk squire, Robert Walpole, then quite unknown to fame. Catherine has been described as of exquisite beauty and distinguished manners, but she was wildly extravagant and of loose morals. The paternity of Horace, her most famous son, is a matter of doubt; Carr, Lord Hervey, has been assigned as his father, and undoubtedly he resembled the Herveys far more than the Walpoles. In either case his paternal relationship would be distinguished, though in very different directions, but the line of descent of Horace Walpole, the third of the *Five Great Gossips*, is here traced through his mother and is unaffected by the doubts as to his paternity. It was on his mother's side that Horace Walpole was related to Henry Seymour Conway, the son of Catherine Shorter's sister Charlotte. Conway is distinguished as being almost the only man of his acquaintance with whom Horace never quarrelled. An altogether estimable character, he had considerable talents as a general, and some as a politician, together with much taste both in literature and in the arts. His daughter, Mrs. Damer, achieved considerable note as a sculptor.

The relationship of three such writers as Dryden, Swift, and Horace Walpole is the most striking that can perhaps be found in any family connection. It may be pure coincidence, but it seems unlikely. Not only were the three men supreme literary artists, but a vein of satire and cynicism, most pronounced in Swift, is to be noted in all three. The original germs may perhaps be traced to the Copes, in which family literary expression, though of a very minor kind, first appears in the connection. In the case of Swift, no other line of any ability can be traced; in that of Dryden only the Pickering family, whose abilities did not turn to literature. The case of Horace Walpole is certainly different. The line of descent is longer and many other influences may have come into play. The Hervey connection, if it really existed, might alone account for Horace, and, as has been remarked, a distant relationship also subsisted between him and Lord Chesterfield, a man whose character and attainments resembled his own to a greater degree than those of Dryden and Swift.

The descent of general ability from a common source is normally far more easy to discern than the descent of specialized ability, but in this particular case there does seem some reason to suppose that the germs of literary power were carried down from the Copes to all those three great writers, John Dryden, Jonathan Swift and Horace Walpole.

AMONG the many Scots who fell at Flodden in the year 1515 was one John Reid, of Aikenhead, leaving by his wife Elizabeth, sister of John Schanwell, Abbott of Cupar, a son Robert. This Robert Reid became a man of mark in his day. Entering the Church, he was, in the reign of James V, Abbott of Kinloss and the special confidant of that monarch. Later he became Bishop of Orkney and died in France, it is supposed by poison, while serving as a Commissioner for the marriage of the young Queen Mary with King Francis the second. One of the last of the Scotch Catholic prelates, the Bishop appears to have been a worthy man, with a love of learning and also of gardening. From two of his sisters some very notable figures, in Scotland and elsewhere, were destined to descend. Alison, one of these sisters, was the wife of Edward Bruce, of a family which claimed kinship with King Robert. Two of her sons, Edward and George, were men of mark. The former, a prominent lawyer, was sent on many missions to Elizabeth's Court by James VI, and, after that monarch's accession to the English throne, was created Lord Kinloss, having obtained temporal possession of the lands of which his uncle had been spiritual head. Kinloss seems to have had but a poor opinion of his master. Asked by Cecil as to the King's character, he replied: " Ken ye a Jack Ape ? If I have him he'll bite you, if you have him he'll bite me."

Christina, the daughter of this somewhat outspoken diplomatist, made a brilliant marriage in England to William Cavendish, second Earl of Devonshire, her prudent father probably taking care that she did not figure as an altogether penniless lass. This Countess of Devonshire, following the tradition first set by her husband's grandmother, Bess of Hardwick, and exemplified more than once in later times in the Cavendish family, proved a brilliant wife to a rather commonplace husband. A great patroness of wits and literary men, she was a most enthusiastic supporter of the royal cause during the Civil Wars, and during the Commonwealth her house at Roehampton was a great centre for Royalist conspirators. After the battle of Worcester she made herself responsible for Prince Charles's effects, and had the satisfaction of surviving to see his restoration.

While Lord Kinloss and his daughter mingled much in public affairs, others of their relatives were distinguished in different fields. Sir William Bruce, a great nephew of Lord Kinloss, was the most prominent architect in Scotland in the time of Charles II, and was responsible for the restoration of Holyrood Palace, which, as it stands to-day, is mainly his work. George Bruce, a younger brother of Lord Kinloss, and also therefore a nephew of the Bishop of Orkney, was an early example of a great industrial magnate; a salt manufacturer, he, in addition, worked extensive coal-fields in the vicinity of Culross. In 1617 King James I descended one of these coal-mines, of which the workings were carried on under the sea. The timid monarch, with visions, no doubt, of the Gowrie Raid, was much alarmed, on being drawn up, to find himself on a small island. He was reassured, however, by his host pointing out to him a " handsome pinnace " duly ready to take him on shore.

George Bruce's grandson, Alexander, created Earl of Kincardine, inherited to the full aptitude for science and industrial pursuits. He also took some part in politics during the reign of Charles II, but being, like most intellectual men, a moderate, he found it difficult to steer his course in times when moderation was at a discount. He was happier in his correspondence with Moray, the first President of the Royal Society, a correspondence which shows the most varied knowledge on the part of Kincardine; chemistry, mechanical appliances of all kinds, horticulture, divinity and heraldry, were among the subjects of which he proved himself a master. During a visit to Holland, one outcome of which was his marriage to a Dutch lady, he was engaged with a famous mathematician, Hugens Zulichen, in an endeavour to improve pendulum clocks for use at sea. Like his grandfather, he was, moreover, much engaged in coal-mining and was also interested in the Greenland whale fishery. Unlike his grandfather, however, Kincardine was unable to accumulate a fortune. Burnet said of him that he was "both the wisest and worthiest man that belonged to this country and fit for governing any affairs but his own, which he neglected to his ruin." It is an oft-repeated story: the grandfather, the specialist, makes money; the grandson, more brilliant and versatile, cannot keep it.

Kincardine left daughters only, and with him we part company with the male line of the Bruces of Kinloss, concerning whom, however, it may be remarked that another line, subsequently Earls of Elgin, were in more recent times destined worthily to maintain the family reputation. The eighth Earl of Elgin, famous for having secured the Elgin Marbles for this country, the ninth and tenth Earls successively Viceroys of India, continued the distinction which has in so many different periods of history attached to the name of Bruce.

Mary, the eldest daughter of the first Earl of Kincardine, married William Cochrane of Ochiltree; her son succeeded to the Earldom of Dundonald, and his son Archibald, the ninth Earl, quite clearly inherited much from his great-grandfather, Kincardine. Like him, he was absorbed in scientific pursuits, particularly relating to chemistry, and like him, he was utterly unable to turn his undoubted aptitudes to financial profit, and died, indeed, in great poverty, having spent his fortune on his experiments. He was father of that brilliant naval officer, Thomas, tenth Earl of Dundonald, who, in his turn, combined great ability and the most romantic gallantry with a certain wrongheadedness which led him into perpetual difficulties.

The Cochranes clearly took after the Bruces in some respects; less obvious resemblance is traceable in the other notable descendants of the first Earl of Kincardine. His daughter Elizabeth married James Boswell of Auchinloch, of an old landed family. Their son Alexander went to the Scottish Bar, prospered thereat and became a Lord of Session under the title of Lord Auchinloch. By no means without ability, a sound scholar and a painstaking judge, Alexander Boswell was, however, on the whole rather a dull dog. With his son, James Boswell, we reach the fourth of the *Five Great Gossips*, one to whose distinguished connections, already outlined, on the side of his paternal grandmother, may be added others on those of the side of his mother, Euphemia Erskine, bringing in a connection with that great Scottish legal family.

We look, however, in vain for literary distinction in any of the more immediate relatives of the great biographer, but, as has occurred in many other cases, a versatile ancestry has proved the best foundation for literary ability. In respect, at any rate, of his intellectual curiosity, James Boswell was probably indebted most to his great-grandfather, Kincardine. One of the most remarkable traits in his character, that singular absence of what may be termed proper pride, we fail to discern among his immediate relatives. This characteristic certainly did not descend to his son Alexander, who, according to Scott, inherited all his father's good qualities, cleverness, good-humour and joviality, without any of the meaner ingredients. Alexander dabbled in literature and was a great supporter of Robert Burns, but he left no immortal work behind him. His younger brother James was a man of very similar calibre to himself, and both brothers were strongly of the opinion that their father had lowered himself by his obsequiousness to Johnson, an opinion shared by their grandfather, Lord Auchinloch, who, on the one occasion of his meeting with the lexicographer, dubbed him, not unfairly, " Ursa Major."

One more descendant of the first Earl of Kincardine's daughter, Elizabeth Boswell, achieved a certain measure of fame. Her younger son, John Boswell, brother of Lord Auchinloch, a distinguished physician in Edinburgh, was father of Robert Boswell, whose daughter Jane married Henry St. George Tucker, a very able financier in India. Their daughter Charlotte published innumerable and very widely-read stories under the penname of " A.L.O.E, a Lady of England." A woman of tireless energy, Charlotte Tucker cannot be described as a great authoress, but certainly few writers have had more interesting connections, and in view of their wide dispersion, her choice of a pen-name, with its special association with England, is somewhat curious. Her Scottish ancestry has already been detailed. Her father's family had long been settled in Bermuda, and another branch of the name of Tucker, as has been seen, attained, and still retain, great distinction in Virginia, while her father and most of her brothers made their careers in India. With a nephew of Charlotte Tucker's, the account of this long line from the Bishop of Orkney's sister may close. This nephew, Frederick Tucker, has married the daughter of General

Booth, of the Salvation Army, has taken the additional surname of Booth, and is very well known in connection with that body. His activities would arouse the interest at any rate of James Boswell, but would hardly, perhaps, meet with the approbation of any other among his relatives of olden times.

IN considering the ancestry of Horace Walpole, reference has been made to Sir Ralph Verney, Lord Mayor of London, to whom was to fall the distinction of being one of the ancestors of those three great men of letters, Dryden, Swift and Horace Walpole. Though the greatest, these, however, are far from exhausting the distinction of the descendants of this Lord Mayor.

Sir Ralph was by trade a mercer, who steered his way through the Wars of the Roses with skill, adopting the Yorkist cause, and receiving from the Yorkist King lands in Buckinghamshire, which his son, Sir John, preserved when Henry VII came to the throne, owing to his fortunate marriage with the daughter of a prominent Lancastrian. From this Sir John Verney descended in the male line that family so well known through the Verney Memoirs, published in the last century by Frances Parthenope, Lady Verney, the sister of Florence Nightingale. The Memoirs deal mainly with the times of the Civil Wars, and show the Verneys of that period to have been, if not men of the highest distinction, at least of the very best type of English gentlemen.

Katherine Verney, grand-daughter of Sir John and great-grand-daughter of the Lord Mayor, married a

Sir John Conway. Their son, a second Sir John Conway, was a prominent military man during the latter part of Queen Elizabeth's reign and sometime Governor of Ostend. Like so many of the men of affairs of his time, Sir John took interest also in religious matters, and wrote *Meditations and Prayers disposed in form of the Alphabet of the Queen, her Most Excellent Majesty's Name*. This somewhat quaint production, written apparently while its author was a prisoner of the Spaniards, consists of a number of prayers each based on a letter, the letters themselves forming the words " Elizabeth Regina." Sir John Conway married Ellen Greville, first cousin of Fulke Greville, Lord Brooke, one of the most prominent of Elizabethans, an able administrator and a poet of no mean rank, a great favourite of the Queen's and the one of all her favourites who " had the longest lease and the smallest time without rub."

Edmund, son of Sir John Conway and Ellen Greville, held many offices under King James I, and was created Lord Conway. He does not appear to have been, however, a man of much distinction, and the King declared that he could not write his name; this was, however, probably a joke on the part of the monarch, no doubt occasioned by the bad handwriting of the Minister.

Lord Conway's daughter, Brilliana, who owed her curious name to the fact that she was born while her father was Governor of Brill, in Holland, married Sir Robert Harley, of Brampton House, in Herefordshire. The letters of Brilliana, Lady Harley, mainly to her son but some to her husband, have been published by the Camden Society, and give a most interesting picture of the early days of the Civil Wars. Possessed of some literary tastes, she figures chiefly as the devoted and essentially religious mother, her pious disposition being no doubt inherited from her grandfather, Sir John Conway. She and her husband, an austere man, were thoroughly Calvinistic in their views, and, of course, took the Parliament side in the disputes. During his absence, her management of his estates was eminently judicious, and she successfully defended Brampton against the Royalist forces. After the siege had been raised, she writes to her son: "I have taken a great cold, which has made me very ill these two or three days, but I hope the Lord will be merciful to me, in giving me my health, for it is an ill time to be sick in." But it was destined to be the last letter she wrote, and she died almost immediately afterwards. Her son, Edward Harley, to whom she was so devoted, proved worthy of her. He played some part in politics during a long period, from the time of the Commonwealth to that of William III, always on the more moderate side. His bent of mind was also essentially religious, and to his filial piety the preservation of his mother's letters is, of course, due. These family characteristics descended also to Sir Edward Harley's son Edward, who published religious works and showed much practical philanthropy, but with his elder son Robert a somewhat different type of character was to appear. This Robert Harley, afterwards Earl of Oxford, was intellectually hardly superior to his immediate ancestors, and it was on the whole his talents for intrigue which brought him to the position of Prime Minister under Queen Anne. Sharing but little the religious principles of his forbears, he inherited to the full their love of literature, and commenced the formation of a magnificent library. To this library his son Edward, the second Earl, practically devoted his life. A man of much natural capacity, he was too indolent to make any attempt to take part in public affairs and cared little for general society. His house was, however, a great centre for literary men, of whom Pope was the most prominent. He practically dissipated his fortune by his purchases. His widow ultimately presented most of his books to the British Museum on its foundation, where they form the well-known "Harleian Miscellany." Many of these books were annotated by the Earl; his notes show much curious knowledge and on the whole sound literary judgment, though he certainly erred when he called Thomas Fuller "a wretched and unfair historian." Unfair at times, perhaps, wretched certainly not.

Lord Oxford's aforesaid widow was Lady Henrietta Holles, the greatest heiress of her time. She herself is described as worthy but dull; however, through her, her descendants could claim a relationship to both Lady Mary Wortley Montagu and Lord Chesterfield, one of her grandmothers having been a Pierrepont, a daughter of "Wise William." Lady Oxford's own vast fortune, which included the princely seat of Welbeck, was unaffected by her husband's lavishness, and descended to their only child, Margaret, celebrated in early life by Prior, another *habitué* of her father's house, "as my noble lovely little Peggy." Lady Margaret Harley married William, second Duke of Portland, grandson of the ablest of William III's Dutch favourites. The Duchess of Portland was perhaps the most notable of the great ladies of her period; making all allowance for flattery she was, without doubt, a woman of the highest culture, with strong literary and artistic tastes. Though hardly herself to be reckoned a " blue stocking," she was to that school the divinity they most respected, and to her lifelong friend, Mrs. Delaney, she was the embodiment of all that was perfect.

Her eldest son, William Bentinck, third Duke of Portland, like his great-grandfather, the first Earl of Oxford, filled the Premiership. It is the fashion to call him a mediocrity, but though not a brilliant man, he was sane and sensible to the highest possible degree, and his conduct throughout his political life was wholly admirable. His Premiership, reluctantly undertaken in old age, was not a success, but as Home Secretary, during a most difficult period, 1794-1801, his judgment was admirable, and to him was largely due the comparatively peaceful passage of the country through a most critical time. The qualities he displayed, sound and sagacious leadership without brilliance, were just those qualities which might have been expected from his ancestry. To a great extent those qualities were inherited by his son, Lord William Bentinck, whose tenure of the office of Viceroy of India was marked by many reforms, the best known being the abolition of suttee. The genesis of the idealism which distinguished Lord William's career can clearly be traced to the line of ancestors whom we have been considering.

With three grandsons of the third Duke of Portland the history of this line closes. Lord George Bentinck was a typical sportsman and a great patron of the Turf, but a man of high moral principles who used his great influence to keep racing and betting straight. In his brief but striking career as a politician, though certainly assiduously coached by Disraeli, he showed an intellectual ability for which he has hardly been given due credit. The recent biography of Henry Chaplin has portrayed his brother, Lord Henry Bentinck, as a sportsman of a similarly high-minded type.

Their first cousin was Charles Greville, the fifth and last of the *Five Great Gossips*, the son of Charles Greville and Lady Charlotte Bentinck, daughter of the third Duke of Portland.

Perhaps of the five Charles Greville was the least of a gossip, and doubtless the least notable as a writer, albeit his pages are eminently readable, and he was certainly a master of good English. A complete man of the world, he posed as a cynic, but possessed in reality the kindest of hearts, and, says Sir Henry Taylor, " was most a friend when friendship was most wanted." An eminently sane outlook and sound judgment were clearly inherited from his maternal grandfather.

It will be noted that the name of Greville has occurred before in the intermarriages of the line we have been considering, and on the paternal side Charles Greville was also related to the great Elizabethan, Fulke Greville, Lord Brooke. But the male line showed little distinction, and the diarist probably derived most of his qualities from the side of his mother. The line from Sir John Conway, or, to go farther back, from the first Sir Ralph Verney, produced no individual of pre-eminent greatness, but, with the one or two exceptions which always mark a long descent, we observe a consistent reappearance of those thoroughly stable English qualities to which the country has owed so much.

CHAPTER VIII

SIX MODERN WRITERS

EARLY in the eighteenth century Aulay Macaulay, the descendant of a line of wild Highlanders, took up more peaceful pursuits and became minister of Lewes, in the Hebrides. His action was typical of the change which took place in the Scottish Highlands at the time. Of Aulay's intellectual attainments we know nothing, but his younger son, Kenneth, was the first of a notable connection to turn to literature. He wrote an account of a religious mission to St. Kilda, on which Dr. Johnson sat in judgment: "Very well written except some foppery about liberty and slavery." Kenneth was not only the first of the family to claim authorship, he was also the first to put forward the views for which the family afterwards became so well known.

His elder brother John was, like his father, a minister, and with his family a definite emergence from obscurity began. A happy accident contributed to this result. Aulay, the eldest son of John, decided, with the concurrence of his father, to take orders in the English Church, and fortune sent him as curate to Rothley Temple, in Leicestershire. There he struck up a warm friendship with Thomas Babington, the squire of the place, a young man of strong religious views. Babington accompanied Aulay on a visit to the paternal manse in Scotland, and fell in love with his sister Jean. A marriage took place, notwithstanding the strong disapprobation of the Babington family, who considered it a distinct *mésalliance*. A curious but eminently sensible arrangement was, however, made. Jean was sent to stay for a time with Babington's sister, Mrs. Thomas Gisborne, there to be instructed in the " polite arts." The plan succeeded admirably, and Jean developed into a woman of great charm and intellectual power.

Thomas Babington and Thomas Gisborne were prominent members of the famous Clapham Sect, and Colin, one of Jean's brothers, no doubt owed his commission in the Indian Army to the Indian influence of some of the members of that body. He became a general and was a most remarkable linguist. More direct was the influence of the " Sect " on another brother, Zachary, who was sent out to Sierra Leone with the special aim of looking after native interests there. Returning to England and settling in Clapham itself, Zachary became a leading member of the " Sect," and devoted himself almost entirely to philanthropy and more particularly to the anti-slavery agitation. A thorough Puritan, Zachary denied himself the pleasures of scientific and literary pursuits, in both of which he delighted, but his literary gifts, if latent, were to appear in full measure in his son, the brilliant historian, (16) in his grandson, Sir George Trevelyan, and in his great-grandson, Mr. George Macaulay Trevelyan.

Zachary's descendants, though the best known, do not by any means exhaust the distinction of the posterity of the minister of Lewes. Two grandsons of Thomas Babington and Jean Macaulay, Charles and Churchill Babington, showed marked intellectual power; both were equally well known as botanists and archæologists, both held professorial chairs, and it was remarked that either could with propriety have held the chair of the other. Another Babington descendant, Sir Henry Babington Smith, had a very distinguished career as an official before and during the Great War, and it is interesting to note that all his four sons have won scholarships at Eton.

Aulay Macaulay, Zachary's eldest brother, to whom, as we have seen, the rise of his family was indirectly due, never achieved any considerable reputation, but was a scholar and antiquarian of distinction. One of his sons became Head Master of Repton; another a Queen's Counsel; a third, Samuel, was rector of Hodnet, in Shropshire, and the father of three sons of intellectual power, two distinguishing themselves as mathematicians and one, George Macaulay, sometime lecturer in English at Cambridge, as a literary critic. George Macaulay married Grace Conybeare, of a family whose intellectual attainments equalled those of the Macaulays, though they failed to produce any one man of world-wide fame like Lord Macaulay.

The Conybeare family is an interesting example of a strictly clerical descent. The first parson of the line of whom there is record was vicar of Pinke, near Exeter. He had the misfortune to see his vicarage wrecked in the great storm of 1703, and he himself ultimately died of illness caught on the occasion. His son John, after achieving considerable note as a preacher at Oxford, eventually rose to the Bishopric of Bristol, having previously obtained the Deanery of Christchurch, largely owing to his *Defence of Revealed Religion*, an answer to Tindal's famous work on Deism. As dean, John Conybeare showed an energy not, as a rule, conspicuous in heads of colleges at that time.

His son William, rector of Bishopsgate, made no particular mark, but the bishop's ability clearly reappeared in the rector's two sons, John Josias and William Daniel Conybeare. Both entered the Church in the early part of the nineteenth century, but it would be safe to say that a hundred years later neither would have done so, for their real interests lay outside theology. John was Professor of Poetry at Oxford, and wrote much on the Anglo-Saxon language, and William was well versed in palæontology. Both brothers, however, made their mark more particularly in geology, of which science they were among the earlier pioneers, William obtaining admission to the Royal Society. His son, William John, vicar of Axminster, had, at his early death at the age of forty-two, made his mark in various directions, as an Edinburgh reviewer, as a writer of sociological works and as the author of a novel called *Persuasion*. His son and grandson have followed him in the Church; the latter, the present Archdeacon of Nottingham, is the seventh parson in a direct succession extending over two hundred years.

Grace Conybeare, who married George Macaulay, is the daughter of William John. Her daughter is Miss Rose Macaulay, the well-known author, the first of the six modern writers of this chapter. No woman novelist of the present day has a more intellectual outlook than Miss Macaulay; none certainly can show ancestors and collateral connections of greater intellectual versatility.

IN the reign of James I a certain Sir Thomas Foster was Judge of the Court of Common Pleas. His son

Robert followed his father on the Bench and attained to greater eminence, obtaining a judgeship in 1640. He, as an ardent Royalist, was removed by the Parliament in 1644, but maintained himself under the Commonwealth by practising as a conveyancer. With the Restoration Robert Foster came again into his own, was appointed Lord Chief Justice, and had the satisfaction of trying various regicides, sullying his reputation, however, by his unmerciful bullying, which was particularly flagrant in the case of Sir Harry Vane. Prior to this, Robert's nephew John, son of his brother Thomas, went to seek his fortune in Jamaica shortly after the conquest of that island. For three generations the family remained in the West Indies, acquiring considerable wealth.

The widow of John, grandson of the first settler, married Henry Barham, another wealthy West Indian proprietor. He left his property to his stepson, Joseph Foster, who thereupon adopted the surname of Barham. This Joseph Foster Barham is described by his grandson as "a most refined and interesting gentleman, who embraced many of the Moravian views of religion." His sister married Florentius Vassal, of another well-known Jamaica family, and her grand-daughter was the celebrated Lady Holland, of the palmy days of Holland House.

Thomas Foster Barham, son of Joseph, settled at Penzance and passed his life there as a wealthy dilettante. He wrote poetry and drama and composed music, but made no particular mark. A man, however, of obvious mental calibre, he was the father of four sons, who all achieved some distinction, though a certain vein of eccentricity impeded their road to actual fame.

Thomas, the eldest, for a time a physician, wearied of this pursuit and gave himself up to theological controversy and the study of Greek. In this language he attained a considerable degree of scholarship and began, but never finished, a translation of the *Iliad*. He invented a religion for himself and wrote on the subject. William, the second son, started his career brilliantly as Second Classic and Chancellor's Medallist at Cambridge; before his early death he had published poetry, but his powers had no time to ripen.

Francis, the fourth and youngest son, became the best known of the family. First a solicitor, and then engaged in various literary undertakings, he devoted the last part of his life to a campaign in favour of phonetic spelling, by printing his works in which he rendered them quite unreadable. He also, like his brother Thomas, busied himself with a new religion, which he called Alism. He founded a Society of Alists, and presumably attracted some disciples, but the Society has by now died a natural death.

Charles, the third son, was the sanest and steadiest of the family. He practised all his life as a doctor in Truro, of which city he was for long by far the most prominent citizen. A man of many-sided culture, he contributed much to the Proceedings of the Royal Institution of Cornwall. He married Caroline, the daughter of Clement Carlyon, who had preceded him as the leading doctor of Truro, and who, also a man of many-sided culture, was a great friend of Coleridge, the poet. Mildred, the daughter of Charles and Caroline Barham, is the wife of George Walpole, Bishop of Edinburgh, and the mother of Mr. Hugh Walpole, the novelist, the second of our six modern writers.

Mr. Walpole bears a famous surname and is directly descended from a brother of the great Sir Robert, but the intervening generations, till we reach his father, the bishop, do not appear to have exhibited any outstanding ability. Whereas in the case of Miss Macaulay we see immediate note on both sides, in that of Mr. Walpole we must look mainly to the maternal as the source of his powers—mainly, but probably by no means entirely. His distant relationship to Lady Holland has already been noted; similarly distant is his relationship to Lady Dorothy Nevill, who was born a Walpole. It is, however, interesting that perhaps the two most famous hostesses of the nineteenth century should have this joint relationship to one of the leading writers of the early twentieth century. And among Lady Holland's entourage the leading place was filled by Thomas Babington Macaulay. One likes to imagine how much interested both hostess and guest would be in the achievements of their relatives of one hundred years on.

TWICE before we have had occasion to visit the West Country in these researches; thither we will return again. Late in the spacious days of Queen Elizabeth, John Chudleigh, a Devon squire, " had a mind to equal the exploits of Drake and Cavendish, but after nearly exhausting his estates in preparation, he ultimately perished in the Straits of Magellan." He had married a daughter of George Speke, of White Lackington, in Somerset, of the same family, which many generations later was to produce the famous explorer. Their son, Sir George, and his son, James, took some part in the

Civil Wars, both veering from the Parliamentary to the Royalist side, but thereafter the name of Chudleigh remained in obscurity till the notorious Elizabeth, great-grand-daughter of a second Sir George. Elizabeth Chudleigh, after marrying the Earl of Bristol, espoused the Duke of Kingston during the lifetime of her first husband, and became the central figure of perhaps the most famous trial for bigamy in all history, that trial so graphically described by Horace Walpole. Elizabeth's character was as profligate as could be, but was probably derived, not so much from the Chudleighs, as from a grandmother who belonged to the notorious Villiers connection. At any rate, very different characteristics passed to another descendant of the Chudleighs, who at the time of the impeachment of his relative had just taken Holy Orders, as had his father and grandfather before him. John Penrose's maternal great-grandmother was daughter of the second Sir George Chudleigh, and whatever he may have thought of the career of his too-well-known cousin, he had no objection to accepting from the " Duchess " the living of Fledborough, to which she presented him in 1783, some years after her disgrace, and in which he passed the remainder of his life. His own tranquil career presented few incidents, but on his brother Charles fell the mantle of his Chudleigh ancestors. He began a highly-distinguished career in the Navy by blocking American trade with the Baltic during the War of the American Revolution, a service singularly reminiscent of recent times, and, after assisting Wellington in Spain with naval operations, ended as second-in-command to Lord Exmouth when he scattered the Algerine pirates in 1816. It was, however, the descendants of

John and not those of Charles who were to make their mark. They had naval traditions on both sides, as John Penrose married Jane, sister of James Trevanon, another naval Cornishman, who, after starting his career as a midshipman in James Cook's last exploration, died in the service of Russia.

To one son and to one daughter of John Penrose and Jane Trevanon it fell to carry on the distinction of the line.

The son, a second John Penrose, was, like his father, a country clergyman all his life, but was indubitably a man of fine capacity; his short biographies of his naval uncles were models of perspicuity, a quality conspicuous also in his sermons. His fame, however, was quite overshadowed by that of his wife, Elizabeth Cartwright, daughter of the inventor of the power-loom, niece of a well-known philosopher, aunt of a distinguished naturalist, and herself not known to the world either by her maiden or married name, but by that of Mrs. Markham, author of the *History* so familiar to children of the nineteenth century, but not so familiar perhaps to the children of the twentieth. " Mrs. Markham " was described by a contemporary as " a most delightful woman, the mother of three promising sons, with a lively, active and accomplished mind, and the most engaging sweetness and simplicity of manners."

Of the three promising sons, two achieved some reputation as schoolmasters; the third, Francis Cranmer Penrose, (17) attained greater fame, but not the fame that he deserved, and is an example of a singularly brilliant all-round man, whose name is, nevertheless, now almost quite forgotten. At Cambridge, in addition to rowing three years in the 'Varsity boat, Francis Penrose invented the system, still in use, for registering the position of the boats in the bumping races. In later life he was almost equally distinguished as an architect and as an astronomer, besides being a skilful painter in water-colours. For many years Surveyor of St. Paul's Cathedral, he was the recipient of the Gold Medal of the Institute of British Architects and was made F.R.S. for his astronomical work. Probably Penrose's fame would have been greater if he had been more of a specialist; he remains a most interesting example of a most versatile man with relatives of distinction in almost every field.

His daughter, Dame Emily Penrose, has worthily continued the traditions of the family. After taking a First in Greats at Oxford, she became Principal of Holloway College and was, till lately, Principal of Somerville College, Oxford.

If, however, the descendants of the second John Penrose, with all their brilliance, failed to achieve general recognition, the case is far otherwise with the descendants of his sister Mary, the wife of Thomas Arnold, the famous Head Master of Rugby. Not much is known of Arnold's ancestry. His father William was a Collector of Customs in the Isle of Wight; his mother belonged to the Delafields, an Irish family. In any case, having regard to Arnold's own ability and to that of his wife's relatives, it might reasonably have been expected that their children would prove to be above the average. This certainly was the case. The eldest son, Matthew Arnold, the distinguished poet and critic, was by far the best known of the family, but at least two of his brothers and one of his sisters showed marked ability. The sister, Jane, wife of William Edward Forster, the statesman, was content to shine behind the scenes; her influence, however, on her husband's political career, was very great. In this respect she resembled her mother, Mary Penrose, who equally had great influence with her husband, the Head Master, and who, during her long widowhood, "held the passionate reverence and affection of her whole family."

William Delafield Arnold, one of her younger sons, had a short but in many ways remarkable career. Entering the Indian Army, he in 1853 published a novel entitled *Oakfield*, which created a considerable sensation at the time. It depicted the difficulties of a young officer in India, obviously Arnold himself, whose tastes were widely different from those by whom he was surrounded. Characteristics which ran more or less through the Arnold family marked this book, distinguished as it is by its high moral earnestness or, as less favourable critics might say, by its priggishness. Matthew Arnold was dubbed " a very superior person," and " superiority," both on its good and on its less good side, was very much in evidence throughout the family. It came out to no small extent in the political career of William Delafield Arnold's son, Oakeley Arnold-Forster, who after his father's untimely death was adopted by the Forsters. Arnold-Forster was a man of great intellectual powers and immense industry, but the inherited air of superiority was perhaps too evident, and undoubtedly militated against the complete success of his career.

Thomas Arnold, the second son of the Head Master of Rugby, was gifted with intellectual powers at least as great as those of any other member of his family; he was, however, a rolling stone who did not gather much moss, and had an inconvenient habit of changing his religion at the wrong time. He lost his position in Tasmania through becoming a Roman Catholic, a mastership in England through changing again to Protestantism; finally he ended up in the Church of Rome. He married while in Tasmania Julia Sorel, whose ancestry was quite extraordinarily different to his own. Her grandfather, William Sorel, deserted his wife while on service at the Cape, and was accordingly in 1816 banished (or promoted) to the Governorship of Tasmania. There his son ultimately joined him and was in his turn deserted by his wife, the daughter of one Anthony Fenn Kemp, for many years termed the Father of the Colony, a man of violent temper who was a thorn in the side of successive Governors.

Curious results might be expected from the mixture of the Arnold and the Sorel blood. Mary Augusta, the eldest daughter, was, however, more of an Arnold than a Sorel. As Mrs. Humphrey Ward, she was for a time unquestionably the leading woman novelist in England, and the lack of success of the father was more than balanced by the quite phenomenal success of the daughter. (18) Her sister Julia married Leonard Huxley, son of the great scientist, and became the mother of Mr. Aldous Huxley, the third of our modern writers. Mr. Huxley's brother Julian has adopted science as a career, and at first sight it would seem that in the brilliant heredity of the brothers science and literature would hold an almost equal place. Thomas Huxley, however, though unquestionably a great scientist, was greater in reality as a writer; it is his power of expression that has made his name survive while those of equal scientific merit are forgotten.

Mr. Aldous Huxley's fame has followed closely on that of his aunt, as hers followed closely on that of her uncle, Matthew Arnold, who just lived long enough to read *Robert Elsmere*. Since the early sixties, indeed, when Matthew first became known, one member or another of this remarkable connection has been continuously before the world, now indeed for a hundred years, excepting the period between Thomas Arnold's death and the emergence to fame of his son Matthew.

It may be deemed, perhaps, that there is more of the Huxley and perhaps more of the Sorel in Mr. Aldous Huxley than there is of the Arnold, and in any case his works would undoubtedly meet with more approval from his distant connection, Elizabeth Chudleigh, than from any of his Arnold forbears.

IN the year 1746 Edmund Maskalyne, a young officer in the East India Company's service, was a fellow-captive in the hands of the French with Robert Clive. They succeeded in escaping together and commenced a friendship which led seven years later to the marriage of Clive and Edmund's sister Margaret. After another eleven years Clive, now a peer and at the height of his fame, took out with him as his private secretary on his last visit to India Henry Strachey, of Sutton Court, in Somerset. Six years later the secretary married Lady Clive's first cousin, Jane Kelsall. Both bride and bridegroom came of families of marked ability. The former's cousin and Lady Clive's brother, Nevill

Maskalyne, was at the time Astronomer Royal, a position which he held for forty-six years. To him we owe the *Nautical Almanack*, and he handed on his scientific talents to his maternal grandson, Mervin Story Maskalyne, a distinguished mineralogist, who was largely instrumental in establishing the study of natural science at Oxford. Henry Strachey, for his part, had also scientific connections. His grandfather, John Strachey, the son of a great friend of John Locke's, was a noted geologist and a Fellow of the Royal Society. Scientific distinction, as we shall see, was destined to reappear again.

Of Henry Strachey's own ability Clive spoke in the highest terms. After his connection with India had ceased, he held various ministerial offices, was one of the Commissioners for concluding peace with America in 1783, and was created a baronet. His eldest son, Henry, lived mostly as a country gentleman at Sutton Court, and is in no way known to fame, but from *The Journal of Clarissa Trant* we learn something of the ability which he undoubtedly possessed, but which, owing to his habits of seclusion, was successfully hidden from the world.

Edward, the second son of Henry Strachey and Jane Kelsall, entered the Indian Civil Service, where he became a close adviser of Mountstuart Elphinstone. A good Persian scholar and a translator from that language, this Edward Strachey was the first of the family to show marked literary tastes. While in India he married Julia Kirkpatrick, described by her friend, Thomas Carlyle, as "a singular pearl of a woman," of a Scottish family to another branch of which the mother of the Empress Eugénie belonged. For three generations her family had achieved some note. Her great-grandfather, James, was the author of poetical and medical works—a somewhat strange combination. The *Middlesex Journal*, on his death, described him as " a gentleman who has left behind him many proofs of a fine imagination in his poetical and of great genius and learning in his physical works." His son, another James, was a colonel in India, the author of a work on cavalry organisation, described by the *Gentleman's Magazine* as " important and very judiciously planned." His son William, Julia's father, was a man of wider note. Serving also in India, he acquired a knowledge of Oriental languages described by Lord Wellesley as unequalled; he occupied the responsible post of Resident at Hyderabad and headed our first mission to Nepal.

The sons of Edward Strachey proved eminently worthy of this distinguished ancestry. It had been intended that Edward, the eldest, should follow his father and both his grandfathers to India, but ill-health prevented the fulfilment of this project. His inherited bent of mind led him, nevertheless, to the acquirement of Eastern languages, his literary tastes being indeed versatile in the extreme. These literary tastes descended to his second son, the late Mr. St. Loe Strachey, so well known as the editor of *The Spectator*, while his eldest son, the present Lord Strachie, has, like his great-grandfather, Sir Henry, followed a political career.

The family connection with India was carried on by two of the younger sons of Edward Strachey and Julia Kirkpatrick, John and Richard Strachey. The career of the former was mainly connected with finance, but he also possessed much literary power and has been described as the literary expositor of the domestic and financial policy of three successive Viceroys. Settling in Italy after his retirement, Sir John Strachey, for a change, devoted himself to art and architecture.

The ablest of all the family was, however, undoubtedly Richard, with whom scientific talent reappeared. An officer in the Royal Engineers, Richard Strachey, not long after his arrival in India, undertook an adventurous journey to Tibet, where he made a great botanical collection. In 1862 he was appointed head of the Indian Public Works Department, which for seventeen years he ruled with a rod of iron. A man of most determined will, he nearly always got his own way; fortunately, his way was generally the right one. After his retirement he continued to devote himself to science, particularly meteorology, and received the Royal Society's medal. He was nearly as expert in finance as his brother John, and, like Francis Penrose in the previous connection, stands out as an eminently versatile man with eminently versatile relatives. It is an interesting coincidence that in each case a daughter attained a leading college position, Miss Joan Strachey, Sir Richard's daughter, being now Vice-Principal of Newnham.

Sir Richard, like his father, married into a distinguished Anglo-Indian family. The Grants of Rothiemurchus derived in a direct line from Patrick Grant, a younger son of the chief of the clan in the sixteenth century. William Grant, younger son of a laird of Rothiemurchus in the eighteenth, married into the Ropers, a family of some naval note. Their son, John Peter Grant, ultimately inherited Rothiemurchus, but preferred the career of a barrister to that of a laird, and attained a judgeship at Bombay, which he resigned, owing to a quarrel with the Governor, and took up practice at the Indian Bar, ultimately obtaining a judgeship again and finally the Chief Justiceship of Bengal. A somewhat singular history, but one which showed him to be possessed of obvious strength of character. His son, a second Sir John Peter, had a still more distinguished personality. His career as an Indian civilian was in all respects brilliant. Secretary for many years to the Government of Bengal, he was equally ready in speech and in writing, and his Minute on the annexation of Oudh has been described as one of the most masterly State papers ever penned. During the Mutiny he did good work at Allahabad, and his secretary was Richard Strachey. Once again, in this family, the secretary married a relative of his chief.

After his retirement from India, Sir John Peter Grant was sent out as Governor to Jamaica under critical circumstances, which had arisen owing to the undue severity with which his predecessor, Edward Eyre, had suppressed a negro rebellion. The appointment, which proved highly successful, was a great compliment, as retired Indian officials seldom indeed receive Colonial Governorships.

Sir John Grant married Henrietta Plowdon, of yet another Anglo-Indian family. Her brother Walter was our first consul in Abyssinia, where he was murdered in 1860, the year after his niece, Jane Grant, was married to Richard Strachey.

One of the sons of Richard Strachey and Jane Grant is the fourth of our modern writers, Mr. Lytton Strachey. Perhaps the most consummate literary artist of his time, Mr. Strachey, as has been shown, descends from ancestors of the most varied possible attainments. The connection with India in every direction is most remarkable, but it hardly seems to have exercised any appreciable influence on the writer. Literary ability, however, has been clearly derived from both grandfathers, not to speak of other relatives, and the scientific bent so noticeable in Mr. Lytton Strachey's connections may be responsible perhaps for the somewhat iconoclastic trend of his writings.

AT the end of the seventeenth and beginning of the eighteenth century, one Joshua Symonds was practising as a surgeon in Shrewsbury, following in that calling his father Richard, who had practised at Atherstone, in Warwickshire. Joshua married Elizabeth, sister of the Rev. John Millington, of Shrewsbury, a strong Tory, Joshua being an equally strong Whig and Nonconformist. The latter refusing in any way to modify his views to please his brother-in-law, he accordingly diverted a legacy of £30,000, which would have gone to the Symonds family, to found the Millington Hospital at Shrewsbury. Joshua, the ancestor of many men and women of note, was clearly himself a man of strong character. His son John continued the family profession and also practised at Shrewsbury, devoting his spare time to extempore prayer and sermon-making. Would-be suitors for his daughter were conducted into an inner sanctum and examined as to their proficiency in these exercises. James Hill, a baker and dealer in horse-corn, passed this test with flying colours, and, notwithstanding his apparently lower social position, was allowed to wed the surgeon's daughter Sarah. From James and Sarah Hill descended one of the most intellectual families that have ever arisen in England. The bright particular star was Sir Rowland Hill, famed for his introduction of the now, alas! defunct penny postage; others were Matthew Davenport Hill, criminal law reformer; George Birkbeck Hill, writer and critic; Rosamund Davenport Hill, the most prominent member of the old London School Board; and, at the present day, Sir Maurice Hill, High Court Judge, and Sir Leslie Scott, late Attorney-General. Though these were the most prominent, they are far from exhausting the list of members of this family, who have shown marked intellectual distinction.

To return to the male line of the Symonds family, the son of the first John, another John, followed his ancestors in the surgical profession, removing, however, to Kidderminster, in Worcestershire, where his sister, Sarah Hill, was also established. This John married Maria, daughter of Stephen Addington, a well-known dissenting minister of his time and a writer of schoolbooks. Notwithstanding this further connection with nonconformity, the family began now to move towards the Church of England and all the three daughters of the second John Symonds and Maria Addington married clergymen of the Establishment. To one of these, Elizabeth, we will return later. Another, Mrs. Stone, was the mother of the author of the famous hymn, *The Church's One Foundation*. The male line, while altering their religious tenets, did not abandon the medical profession, and a third John Symonds practised as a surgeon, this time at Oxford. A gentle, rather melancholy man and a fine classical scholar, the

Oxford John Symonds, like his predecessors, made no particular mark in the medical profession. It was otherwise, however, with his two sons, Frederick the younger, (19) a notable social figure and the great surgeon of his day in Oxford, and John Addington Symonds the elder, who first brought the family name into real prominence. Establishing himself at Clifton, John Addington Symonds obtained an enormous practice, and was equally adored by fashionable ladies and by the poor. He wrote much, particularly on the relation of mind and muscle, possessing, indeed, omnivorous literary tastes, the indulgence in which sometimes worried a conscience inherited from his Puritan ancestors. Literature for the first time in the family was adopted as a profession by his son of the same name, the second John Addington Symonds, the famous writer and critic, and was continued by Mr. St. Loe Strachey, whose mother was the daughter of the Clifton physician, and who, as we have seen, derived his gifts from his father's side also. Literary ability also descended to the late Mrs. Margaret Vaughan, a daughter of the second John Addington Symonds, while another daughter, Dame Katherine Furse, made her mark in a different direction as Commandant of the V.A.D.'s in the late war.

It will be seen already that the distinction of the descendants of Joshua Symonds is considerable and varied, but neither the extent nor the variety is yet exhausted. Reference has been made to Elizabeth, the daughter of the second John Symonds and Maria Addington. She married John Mackenzie, who claimed descent from the Mackenzies of Scatwell, but whose immediate ancestors were shipbuilders. John, however, deserted that calling, went into the Church and set up a school at Huntingdon, the ruling spirit of which was his wife Elizabeth; he himself was more the scholar and the book-lover. A daughter married James Miall, and their son Louis, a zoologist of note, added the distinction of F.R.S. to the many others achieved by this connection.

The three sons of John Mackenzie and Elizabeth Symonds were John Morell, Stephen and Charles. John Morell entered the Church, and a promising career was cut short by a tragedy which made a great sensation at the time, the wreck of the *Pegasus*, which ran on the rocks off the coast of Northumberland on July 19, 1842. Most on board perished, including John Morell Mackenzie. A survivor related: "I saw the Rev. Mr. Mackenzie on the quarter-deck praying, with several of the passengers on their knees around him. Mr. Mackenzie seemed calm and collected. All those around him were praying, too, but Mr. Mackenzie's voice was distinctly heard above them all."

Stephen, the brother of this very gallant gentleman, followed the calling of his maternal ancestors. A very handsome man and a most fastidious judge of literature, he was considered to be "thrown away as a doctor in a London suburb." He also met a tragic end, killed in early life by being thrown out of his gig. His widow, left in straitened circumstances, set up a school, and was glad to get her son Morell into an office. The boy, however, had inherited strong medical tastes, and through the help of an aunt was enabled to qualify, and lived to become the famous throat specialist, Sir Morell Mackenzie. Successful to the last degree till middle life, his later years were clouded by the controversy occasioned by his attendance on the Emperor Frederick. Sir Morell was not himself altogether judicious, but the jealousy of the German medical fraternity was undoubtedly at the root of the trouble which ensued. Sir Morell Mackenzie also shared the literary tastes of so many of his relatives, and had singular gifts as a lecturer and a writer. Two of his nephews now living have achieved distinction in different fields, one, Sir Francis Aglen, (20) as Inspector-General of Chinese Customs, another, Dr. Albert Cooke, as Regius Professor of Hebrew at Oxford.

Many and various as were the achievements of the members of the Symonds connection, by far the greatest break with the past was furnished by Charles Mackenzie, the youngest son of John Mackenzie and Elizabeth Symonds. Placed in early life in an office, Charles, like his nephew Morell after him, detested the calling, and it is notable that not one member of the connection has ever made a success in commerce. Charles's heart was set on the stage, and on the stage he went, with the strong disapproval of his puritanical relatives. This disapproval led him to the decision of changing his name, and he adopted that of Compton, which had been his paternal grandmother's. He, moreover, made a further alteration, the occasion whereof was said to be as follows. Some of his colleagues asked for his Christian name; he suggested that they should guess. They never thought of Charles, but suggested Harry. He then smiled at their not having lighted on so ordinary a name as Charles, whereupon someone said, " Harry it is." He accepted the position, but later changed it to Henry.

As " Henry Compton " he made a great name for himself. Possessed of an irresistibly dry and quaint humour, he played chiefly the comic parts in Shakespeare and in the legitimate drama generally. He was associated chiefly with the old Haymarket, where he played practically continuously from 1853 to 1870. For an actor, Henry Compton was very reserved in his manner, and in many respects was as much of a Puritan as his ancestors. He was, however, much loved by those who knew him best. An enthusiastic admirer said of him: "He was not only the wittiest and wisest and best-tempered man it ever came to us to behold, but he was also the strongest and the best horseman and the best boxer." He was, indeed, a remarkable all-round athlete, and, in addition, a useful chess-player. A fine example of the *mens sana in corpore sano*.

Henry Compton cemented his connection with the stage by marrying into "the profession." His wife Emmeline was daughter of Harry Montague, a comedian who was known as "Bath" Montague, from his acting chiefly in that city. Emmeline herself was for a time on the stage, making her debut as Juliet; she is the Ophelia in Maclise's well-known play scene from *Hamlet*, now in the National Gallery.

Henry Compton, notwithstanding his success on the stage, was very chary of recommending anyone to follow so precarious a calling, but his own family took to it as ducks to water. His daughter Katherine, who married the well-known dramatist, R. C. Carton, had a long career before the footlights; his son, Edward Compton, though he acted frequently, was best known as a manager; with his wife he for many years ran the Compton Comedy Company. That wife, Virginia Bateman, herself came of a family with most interesting dramatic connections. Her maternal grandfather, Joseph

Cowell, is said to have been a nephew of Admiral Sir James Hawkins Whitshed; he at any rate commenced his career as a midshipman, in the course of which he was nearly court-martialled for striking a superior officer, but owing to bravery in a subsequent action received an honourable discharge. Cowell next tried painting, but in 1812 definitely became an actor, and succeeded from the first. Though taking almost every kind of part, he preferred comedy. Much of his career was passed in the United States, where he made a great reputation. He put his son Samuel on the stage at the age of nine, from which time the latter earned his own living. On one occasion the father and son played the two Dromios, the former declaring that " Sam is me at the wrong end of the telescope." The illusion, however, cannot have been very great. Samuel Cowell later took up character-singing, and may be regarded as the founder of the modern music-hall entertainment. A typical Bohemian, Sam Cowell was equally popular and improvident. He was grandfather of the well-known actress, Miss Sydney Farebrother.

Joseph Cowell's sister, Sidney Frances, married Hezekiah Bateman, an American of a family long settled at Baltimore. Like Henry Compton, Bateman was brought up in a most puritanical atmosphere, his parents being strict Methodists. He and his wife, however, devoted themselves exclusively to things theatrical. She wrote several plays; a comedy, *Self*, and a tragedy, *Geraldine*, long held the boards. Their three daughters were all brought up to the stage, and, following the example of their uncle, Samuel Cowell, made a great reputation when very young, being known far and wide in America as the " Bateman children."

Hezekiah and Sidney Bateman, after managing theatres

successively in St. Louis and New York, came to London in 1870 and took over the Lyceum Theatre, where they had the great distinction of bringing forward Henry Irving. Hezekiah Bateman may be regarded as the first of the long series of American impresarios. After his death his wife essayed the management of the once-famous Sadler's Wells Theatre, but in this she was unsuccessful and lost all her money. Of the "Bateman children," Ellen early left the stage, but Kate made a great reputation as an actress in the seventies. The third daughter was Virginia, Mrs. Edward Compton; and her daughter, Miss Fay Compton, is now, as is well known, one of the two or three leading actresses on the London stage. Her brother is Mr. Compton Mackenzie, the novelist, who has reverterd to the real family surname, and who is the fifth of our six modern writers. As will be seen, Mr. Compton Mackenzie's immediate connections are entirely with the stage, and with novels in connection therewith he first made his reputation. A harking back to other ancestors is, however, visible in his later writings, and, in any case, no present-day novelist can boast a more varied collection of relatives of interest. With the one exception of commerce, there is practically no field in which distinction has not been achieved, though the variety is almost entirely on one side, that of Henry Compton.

IN the year 1717, shortly after the advent of the Hanoverian dynasty, one John Baring, posthumous son of a Lutheran minister at Bremen, and thus, as it were, a neighbour of King George I, came over to England. All knew the King, few knew John Baring; but the

House of Baring was destined to become almost as celebrated, and far more distinguished, than the House of Guelph.

The Baring family had been, however, by no means entirely obscure in the Fatherland. They can be traced back to one Franz, who at the Reformation left the cloister to which he was destined, married, and became a Protestant Doctor of Theology. From him the line to John passes through pastors and notaries, with intermarriages into commercial families.

John Baring was apprenticed at Exeter to one Edward Cook, to learn the trade of a serge-maker. Naturalized in 1722, John in 1729 married Elizabeth, daughter of John Vowler, probably of Dutch extraction. She was a woman " of a shrewd wit and excellent business talents," and the pair prospered exceedingly in the wool business which they set up. It is rather quaintly remarked that at one time only the Bishop, the Recorder, and the Barings kept carriages in Exeter! Three sons of this successful couple may be noted. John, the eldest, carried on the Exeter business and also founded a bank. He was well known locally as " Old Turkey Legs." His line died out. Charles, the youngest, who married an heiress, adopted the additional surname of Gould, and was ancestor of many men of note, among others that very versatile writer, the Rev. Sabine Baring-Gould; the less versatile, but more distinguished writer, the historian, Samuel Rawson Gardner; Stafford Northcote, Earl of Iddesleigh, well known in the politics of the last generation; and Sir Hilton Young, who is making his political mark in the present day. The last named, whose financial ability is well known, alone in this branch seems to have inherited that remarkable trait of the Barings.

It was Francis, the second son of John Baring and Elizabeth Vowler, who first made the family name of world-wide fame. Coming up to London and entering finance, he founded his fortunes by the ability with which he executed some commissions sent to him by the great house of the Hopes of Amsterdam. (21) Founder of Baring Brothers, Sir Francis was at his death, in the words of Lord Erskine, " the first merchant in Europe." It was remarkable that he was deaf from his youth, but though he read little, he had a great fund of conversation. His indefatigable industry was carried into the minutest details of family life; he is said to have even ordered his daughters' frocks and shoes. (22) In these matters he was perhaps not much helped by his wife, Harriet Herring, who, though the cousin of an Archbishop of Canterbury, seems herself to have had but little ability of any kind; she is described as " a vain, worldly, fine woman, whose life was devoted to fashionable society."

In connection with the marriage of their daughter Dorothy, a story has often been told, but may perhaps bear re-telling. In the house of Hope, of Amsterdam, Sir Francis's correspondents, there was, early in the nineteenth century, a young clerk named Pierre Labouchere, a refugee from France. Frequently sent over to do business with the Barings, Pierre met Dorothy, and, desiring marriage with her, approached her father. The latter would have none of it. Labouchere's position was by no means good enough.

" Well, sir," said the young man, " would it make any difference to your decision if I were a partner in Hope's ? "

" Undoubtedly it would," replied Sir Francis.

Labouchere forthwith repaired to Mr. Hope and

suggested that he be taken into partnership. On the idea being repudiated, "Would it make any difference to your decision, sir, if I were engaged to Miss Dorothy Baring?"

Mr. Hope admitted that it would.

"Well, then," said Labouchere, "I am engaged to Miss Dorothy Baring"; and forthwith he wrote to Sir Francis that he was a partner in Hope's and claimed his bride. The marriage duly took place. History does not relate whether Baring and Hope ever discovered the deception; if they did they probably came to the conclusion that a man of Labouchere's resource would be useful to them alike as son-in-law and partner. And so it actually proved; an excellent man of business, Labouchere made a large fortune. His wealth, and also his resourcefulness, descended ultimately to his grandson Henry, the universally known "Labby," if not the greatest, without doubt the most interesting, personality of all the Baring connection.

Of the three sons of Sir Francis Baring, Sir Thomas, the eldest, showed no particular ability but much religious zeal, and was too frequently the victim of impostors. The financial skill of the family reappeared, however, in his son Thomas Charles, long the head of Baring Brothers, while a grandson, the first Earl of Northbrook, was an efficient, if perhaps rather mediocre, politician who filled the office, *inter alia*, of Viceroy of India.

By far the most brilliant of Sir Francis's sons was the second, Alexander; in this generation, as in the last, it was the middle son who achieved most prominence. Alexander, eventually Lord Ashburton, was head of Baring Brothers between his father and his nephew, Thomas Charles, and raised the position of the firm to its greatest pitch of splendour. Entering politics, he achieved therein less note than in business, mainly, however, owing to his intellectual honesty, as he was quite unable to adapt himself to the strict party game. John Louis Mallet, who knew him well and who was anything but a flatterer, said of Lord Ashburton: "I do not know any man of a more easy and agreeable temper, more communicative and with a better taste and judgment in conversation."

Henry Baring, Lord Ashburton's younger brother, married for his second wife Cecilia Windham, of an interesting family which bore but little resemblance to the Barings. She was great-niece of William Windham, that statesman of the early nineteenth century who was born out of due time; his proper period would have been the Elizabethan. To quote Lord Rosebery, "At once a statesman, an orator and a mathematician and the most fascinating talker of his day." His brilliant talents were, however, greatly marred by the vacillation of his character—a vacillation which clearly comes out in his *Diary*, published many years after his death by Mrs. Henry Baring.

William Windham left his estates to his nephew, William Lukin, who took the surname of Windham. This second William Windham, who attained the rank of admiral, was father of General Sir Charles Windham, who achieved great distinction in the Crimea, particularly for his conduct at the assault on the Redan, after which he was for a moment perhaps the most popular man in England. Later, in the Indian Mutiny, he was less successful, though his failure to relieve Cawnpore was mainly owing to misconduct on the part of a subordinate, whom he chivalrously shielded. His later years were saddened by the doings of a scapegrace nephew, the heir of the Windhams, who completely dissipated the family property and ended his life as the driver of the Cromer coach. Sir Charles came to see him on his death-bed, but he was no more when he arrived, and the uncle could but murmur : " Poor boy, I have tried to save you, and I have tried to save the property, and now both are gone."

The mother of Sir Charles and of Mrs. Henry Baring was daughter of Peter Thelussen, the Swiss who acquired a great fortune in England, but who lives chiefly as the maker of the famous will, by which he endeavoured to accumulate his estate for several generations—a will which led to special legislation to stop such practices in the future.

The children of Henry Baring and Cecilia Windham had a brilliant heredity. By far the most distinguished of the family was Evelyn, subsequently Lord Cromer, in whom the gifts of the Barings and the gifts of the Windhams were combined with the happiest results. Though mainly, of course, of English descent, it is not a little curious that this typical English pro-consul should have had German, French-Swiss, probably also Dutch blood. Lord Cromer's eldest brother, created Lord Revelstoke, became head of Baring Brothers on the death of Thomas Charles Baring, but in his day occurred the great catastrophe which nearly brought that famous House to the ground. The position has, however, been rehabiliated largely owing to the abilities of his eldest son John, the present Lord Revelstoke, who, though but little known to the general public, is one of the financial geniuses of the present time. In him the special family talents have fully reappeared.

His younger brother, Mr. Maurice Baring, is the sixth of our modern writers. The great ability on his father's side has been shown ; there has been scarcely less on that of his mother's mother, a daughter of the Prime Minister, Earl Grey, of a family whose name is writ large in our political annals, and to whom reference has been made in another chapter. In almost every direction Mr. Maurice Baring is related to statesmen and in one direction to financiers, but except in the case of his distant connections of the Baring-Gould branch, literary ability has not heretofore appeared among the descendants of John Baring, of Exeter. The connections of Mr. Maurice Baring and Mr. Compton Mackenzie were widely different in their activities, but are alike in the clear possession of hereditary ability.

SUCH ability has, however, clearly persisted for many generations in the case of, at any rate, some lines of the ancestry of all the six writers who have been considered. In each instance some literary relatives can be found, but literature, as will have been seen, is far from playing an exclusive part. Science figures largely, administration, politics and the law to a considerable extent, art much less. While there are one or two architects, there is no painter of any note and no musical composer, while the stage is represented only in the Mackenzie connection. This is in accordance with a general law that those who have won prominence in the arts have, as a rule, far fewer relatives of distinction than those who have won prominence in public affairs, in literature or in science. For some reason or other, not very easy to explain, artistic gifts seem to be more concentrated in the individual, while other gifts are apt to be more diffused among the family.

CHAPTER IX

SCOTLAND AND THE SOUTHERN STATES

IT is curiously seldom that any family connection has achieved any striking distinction alike in Great Britain and in the United States. Reference has already been made to the Tucker family; there is also the Scottish family of Dallas, and more recently the English family of Mayo, with its distinguished physicians in both countries. (23) General Robert Lee, moreover, could show a descent from the Scottish family of Spottiswoode, which produced an Archbishop and other men of note in the seventeenth century, and were later well known as the Royal Printers. The American Livingstons were far more notable than their Scottish relatives, though these were not wholly undistinguished, and the Randolphs, as we have seen, had, at any rate, one well-known English relative. These, however, so far as the writer is aware, practically exhaust those connections who have really achieved fame on both sides of the water, with the exception of that connection which was by far the most notable and which will be considered in the following pages.

Its ultimate ancestor was the John Reid whom we have already met, the father of the Bishop of Orkney and of a daughter from whom James Boswell was descended. Janet, another daughter of John Reid, married Gilbert Robertson, a cadet of the family of Robertson of Struan. From her, in the third generation, descended one William Robertson, who late in the seventeenth century was seated at Gladney, in Fifeshire, and was probably what was called in Scotland a pocket laird. This William Robertson married the daughter of a Dr. Michell, but no characteristics either of himself or of his wife seem to have been preserved. This is a pity, having regard to the eminence reached by their descendants, but we may well surmise that they were steady God-fearing people, and that their intellectual attainments, if hidden under a bushel, were nevertheless of a high order. The lines descending from one son and two daughters of the laird of Gladney fall to be considered. The son, another William Robertson, became a minister of the Established Kirk; of the daughters, Mary married an architect of the name of William Adam, and Jean married one Alexander Henry; both Adam and Henry were, like their wives, Scottish.

The eldest son of William Robertson, the minister, another and more famous William Robertson, followed his father in the Church. Shortly after his induction into the living of Gladsmuir, in Haddington, both his parents died and his younger brothers and sisters were left on his hands. In eight years he had placed them out in the world, his own income being sixty pounds a year. Then he married. For another eight years, still with the same income, he, in addition to his cure of souls, diligently prosecuted historical studies, and finally, in 1759, he published his *History of Scotland*. No man better deserved success than William Robertson, and success he achieved in full measure; he, quite as truly as Byron, "awoke one morning and found himself famous." His *History* not only brought him immediate pecuniary success, but obtained for him the incumbency of an Edinburgh church, and later the Principalship of Edinburgh University in addition to the post of Histriographer to the King of Scotland. The rest of his life was smooth and prosperous; his later histories of America and of Charles V were equally popular, and he made a great figure in the General Assembly of the Church of Scotland, where his eloquence was much appreciated. In all relations of life, Principal Robertson was an estimable figure, and no man that ever lived more fully reaped the rewards of virtue, no career would more fittingly adorn a moral tale.

The historian's favourite sister Mary helped him greatly during his early struggles. She married another minister, James Syme by name, and had one child, Eleanor, who married Henry Brougham, of an old but hitherto undistinguished Cumberland family. On her eldest son, to become so well known as Lord Brougham, the ability of this line was concentrated. Lord Brougham in his *Autobiography* informs us that before meeting Eleanor Syme his father had been engaged to a Miss Mary Whelpdale, who, however, died before the marriage could take place. "If I had been her son," he remarked, "I should probably have remained mediocre." There can be no question, indeed, that the future Lord Chancellor owed his ability to the maternal side. For his grandmother he had an unbounded admiration. He says of her that she was "remarkable for beauty but far more for a masculine intellect and strong understanding," and "to her I owe my success in life."

Brilliant to the last degree up to a point, Brougham's later career was disappointing. Extraordinarily industrious, taking all knowledge for his province, a very

SCOTLAND AND SOUTHERN STATES 173

effective speaker with great powers of sarcasm, and an unfailing gift of humour, Brougham nevertheless showed a marked lack of balance which in his later years developed into positive eccentricity. These last characteristics were almost certainly derived from other sources and not from his Robertson ancestry, and they made him, on the whole, a failure—albeit a splendid failure. None of his three brothers attained any distinction.

Brougham was by far the most notable of Principal Robertson's more immediate kin, but the historian's own descendants have not lacked talent. One of his sons became a Scottish Lord of Session; another, a colonel, raised the first Malay Regiment in Ceylon. His daughter Mary married Patrick Brydone, a man of considerable scientific attainments, who published in 1773 an extremely readable account of Sicily and Malta, the first really good narrative of travels in those islands. Their daughter Mary became the wife of Gilbert Elliot, second Earl of Minto, of a line which for generations married into families of note, and which kept up its own distinction for a proportionately long period. Lady Minto is described as " very good-looking, regular features and beautiful skin, a soft rose-colour in her cheeks, very even-tempered and gentle, but capable and reliable." A worthy granddaughter of Principal Robertson.

Her descendants have filled many and various positions. One grandson, the late Lord Minto, was successively Governor-General of Canada and Viceroy of India, most popular in both capacities; another, Arthur Elliot, was editor of the *Edinburgh Review*. A son, Sir Henry Elliot, was Ambassador at Constantinople. Sir

Gerald Portal, son of Lady Minto's daughter Charlotte, had a singularly brilliant career in diplomacy, cut short by an untimely death. In 1887, in Abyssinia, and in 1892, in Uganda, he showed great abilities, and received the K.C.M.G. at the exceptionally early age of thirty-four. Had he lived, Gerald Portal would undoubtedly have gone very far. Frances Elliot, daughter of Lady Minto, became the wife of Lord John Russell. She combined great ability with an extremely attractive character. Justin McCarthy, who knew her well, was unstinted in his admiration for her. "I have no words," he says, "literally none, in which to express adequately the admiration, the affection and the devotion which I felt for Lady Russell. No higher type of womanhood has yet been born into our modern world." He adds that she was one of the best conversationalists that he had ever known. She had strong Liberal opinions, which went far beyond those of her Whig husband; these views, together with her ability, were inherited by her son, Lord Amberley, and by her grandson, Mr. Bertrand Russell. The last named, one of the greatest mathematicians of the present day, is, in the realm of pure intellect, probably the most distinguished of the descendants of Principal Robertson.

Let us now turn to other descendants of the first William Robertson, the grandfather of the historian. Reference has already been made to his daughter Mary, who married William Adam. This William Adam was the best known and most widely employed architect of his day in Scotland and filled the office of Master Mason in that country to the Board of Ordnance. In varying degrees his gifts descended to all his four sons, John, Robert, James and William. Of this notable

SCOTLAND AND SOUTHERN STATES

brotherhood, Robert was the most famous. In early life he travelled on the Continent, and Lady Mary Wortley Montagu, who met him, described him as a man of genius. Returning to England, Robert Adam's fame as an architect quickly followed that of his cousin, William Robertson, as an historian. He and his brothers planned much notable work, but are now best remembered as the architects of the Adelphi buildings in London, so called after the Greek word for brothers.

Robert Adam was buried in Westminster Abbey, and the *Gentleman's Magazine* of 1792 compared him, as an architect, with Reynolds as an artist, Sir Joshua having died in that same year.

John Adam, who played throughout a somewhat secondary part to his brother Robert, was the father of Sir Charles Adam, a man of much note in his day. A great friend of Charles Fox, whose political views he shared, Charles Adam played a leading part in the impeachment of Warren Hastings, on which occasion he made a speech of great power. Later, filling a Scottish judicial position, Charles Adam became best known by his formation of the " Blair Adam Club," which met weekly at his residence for antiquarian research, and to which many eminent men belonged. Walter Scott was a member, and it was at one of these parties that the plot of his novel, *The Abbot*, was suggested.

Two of Sir Charles Adam's sons rose to distinction in the Navy and Army respectively. The latter, Sir Frederick, commanded the brigade at Waterloo which finally checked the advance of Napoleon's " Old Guard." A daughter of Sir Charles married John Loch, of a family which had a connection with the

Erskines; their son, James Loch, adopted yet another career, becoming the best-known land-agent of his time, acting for the Sutherland, Bridgewater, Dudley and Carlisle estates, and being concerned in the management alike of agricultural and pastoral land, of mines, of factories and of canals. It was he who superintended the much-discussed " Sutherland Clearances," by which tenants living miserably in the interior of that wildest of Scottish counties were removed to more suitable locations by the sea. These proceedings caused a great outcry at the time, but were abundantly justified by the result. In 1812, at the commencement of James Loch's Sutherland agency, there was not a single road in the county; in 1833 there were four hundred and fifty miles of road and a hundred and thirty-four bridges.

Granville and Henry Brougham Loch, the sons of this great public benefactor, saw service in many parts of the world. Granville, who was in the Navy, was distinguished in two countries at the moment much in the public eye: in 1841 he fought as a volunteer in China and published an account of his experiences; in 1848 he commanded a remarkably successful little expedition to Nicaragua, to obtain satisfaction for various outrages committed by that turbulent little country. He fell at a comparatively early age in an expedition in Burma. Some twenty years after, his brother, Henry Brougham Loch, also saw service in China, where, as a military member of Lord Elgin's expedition in 1860, he had the misfortune to be captured by the Chinese and to be subjected to torture, barely escaping with his life. In later years, after a peaceful time as Governor of the Isle of Man, Henry Loch was High Commissioner for South Africa in the difficult years of 1889–94, when trouble was brewing. There he worked with Rhodes in his imperialistic projects, but was hardly perhaps to be accounted a great administrator. His nephew, Arthur Nicholson, now Lord Carnock, son of his sister Clementina, has been Ambassador in St. Petersburg.

An interesting figure at Sir Charles Adam's parties at Blair Adam was his cousin, John Clark, whose mother, Susannah, was a sister of the architect. John Clark was a great figure at the Scottish Bar; at one time he was said to have had half the total practice. A man of rough and sarcastic humour, he dominated the judges as he thought fit. His appearance was plain, and he was also lame, and on one occasion a lady passing him said to a friend: "There goes Johnnie Clark, the lame lawyer." Clark, overhearing, turned round and said: "No, madam; a lame man but not a lame lawyer."

For the American side of the Robertson connection we must turn to Jean, another of the daughters of the laird of Gladney, who married Alexander Henry. Two of her sons, John and Patrick Henry, emigrated to Virginia in the third decade of the eighteenth century, Patrick, notwithstanding his Presbyterian relatives, becoming an Episcopalian rector. This Patrick Henry made no mark in history, but it was otherwise with his nephew of the same name, the son of John. The second Patrick Henry probably owed much of his talent to his maternal as well as to his paternal descent; his mother is described as a woman of unusual intellectual gifts, with great linguistic ability. Patrick, after a short career in business, was called to the Virginia Bar, and soon acquired a large practice. His remarkable gifts for public speaking were early displayed, and when the revolutionary period dawned, if it found in Washington its soldier and in Jefferson its statesman, it emphatically found in Patrick Henry its orator. His surpassing eloquence was "due primarily to the greatness of his emotion and to the versatility which enabled him to assume at once any emotion that suited his ends," but he possessed also every physical adjunct, marvellous voice production and a complete control over intonation, pause, gesture, and play of countenance. Patrick Henry rose to distinction a little later than his relatives, William Robertson and Robert Adam, with whom, however, he was in the main contemporary, but his own attainments clearly bore a closer resemblance to those of his somewhat more distant relative, Brougham, whose fame belonged to a subsequent generation. Although Henry, as we have seen, may have owed something to his mother's side, one can hardly but think that these two great orators must alike have derived their special powers from their common descent. But history is mute as to the ability in this sphere of the laird of Gladney or of his father-in-law, Doctor Michell.

Brougham and Patrick Henry had other resemblances than their oratorical skill. Both alike, in their earlier years at all events, held strong Radical opinions, but while Brougham was enabled to play an important part in the abolition of slavery in the British Empire, Patrick Henry was only in the position of a strong advocate of the abolition of slavery in the United States. But when the great struggle came, most of his kinsfolk were to be found on the other side, and it is possible that Henry himself, had he been forced then to make his choice, would likewise have stood by his State.

It was from two sisters of the orator that most of

these kinsfolk of distinction sprang. Elizabeth Henry married William Campbell, who highly distinguished himself in the War of Independence, and her daughter Sarah married Francis Preston, of a family of Ulster origin, which carved its name deeply in the annals of the South. Three sons of Francis Preston and Sarah Campbell played leading parts in the troublous times before the Civil War. William, the eldest, settled in South Carolina, the most fiery of all the Southern States, and adopted to the full its fiery spirit. An ardent advocate of State Rights and a leader of the "Nullification" party, the mantle of Patrick Henry as an orator descended on this great-nephew, who was, in addition, a fine classical scholar, an attainment by no means so common in the South as powers of speech. William Preston died just before the war broke out. When on his death-bed, a friend said to him: "I envy you, Preston; you are leaving it, and I shall have to stay and see it all." With a sigh of relief, the dying man signified that this was true. But he, at least, had done much to bring it about.

If William Preston escaped the war, his younger brothers, Francis and Thomas, did not, and both held high commands therein. Francis had previously also taken a strong political line in Louisiana, where he spent a fortune, gained as a sugar-planter, in the purchase of works of art, continuing the culture derived from many of his ancestors. After the war Francis Preston retired for a time to England, but returning eventually to America, he, quite unrepentant, created a great stir by a speech to the University of Virginia in which he still advocated the right to secession.

Thomas, the younger brother, who had previously devoted himself almost entirely to commerce, served during the war on the staff of his relative, General Johnstone. Joseph Egglestone Johnstone was the greatest of the connection in America since the days of Patrick Henry. His mother, Mary, was the daughter of Valentine Wood and Lucy, another of the Henry sisters. Lucy Wood is described as equalling her brother Patrick in mental endowments and as having been as great a conversational force in society as he was on the hustings. Her daughter, Mary Johnstone, inherited all her ability, and herself educated her sons for college. These sons, mainly as lawyers and journalists, showed considerable talents, though none but Joseph came markedly to the fore. The last named entered the United States Army and served with great distinction in the war with Mexico, when he successfully conducted that most difficult of all military operations, a retreat in face of superior forces. In 1861 he was Quartermaster-General and was the highest in army rank of those who joined the Confederates. Lee was, however, perferred to him for the supreme command, and rightly so, for Lee had genius, Johnstone no more than talent. Under most difficult circumstances, however, Johnstone put up a wonderful fight against Sherman in the latter days of the war, and, like Lee, he gained the deep affection of his men. Many years after, in 1890, an unforgettable scene occurred in Savannah, when the old general attended the memorial exercises, his veterans flocking round him and insisting on drawing his carriage. His great opponents, Grant and Sherman, both became his personal friends, and he was one of the pall-bearers at both their funerals.

At the present day the most notable of the relatives of Patrick Henry are perhaps the Breckinridges, whose grandmother was a sister of the Preston brothers.

Henry Breckinridge, a lawyer by profession, was Assistant Secretary of State for War in 1917 and later on the staff of the American Army in France; he was, until recently, President of the American Navy League. His cousin, Dasha Breckinridge, is a well-known editor, and the latter's sister, Sophinisba, a prominent writer on social science, is one of the few women who have tackled currency problems. In this, as in so many other family connections, it is only in recent times that we find the women attaining any prominence, but again, in this as in so many others, it was clearly want of opportunity rather than want of ability which kept them in the background.

The descendants of William Robertson, of Gladney, have not, perhaps, produced any actual genius, unless Brougham can be considered entitled to that elusive appellation. But marked ability in the most varied fields and in the most varied regions has been eminently their characteristic. Two great orators in Patrick Henry and Brougham, a great historian in William Robertson, a great general in Joseph Johnstone, and, one may add, a great man of business in James Loch, these form a singularly notable galaxy, not to speak of the lesser lights, particularly in advocacy, in administration and in diplomacy. Another most striking characteristic of the connection deserves, however, special mention, their high moral worth and the general likeableness of their characters. To the latter unquestionably, and to the former on the whole, Brougham was an exception, but these traits are most conspicuous in the great majority of cases, and a certain unctiousness, rather too obvious in some other connections of equal moral worth, was noticeably absent from this relationship of Scotsmen, Englishmen and Americans.

CHAPTER X

THE CELTIC TOUCH

THE number of Irish connections of Celtic origin which have achieved varied prominence are not numerous, a very large proportion of the more notable Irish families being of Anglo-Irish origin. A striking exception is that of the Sheridans, who are almost certainly of Celtic descent in the male line; another is furnished by the Doyles.

This last-named family had long been seated in Wicklow, and were in times past one of the disorderly Celtic septs who frequently descended from their mountains and plundered Dublin. In the seventeenth century, when these marauding habits had perforce to come to an end, a branch migrated to Carlow. During that century they were certainly still Catholics, but during the eighteenth, Protestantism was adopted, probably first by Charles Doyle, of Bramblestown, the son of William Doyle and Jane, daughter of Cormac Egan, who, judging from his name, must most certainly have been a Celt.

Charles Doyle, the common ancestor of all the notabilities referred to in this chapter, married Elizabeth, daughter of the Rev. Nicholas Milly, a Protestant rector. The pugnacious spirit of the older Doyles was destined soon to emerge again in the male line. Of the four sons of Charles and Elizabeth Doyle, two, John and Welbore, entered the army; a third, William, the law; and the fourth, Nicholas, the Church; while

Catherine, the only daughter, married a parson, the Rev. Thomas Bushe. The professions, rather than commerce, attracted this intensely Hibernian family.

Of the four sons, John attained the greatest distinction. He comemnced his military career in the American War, and during the period of peace which followed served in Grattan's Parliament, distinguishing himself by his eloquence, which was specially exerted in favour of the Irish soldiers, whose pay at that time was less than the English rate. A man of liberal opinions, Doyle was in favour of Catholic emancipation. During the later wars he served with distinction in the Egyptian campaign, and subsequently was very nearly appointed to the command in the Peninsula, actually given to Arthur Wellesley. At this time Sir John, as he had now become, was Governor of Guernsey, a post he held all through the difficult period of the later Napoleonic wars. A typical Irishman, a most brilliant and witty talker, and boundlessly hospitable, Sir John Doyle was to the last degree a favourite during his Governorship; he was known as "Popularity Jack," and on his retirement received a special vote of thanks under the Great Seal, an unprecedented occurrence. Later, a column was erected to him with the simple inscription, "Doyle, Gratitude." During the latter part of his life Sir John's own extravagance, coupled with the help he gave to troublesome relatives, greatly impaired his financial position.

His youngest brother, Welbore Doyle, entered the army still earlier, and probably, had he lived, he would have gone farther than John. Less lovable than the latter, Welbore was a most able and determined man. A major-general at thirty-six, he died at the age of thirty-nine of a fever in Ceylon, of which island he was then Governor. Earlier in his career he had been military attaché in Poland, and was there connected with a curious incident. A Polish girl about to be married came to Welbore Doyle and asked him to take charge of a document which, on examination, proved to be a protest against the marriage into which she was about to enter. She informed Doyle that this was merely a precautionary measure and that the protest might prove useful if, in the course of time, she might wish to apply for a divorce. (24)

Welbore Doyle's two sons pursued very different careers. Charles Joseph, the younger, known as Carlo, had a long military service, first in the Peninsula and later in India. A great dandy, he was considered the best-looking man in the army, and had, moreover, considerable artistic powers, remarkably illustrated by his production of a picture upon a pocket-handkerchief of Lord Hastings's entry into Oude. Like so many of his family, Carlo Doyle, at the end of his life, experienced great financial difficulties. His elder brother, Sir Francis Doyle, though early in life also in the army, was later Chairman of the Board of Excise. He had a great reputation in his time as a man of the world, and was called upon to arbitrate in two famous marital quarrels, those of the Byrons and of the Lyttons (the latter, as we shall see, his relatives), but with all his tact he found the husband in the first case and the wife in the second quite unmanageable. His son, another Sir Francis Doyle, was an intimate friend of Gladstone's, with whom he was in " Pop " at Eton and at whose wedding he was best man. He combined a Receivership of Customs with the Professorship of Poetry at Oxford, his own poems, particularly his ballads, being of considerable merit. Though not a military man himself, the younger Francis Doyle was permeated with the spirit of his military relatives, and his best work was done on martial themes. *The Private of the Buffs* is universally known, and *The Red Thread of Honour* was translated into the Pushtu language, and became a favourite among the natives on the North-West Frontier of India.

Let us now return to William Doyle, the eldest son of the progenitor, Charles Doyle.

William became a King's Counsel, and, like his brother John, was celebrated both for his wit and his extravagance. A noted duellist, on one occasion he, owing to the gout, was carried to the scene of action in a sedan chair. He, of course, died insolvent. His son, Sir Charles, had a long military career and served throughout the Peninsular War. Military historians, particularly Fortescue, have laughed at his extravagant and theatrical conduct, and have regarded him as little better than a mountebank; he had, however, great influence with the Spaniards and raised several Spanish regiments. One of these, called *Tiradores de Doyle*, was in existence till recently, and some of his regiments still survive. Sir Charles Doyle's strongly Irish characteristics would naturally make him *simpatico* to the Spaniards; in addition he had an Austrian mother.

The last of the military Doyles of note was Sir Charles's son, Sir Charles Hastings Doyle, who commanded the troops in Nova Scotia during the period of the American Civil War, and was specially thanked by both the British and American Governments for the great tact he exhibited in difficult circumstances.

Perhaps, however, the most romantic history of all the Doyles was that of Sir John Milly Doyle, son of Nicholas, the parson son of the first Charles. While in the Peninsular War, his cousin, Sir Charles, commanded Spanish troops, Sir John Milly commanded Portuguese, and later in life returned to the scene of his former exploits to assist the young Queen Maria against her uncle Miguel. Captured by the latter and left for a time in a loathsome dungeon, he was ultimately ransomed by his uncle, Sir John, the ex-Governor of Guernsey, and, nothing daunted, returned to fight for Queen Maria, and played a considerable part in placing her upon her throne. But when it came to a question of payment there was nothing doing. Sir John Milly Doyle was largely instrumental in getting a Committee of the British House of Commons to sit on the claims of those officers who had served Portugal, and in the end everyone was paid except himself. As his biographer and relative, Colonel Arthur Doyle, caustically remarks: " The moral of this is, if you go out to place a wandering princess on her throne, have a stamped agreement, or, better still, get paid in advance."

Sir John Milly Doyle sank into complete poverty and ended his days as a Military Knight of Windsor. From him Thackeray may well have drawn his character of Colonel Newcome.

The Doyles, one and all, exhibited Irish characteristics to an extent which, if set out in fiction, would be regarded as exaggerated, and as improbable of occurrence in so many different individuals. Gallantry, wit, extravagance, popularity, all are there in a greater or lesser degree in every one.

Anne, sister of Sir John Milly Doyle, married an

Irish squire named Francis Wheeler, an easy-going man, incompetent in money affairs. Of him and his incompetence she tired, and took up her abode, together with her two daughters, with old Sir John Doyle, at the time Governor of Guernsey.

One of these daughters, Rosina, tells us in her memoirs of how she loved the pomp and state which Sir John kept, and regarded him himself as the dearest and kindest of all created beings. A singularly brilliant and a singularly beautiful girl, Rosina Wheeler attracted the equally brilliant young author, Edward Bulwer Lytton. But the marriage of these two, dowered as they were with all the gifts of the gods, proved singularly unsuccessful. When they finally separated there were undoubtedly faults on both sides, but while the husband subsequently bore himself with dignity, the lack of balance which obviously existed in the Doyles reached a fatal pitch in the wife, whose later career was unedifying to the last degree. Many tried to help her, but, except for her faithful biographer, she was found by all to be impossible. Robert, the only child, saw her only once, though his attitude towards her throughout life was always chivalrous.

Robert, afterwards first Earl of Lytton, whose descent on both sides was extraordinarily interesting, had indeed an intensely chivalrous nature; his career has often been compared to that of an Elizabethan noble. As might have been expected from his descent, he was versatile to the highest degree, diplomatist, administrator, poet, a most brilliant talker and strikingly good-looking. It was from his mother's side undoubtedly that he inherited that undue optimism in money matters so characteristic of the Doyles. As

Viceroy of India, his politics, though magnificently conceived, have been severely criticized, but as to his social qualities in that position there was never any disagreement, and these same qualities fitted him better still for the Embassy at Paris, in which he died. As a poet he stands high in the second rank, but the dazzling glitter of his verses fatigues in time. In most respects he greatly resembled Lord Dufferin, his successor both in India and at Paris; but if Lytton had the greater brilliancy, Dufferin had the greater tact, Lytton's unconventionality frequently deeply offending the dull of wit. Lord Dufferin's mother, it is interesting to recall, was a Sheridan, and there was something in him, too, of the Celt.

The first Earl of Lytton's wife, Edith Villiers, niece of the Lord Clarendon so well known as Foreign Secretary in the middle of the nineteenth century, came of a family with abilities almost equal to those of the Lyttons, allied, however, with more solid qualities. Lord and Lady Lytton's children have shown marked versatility. The present Earl, well known in his Cambridge days as a leading light of the A.D.C., has been a successful Governor of Bengal during a most difficult period. His brother, Mr. Neville Lytton, writer, painter and amateur champion at "royal" tennis, has exhibited very diverse talents, while one of the daughters, Lady Constance Lytton, became very well known indeed at the time of the Woman Suffrage agitation. Her brother Neville's book, *The English Country Gentleman*, contains a most interesting study of his sister, who inherited the intensely artistic and emotional disposition of so many of her ancestors. Mr. Neville Lytton's own wife is daughter of that curiously interesting personality, Mr. Wilfrid Blunt, and on her mother's side is descended from Byron. Their children can boast a most exceptional number of interesting relatives in almost every direction, both in the immediate and the remoter past. So also can their cousins, the present Lady Lytton belonging to the Anglo-Indian family of the Plowdens, to whom reference has been made in another chapter, while Lady Betty Lytton married Mr. Gerald Balfour, Lord Balfour's brother, and Lady Emily Lytton Sir Edwin Lutyens, the leading architect of the present day.

We have now traced the descendants of chief note of the sons of the first Charles Doyle and Elizabeth Milly, his wife, and we will next turn to the descendants of their daughter, Catherine Bushe. While the " Celtic touch " is clearly to be discerned in these descendants, other characteristics, not so recognizably Hibernian, also appear. Charles Kendal Bushe, the only son of the Rev. Thomas Bushe and Catherine Doyle, was very prominent in the famous College Historical Society of Trinity, Dublin. Grattan, who heard him there, remarked : " Bushe spoke with the tongue of an angel." Acquiring a large practice at the Bar, Bushe rose to be Chief Justice of Ireland, and filled that office " with a character the purest and most unsullied that ever wore the ermine." An altogether admirable man, the Chief Justice seems to have escaped the weaknesses noticeable in so many of his maternal relatives, but, like them, he was a delightful companion and a wonderful *raconteur*. His wife Anne was sister of Sir Philip Crampton, the leading Dublin doctor of his time, and from the Crampton strain is probably derived the scientific abilities which were to reappear in some of Mrs.

Bushe's descendants. Her daughter Charlotte married John, third Lord Plunket, whose father, the first Baron, had been Lord Chancellor of Ireland at the time when Charles Kendal Bushe was Chief Justice. An even greater orator and an equally brilliant wit, the Lord Chancellor is better known to fame than the Chief Justice, but was hardly perhaps a greater man.

Their grandchildren proved worthy of their distinguished grandfathers. William, fourth Lord Plunket, took orders in the Irish Church and rose to be Archbishop of Dublin. Hardly as great an orator as either of his grandfathers, the Archbishop possessed, however, a singularly charming voice, and his wise statesmanship was of the greatest value to the Church during the difficult period after Disestablishment. Like another Archbishop of more recent times who also belongs to a most distinguished connection. (25) Archbishop Plunket had a positive genius for compromise and was the very antithesis of the narrow-minded type of ecclesiastic. Possessed of much wit in private, his appearance in public was, however, almost lugubriously solemn. His wit was clearly inherited from every direction, not least from his mother, to whose inveterate habit of punning he playfully alluded in verse.

His younger brother, David Plunket, was in many respects more brilliant, but did not go so far. Inheriting to the fullest degree the family eloquence, he, when Member for Trinity College, always filled the House when he spoke, but after serving for a time in one of Lord Salisbury's Cabinets, he faded out of public life. His social successes remained with him to the end, his popularity was unbounded, and in the palmy days of the diner-out no one was more in request than David Plunket, ultimately Lord Rathmore.

Two sisters of the Archbishop and Lord Rathmore published books of amusingly contrasted types. Miss Emmeline Plunket wrote learnedly on *Ancient Calendars and Constellations*, while her sister, Mrs. Richard Greene, produced children's stories, one at least of which, *Cushions and Corners*, was long widely popular. One of Mrs. Greene's sons, Sir Conyngham Greene, has been ambassador to Japan; another, Mr. Plunket Greene, is the well-known vocalist. Great singers have not, as a rule, had many notable relatives in other fields, but to this rule Mr. Plunket Greene is most certainly an exception.

Sir Dunbar Barton, son of another sister of Archbishop Plunket, after a distinguished career as an Irish judge, has occupied his leisure in writing an exceedingly interesting life of that remarkable personality, Marshal Bernadotte. (26)

The scientific ability already referred to as probably emanating from the Cramptons has been inherited by two grandsons of Anne Bushe, another daughter of the Chief Justice. One of these grandsons, Sir Bertram Windle, an F.R.S., and one of the leading anthropologists of the day, is at present a professor at Toronto University, while his cousin, Admiral Boyle Somerville, a great authority on tides, has, in addition, published dictionaries of native languages in the Pacific. Miss Edith Somerville, sister of the latter, is the well-known authoress of the *Adventures of an Irish R.M.* Few writers have shown greater insight into Irish character than has Miss Somerville; her descent is Irish in every direction, but one may well imagine that she owes most to the line emanating from the Doyles. (27)

The amazing versatility of the descendants of that obscure Irish squire, Charles Doyle, is sufficiently manifest. Half a dozen generals of note; an Archbishop; a Chief Justice and another judge; a Cabinet Minister; a Viceroy of India and another Governor; two ambassadors; a Fellow of the Royal Society; a biographer, two poets, two novelists, a writer of children's stories, a singer and a tennis champion; it is a sufficiently varied list. None stand perhaps quite in the first rank, but many stand high in the second; this is a characteristic we have met with in many similar instances. Intermarriage into other able families, notably the Lyttons, the Cramptons and the Plunkets, has doubtless been of great advantage, but there must clearly have been much latent ability in Charles Doyle or in Elizabeth Milly, or some probably in both. And that ability has taken, as we have seen, a distinctively Irish turn, for in almost all the members of the connection obvious Irish characteristics are observable. There are Irish families that can show one or two greater men, but for all-round brilliance none can vie with the descendants of Charles Doyle, of Bramblestown.

CHAPTER XI

TWO RENEGADES

THE origin of most of the leading Scottish families is rooted very far back in Scotland's past. This, however, is not the case in one of the most conspicuous of such families—a family which, producing many men of note in the male line, is even more remarkable for the descendants of its founder in female lines.

When in 1537 the lovely but ill-fated Madeline of France landed in Scotland as the bride of King James V, a certain John Hope came over in her train. Hope is said to have been a domestic, but after the death of his young mistress he, staying in Scotland, took up mercantile pursuits, and did well therein. He dealt mainly in the importation of silks and velvets from France, and in this business he was succeeded by his son and eventually by his grandson, Henry Hope, who, in the course of a visit to France on business, met and married Jacqueline de Toit, who, like himself, belonged to the Reformed Faith. From Henry Hope and his French wife sprang a most extensive connection, numbering, among others, a Prime Minister, Lord Rosebery; a Lord Chancellor, Lord Erskine; the present Archbishop of Canterbury; three Viceroys of India, the first and fourth Earls of Minto and Lord Auckland; a great philosopher in Sir William Hamilton, a great novelist in Robert Louis Stevenson, and a famous banker in Thomas Coutts. Here it is proposed to trace from Henry Hope two lines of descent, in themselves of interest in almost every direction, and ending in two of the most singular characters of recent times, men gifted with great abilities, who for causes almost inexplicable saw fit to pursue lines of action at total variance with what should have been their natural instincts.

Thomas, the youngest son of Henry Hope and Jacqueline de Toit, was the first, but by no means the last, of his family to make a name in the legal profession. As a young man, in 1616, Thomas Hope first came to the fore by his brilliant defence of certain Presbyterian ministers accused of treason—a treason which existed only in the bigoted imagination of King James I. Hope lost his case owing to the subservience of the Bench, but he made his reputation and in time a large fortune. For many years Lord Advocate, his influence at the beginning of the troubles under Charles I was always exercised on the side of moderation, but he was unable to control the furious passions of the times. Never himself elevated to the Bench, he had the curious experience of seeing two of his sons Lords of Session, a position ultimately attained also by a third. It has been said that the custom of the Lord Advocate wearing his hat while pleading arose from the feeling of impropriety evoked by Sir Thomas Hope addressing his sons with uncovered head.

Sir Thomas kept a diary, consisting mostly of entries of a somewhat bald nature, but at times mentioning curious incidents. On the marriage of his daughter Mary to Sir Charles Erskine, Sir Thomas borrowed jewellery for the bride from his daughter-in-law and notes as follows: " From Anna Foulis the jewel for Mary at her marriage, and I gave her a ticket to give it back or else good before Whitsunday next." Anna

TWO RENEGADES

Foulis seems to have been a business-like lady. A considerable heiress, she brought her husband, Sir James Hope, lead-mines near Leith, which he worked successfully, in addition to attaining a considerable reputation as a judge—"a pious and prudent man," says the annalist Nicholl. He was ancestor of the later Earls of Hopetoun.

His two elder brothers, John and Thomas, both, as has been mentioned, also judges, took the Parliament side in the Civil Wars, John sitting, in Cromwell's time, in the English House of Commons. His son Archibald eventually reached the Bench, and even this did not exhaust the legal distinction of the immediate descendants of Sir Thomas Hope. Margaret, daughter of John and sister of Archibald, married Sir Robert Pringle, and their son, Walter Pringle, was in the time of Queen Anne the leading advocate at the Scottish Bar. He was not raised to the Bench till late in life, but in such high consideration was he held, that on his death all the judges attended his funeral in their robes of office, a tribute unique at the time.

With Walter Pringle legal distinction ends in the line which we are considering, to be replaced, however, by distinction as great in another field. His nephew, Sir John Pringle, rose in the middle of the eighteenth century to be perhaps the greatest physician of his time. Commencing his career as an army doctor, he served at the battle of Dettingen, and by his writings laid the foundation of the scientific treatment of those diseases which are specially liable to be contracted in campaigns, a subject which had been much neglected till his time. Acquiring later an extensive civilian practice, he served for six years, 1772–78, as

President of the Royal Society, to which body he read papers on the most varied topics, by no means confined to medical matters, but including such subjects as natural history, the reflecting telescope and the theory of gunnery. Sir John Pringle took, indeed, all science as his province; his biographer informs us that he did not care for art or poetry, but was fond of music, " though," he continues, " this (music) is often neglected as persons advance in years, and this I think was the case with my friend, Sir John Pringle."

Some of the gifts of this great but now almost forgotten worthy descended on one who was doubly his great-nephew. The physician's sister, Margaret, married a Sir James Hall, and their son, Sir John Hall, married his first cousin, Magdalen Pringle, daughter of Sir John Pringle's brother Robert. Sir James Hall, son of Sir John Hall and Magdalen Pringle, achieved a great reputation as a geologist in the early days of that science, was President of the Royal Society of Edinburgh, and was also a leading authority on Gothic architecture, constructing a remarkable model of a Gothic cathedral in wattle-work. In early life Sir James Hall was sent to the Military School at Brienne, in France, where he was contemporary with, though senior to, Napoleon Bonaparte, a fact afterwards recalled to his son at St. Helena, when the ex-Emperor made special mention of the Scotsman's mathematical abilities. Sir James Hall was then still alive, and curiously different had been his quiet career to that of the pupil who was probably considered in those early years as greatly his inferior in mental attainment.

Sir James Hall married Lady Helen Douglas, herself descended from Sir Thomas Hope, the Lord Advocate, and sister of a most interesting character, Thomas Douglas, fourth Earl of Selkirk. A born idealist, Selkirk, in 1802, perceiving the wretched condition of much of the Highlands at the time, took an active part in settling denizens of that region in Prince Edward Island, in Canada. This was successful, but a further and more ambitious effort led the Earl into many and great difficulties. Determining to send settlers to the Red River, in Western Canada, now the Province of Manitoba, but then an uninhabited wilderness, Selkirk purchased a controlling interest in the Hudson Bay Company, which was supposed to own that region. In 1811 he sent out his settlers, but these first of all suffered great hardships owing to rascally conduct on the part of the Earl's agents, and subsequently another organization, the North-Western Company, claimed control of the Red River district, and what was practically a state of civil war ensued in this remote region. Selkirk in 1815 went out and re-established his settlers, who had been evicted by the rival company; for this he was prosecuted in the Canadian courts and heavily fined. Worn out with worry and broken in health, he returned to Europe, only to die. Walter Scott said of him: "I never knew a man of a more generous and disinterested disposition." Soon after his death the two companies amalgamated, a course which, if earlier adopted, might have saved him all his trouble, but his name is, at any rate, held in honour in Manitoba, where the town of Selkirk is called after him.

The name of his nephew, Basil Hall, son of Sir James, was, just a hundred years ago, exceedingly well known to readers, particularly to those of the younger generation. During a long career in the navy, Hall was fortunate enough to see service in many remote parts of the world, and wielding, as he did, a skilful pen, his books on the Loo Choo Islands and on the West Coast of South America were particularly delightful. It was on his return from the China Seas that he landed in St. Helena, on which occasion that interview with the ex-Emperor took place to which reference has already been made. Hall naturally thought it remarkable that Napoleon should remember his father so well, considering all that had happened since.

"Not at all," was the reply. "Your father was the first Englishman I ever met, and I have remembered him all my life on that account." Napoleon further inquired as to the opinion Sir James held of him. Basil tactfully replied that his father had always spoken well of the encouragement which the Emperor gave to science.

Basil Hall, in addition to his literary, possessed considerable scientific attainments, and was elected a Fellow of the Royal Society. This distinction had fallen also to an elder brother, to his uncle, Lord Selkirk, to his father, Sir James, and, with the Presidency, to his double great-granduncle, Sir John Pringle. A very remarkable succession.

Basil Hall's daughter, Eliza, married Rear-Admiral William Chamberlain, of a famous Service family. Two of his brothers, Neville and Crawford Chamberlain, were highly distinguished in the Indian Army, Neville, in particular, being the typical *beau sabreur*, the very soul of chivalry. Neither of the sons of Admiral William Chamberlain and Eliza Hall themselves adopted, however, a Service career. The elder, Basil Hall Chamberlain, followed in the footsteps of his maternal grandfather to the Far East, settling, however, in

Japan, a country strictly closed to all Europeans in the grandfather's days. For many years Professor of Japanese at Tokio University, Basil Hall Chamberlain is the greatest living European authority on that country, and his best-known work, *Things Japanese*, is a classic.

His younger brother, Houston Stewart Chamberlain, was also destined to pass the greater part of his life outside his native land. He is the first of the *Two Renegades* who give the title to this chapter. Named after a well-known admiral, under whom his father had served, he was, when his health broke down in boyhood, given a German tutor, who no doubt first implanted in him a love of Germany. Settling in that country and marrying a German wife, Chamberlain gradually became less and less English in his views. He sprang first to fame in 1899 by his work, written in German, *The Foundations of the Nineteenth Century*. Showing considerable learning and a very fair style, this book has been described as a glorification of Germany alone, but this is hardly correct; it is rather a glorification of the Nordic, or, as it was then called, the Teutonic race, and Chamberlain is careful to say that he does not identify Teutons exclusively with Germans. There is, in fact, nothing particularly anti-English in the book, and Chamberlain's other writings before the war were chiefly in connection with Wagner, the daughter of which great composer he took for his second wife. When the war came, however, he, as is so well known, threw himself entirely on the side of his adopted country, and, far from maintaining silence, an at any rate possible course, wrote extensively against England. In one of these writings he permits himself to remark on the total want of intellect in the English character. And this, to go no farther, with the example of his own ancestors before his eyes. Almost wholly English on his father's side, almost wholly Scottish on his mother's, Chamberlain's conduct was in flat defiance of all natural instincts. Subjected, no doubt, to strong pressure, local and domestic, there still remains a curious kink in his character, the origin of which, among his most variously distinguished ancestors, it seems impossible to discern.

FOR the descent of the second of the *Two Renegades* we must go back to Henry Hope, the Edinburgh merchant, and Jacqueline de Toit, his wife. In addition to Thomas, the Lord Advocate, Henry and Jacqueline had other sons, one of whom founded the great financial house of the Hopes of Amsterdam. Another, Henry, carried on the family business in Edinburgh, which business descended to his only child, Anna. Anna Hope married James Stewart of Coltness, who was himself connected with financial affairs and became Lord Provost of Edinburgh. Anna, however, was quite capable of carrying on her own business herself; according to her grandson, she "made few demands for family expenses, but answered most of these from her profits in her own way." The same narrator tells us further of Anna: "If she had any fault it was in being too anxious, either when she imagined her husband in any danger or upon his necessary absences abroad. No occasion of writing was to be omitted, else it was next to death." Capable, warm-hearted and full of nerves, admirable and lovable, but also, no doubt, sometimes a little trying, Anna Hope's type is still with us, perhaps even more so now than in that day.

Two of the sons of James Stewart and Anna Hope, Henry and Robert, carried on alike the mercantile traditions and the connection with France by engaging, with success, in the wine trade with Bordeaux. Robert, who purchased the estate of Allenbank and was created a baronet, had many descendants of interest. Two may be mentioned here as representing almost the opposite poles of activity: Thomas Coutts, founder of the famous bank, was a great-grandson; Jean Elliot, authoress of the pathetic ballad, *The Flowers of the Forest*, was a grand-daughter. The talents of Thomas Coutts are more clearly referable to the Hope descent than are those of Jean Elliot.

James Stewart, another son of the Lord Provost and Anna Hope, passed an interesting and varied career. Called to the Scottish Bar, he in the reign of Charles II had to fly the country, owing to his opposition to the Government, and hide himself in London, where, under an assumed name, he eked out a livelihood by giving legal advice at half the usual fees. On one occasion he emerged to assist in a debate between English and Scottish bishops, when he was described as " a man in a very negligent mean habit, who astonished the prelates by his learning." Ere long he was forced to seek a more secure refuge in Holland, but with the advent of William III his prospects changed completely. In 1692 he was made Lord Advocate, and held that office for many years. A most rigid Presbyterian, Sir James Stewart was, as was natural, also the strictest of Sabbatarians. An interesting account of the Sundays of his household has been given by a grand-daughter: "After prayers by the chaplain at nine o'clock, all went together to church at ten, the women in high dress. Half after twelve they came home, at one had prayers again by the chaplain, after which they had a bit of cold meat and an egg, and returned to church at two, were out again by four, when everyone retired to their private devotions except the children and servants, who were convened by the chaplain and examined. This continued till five, when dinner was served. A few friends partook of the meal, which continued till eight, after which prayer was performed by the old gentleman himself, when all retired." The three hours' dinner seems to have been the only respite.

One rather suspects that the writer of this account, Agnes Mure, was beginning to revolt against this austerity, which would, however, undoubtedly have appealed to her mother, Anna Stewart, the wife of William Mure of Caldwell, a lady of strong religious views who in 1723 made a Covenant with God, referring to various similar Covenants made in previous years, all very much in the style of a legal document. In 1728 she renewed this Covenant, being apparently somewhat afraid that her former efforts might be considered out of date. A legal trend of thought was evidently inherited by this Mrs. Mure, who withal was a woman of sound practical sense, as evidenced by the advice she gave her son William anent his marriage: "In your choice of a wife, first seek God's direction, which only can keep you from erring; next seek her out of a good family and a good mother, which we reckon still a good Scot's mark for a good wife. Let not money be your only care; a good woman will soon make up her tocker." This son, William

Mure, married according to his mother's directions, became himself a Scottish judge, and was grandfather of another William Mure, the historian of Greek literature. This last William Mure was a man in whom pride of birth and pride of intellect struggled for first place, with the rather unfortunate result that he is said to have "despised historians because they were not country gentlemen, and country gentlemen because they were not historians." From the Mures of Caldwell the present Archbishop of Canterbury is descended.

The son of the Sabbatarian Lord Advocate, a third Sir James Stewart, became Solicitor-General for Scotland; he married into the great legal family of Dalrymple, and thus his children had a singularly brilliant heredity. Particular mention may be made of the son and of two of the daughters. The son, a fourth Sir James Stewart, was forced to leave Scotland owing to being concerned in the rising of '45, and spent many years on the Continent, maturing during his exile a work on political economy, which he eventually published when allowed to return to his native land. His was perhaps the first publication of importance on the subject; it was not without merit, but, unfortunately for the author, was almost immediately superseded by the superior work of Adam Smith. A man of great culture, beloved by all who knew him, Sir James Stewart was held in specially high regard by Lady Mary Wortley Montagu, who made his acquaintance during their joint wanderings, at about the same time as she met his young compatriot, Robert Adam. Whilst residing at Spa, in the Netherlands, Sir James Stewart was visited by his sister Margaret, Mrs. Calderwood, who, with her husband, took the opportunity of making a somewhat prolonged tour in that part of the world. Fortunately for posterity she left a journal, not separately published till the seventies of last century. It is a fascinating work, written in a simple and downright but most attractive style. Places and people are alike described in an extremely vivid manner, and the character of the authoress herself is writ large before us, intensely practical, shrewd and business-like, with a strong Scottish Presbyterian dislike of Catholicism, the good points of which, however, she was always fair enough to recognize. Except for the exercise of linguistic talents which his wife lacked, Mr. Calderwood seems to have played a singularly subordinate part in these travels—she managed everything. Either, however, through his insistence, or more probably through her forbearance, he is found occupying a cabin to himself on the voyage across, while she occupied one with a most miscellaneous horde, male and female, notwithstanding which, in describing her night's experience, she informs us that she undressed, being assisted in her toilet by her footman!

Agnes Stewart, the sister of this very strong-minded lady, married Henry Erskine, tenth Earl of Buchan. He was her distant cousin, being himself descended from the Hopes; his great-grandmother was that Mary Hope who married Charles Erskine, on which occasion, as has been already related, her father, Sir Thomas Hope, borrowed for her a jewel. In another direction Lord Buchan descended from Sir Thomas Browne, the famous author of that curious production, *Religio Medici*, but he does not seem himself to have been a man of any special capacity, and, like Mr. Calderwood, played second fiddle to his brilliant wife. Lady Buchan, in addition to mathematical gifts most unusual among women, was, like her sister, a notable housewife. Though the Buchans were very poor for their rank, they entertained all the best of Edinburgh society, generally over a "cosy dish of tea," the general standard being pleasantly inexpensive. Under this regime of plain living and high thinking were brought up the three sons with whom the distinction of this line culminated. The least notable was the eldest, David, afterwards eleventh Earl of Buchan, in whom much natural ability was marred by a colossal vanity. Passing as a patron of literature, Buchan carried on an extensive correspondence with literary men. Very good-looking, he was a sad dog with the ladies, and showed singularly little consideration for his wife by his oft-repeated remark to the pretty girls he met: "Good-bye, my dear, and pray remember that Margaret, Countess of Buchan, is not immortal."

His next brother, Henry Erskine, was a far more worthy member of society. At the Scottish Bar he had for many years the leading practice, but, unlucky in his politics, a Whig when his party were hardly ever in the ascendant; he filled, for two short periods only, the office of Lord Advocate, previously occupied by so many of his relatives. Henry Erskine was universally popular and was considered the wittiest man of his day. On the first occasion of his attaining the position of Lord Advocate, his predecessor, Dundas, conceiving rightly, as it turned out, that Erskine's tenure would be but short, offered him the loan of his gown of office. "No, thank you," was the reply; "it shall never be said of Harry Erskine that he adopted the abandoned habits of his predecessor."

The career of his younger brother, Thomas, by far the most notable of the family, reads like a romance.

In 1764, at the age of fourteen, he left Scotland to join the navy, and actually never revisited his native land for more than fifty years. Detesting the service afloat, he spent a small legacy in purchasing a commission in the army, in which career, however, he found himself no better suited. Visiting on one occasion an Assize Court, he got into conversation with his compatriot, the great Chief Justice, Lord Mansfield, who, struck with his talents, advised him to go to the Bar. Selling his commission, Erskine, who had already married, lived with the greatest economy while studying for that profession, but his resources were practically at an end at the time of his call. Shortly after, he happened to meet a certain Captain Baillie, who was at the time bringing an action against Lord Sandwich, the First Lord of the Admiralty. (28) Erskine was unaware of the fact, but, as it happened, inveighed against Sandwich's general conduct. Baillie forthwith gave him a retainer, and Erskine, seizing the opportunity, pleaded the cause so brilliantly that his career was made. For many years thereafter he was by far the leading advocate at the English Bar. Inheriting the strong Whig traditions of his ancestors, his greatest fame was obtained by his defence of those prosecuted during the reaction after the French Revolution, when his eloquence extorted the unwilling admiration of those most opposed to his political views. Although attaining the Chancellorship, Lord Erskine, like his brother Henry, and for the same reason, was in office for a short time only, but he had, in any case, few qualifications as a judge. Like his eldest brother, his character was greatly spoiled by colossal vanity, but yet, like Brougham, whom in many respects he resembled, he studied the doings of his ancestors and acknowledged his debt to them. "Since," he said, "I am come lineally and directly from so many great lawyers in Scotland, I am forced to see that I owe my success entirely to the breed and not to any merit in myself."

Mary, daughter of Lord Erskine, married Edward Morris, a Master in Chancery, and their daughter Frances became the wife of Thomas Barton, an Anglo-Irish squire. The history of the Barton family presents features of interest. They derive originally from one Thomas Barton, of Norwich, who, going over to Ireland in the reign of James I, was one of the burgesses of Enniskillen at the time when a charter was first granted to that city in 1611. His descendant, another Thomas Barton, established in 1725 a wine business at Bordeaux, made a fortune and purchased an estate in Co. Tipperary. The Bordeaux business was continued during the eighteenth century, and Hugh Barton, grandson of the second Thomas, was, when the French Revolution broke out, at its head. During the Reign of Terror he barely escaped with his life, and was only saved through the exertions of his wife, born a French subject, though of Scottish origin. Though forced to flee from France, Hugh Barton was able, all through the period of the wars, to conduct his business through his French partner, Daniel Guestier. Hugh was father of the Thomas Barton who married Frances Morris, and while the immediate ancestors of the husband were concerned in the Bordeaux wine trade, curiously enough, as has been seen, remote ancestral connections of the wife had also been connected with that trade. Their daughter Anna married Robert Cæsar Childers, a brilliant Oriental scholar who died in the prime of life, and she was the mother of Erskine Childers, the second of the *Two Renegades*, whose strange and tragic career will be generally recollected. A man of brilliant literary gifts and much personal charm, Erskine Childers's extreme attitude during the recent Irish troubles remains wholly inexplicable, though, as in the case of Houston Chamberlain, *cherchez la femme* may afford some clue. While Chamberlain could, however, show no German descent at all, Childers could show a little Irish, but it was very little. Of his eight great-great-grandparents, four were of English origin, two of Scottish, one of Jewish and one only of Anglo-Irish. The Jewish origin, which may possibly account for some of the curious complications of his character, was derived by descent from Sampson Gideon, a well-known Hebrew financier of the eighteenth century. The Bartons, as we have seen, were themselves by no means specially Irish; of original English ancestry, their intermarriages had throughout been with similar families. Erskine Childers's descent was shared in all respects by his double first cousin and faithful follower, Robert Childers Barton. The cousins, with this slight Irish connection, took, as is well known, a course which led them far beyond the opinions of the majority of ultra-Celtic Hibernians. Erskine Childers's most famous book was *The Riddle of the Sands*, and the "Riddle of Erskine Childers," like the "Riddle of Houston Chamberlain," remains insoluble by heredity. Heredity can account for the gifts of both men, but not for the perverseness with which those gifts were used. That the two most notorious renegades of recent times should be distantly related is, no doubt, merely a coincidence, but it must be admitted to be, at any rate, a coincidence of remarkable interest.

CHAPTER XII

MOUNT EVEREST

FROM the fifteenth to the seventeenth centuries the family of Waller was of much consideration in the county of Kent. The first Waller of note was a Sir Richard, who fought at Agincourt and to whose custody the Duke of Orleans was committed during his captivity. Sir Richard's daughter Alice married Sir John Guildford, and from her descended the Dudleys and Sidneys. Edmund Waller, the poet, derived from Sir Richard through a junior line seated in Bucks; he was fourth cousin of two notable military leaders, Sir William and Sir Hardress Waller, who belonged to the main line settled in Kent; they were alike grandsons of a Sir Walter Waller. Sir William, who adopted the Parliamentary cause during the Civil Wars, was, till the advent of Cromwell, perhaps the most distinguished commander on the Roundhead side. From his daughter, who married into the Harcourt family, descended a notable line, of whom Simon, Lord Harcourt, was Lord Chancellor in the early years of the eighteenth century, and Sir William Harcourt only just missed the Premiership at the end of the nineteenth.

We are here, however, concerned with Sir Hardress Waller and his descendants. Hardress in 1630 settled in Ireland, where he married Elizabeth Dowdell, who brought him an estate in Co. Limerick. On the outbreak of the Civil War in 1641, he, in common with most of the Irish Protestants, was at first more concerned in attempting to suppress the Catholics than in definitely taking the side of either King or Parliament, but a visit to England, and probably the influence of his cousin, Sir William, brought Hardress decisively to the Parliamentary side, in which, for a time, he took an active and leading part. He was one of the King's judges and signed his death-warrant, subsequently becoming Cromwell's right-hand man during his reconquest of Ireland. During the Protectorate, however, Hardress Waller curiously enough received no preferment, and though before the Restoration he made some effort to change sides, his position as a regicide rendered all attempts at reconciliation impossible. In October 1660 he stood his trial, and though, thanks to strong influence exerted in his favour, he escaped the death penalty, he ended his life in confinement. His son was, however, allowed to retain the Irish property, and his descendants in the male line were associated with Ireland till recent times.

It is to the daughters of Sir Hardress that we must turn for further distinction. Both married in Ireland, Anne, the elder, first to Sir Maurice Fenton and secondly to Sir William Petty, Bridget, the younger, to Henry Cadogan. Anne Waller had a curiously interesting career, touching history at many points. She married Maurice Fenton in 1653, at the time of her father's greatest prosperity, Fenton himself being connected with the great Boyle family, whose influence at that time permeated all Ireland. Cromwell created Maurice Fenton a baronet, which baronetcy was, of course, forfeited at the Restoration, but, singularly enough, Charles revived it in his favour, although his father-in-law was at the time lying in gaol as a regicide! Fenton did not long survive, and his widow shortly after took for her second husband Sir William Petty, one of the most remarkable men of his time. The son of a clothier, born with a genius for mathematics and mechanics, Petty was in 1649 an Oxford Professor and a member of the club which was the precursor of the Royal Society, of which body he was later to be a founder. In 1651 Petty, who was ready to turn his hand to anything, became physician to the forces in Ireland. His presence in that country led to his appointment of surveyor of forfeited lands. This survey he executed with consummate skill, incidentally acquiring for his own use no inconsiderable portion of the said lands, particularly in the county of Kerry. At the time of his marriage to Anne Waller, Lady Fenton, Petty was a rich man, but he himself cared little for spending; his tastes were simple, and his published letters show an amusing disinclination to disburse small sums, a trait which must often have brought him into conflict with his wife, whose outlook was widely different. John Aubrey, a great friend of both husband and wife, describes her as " an elegant lady who could endure nothing mean or that was not magnificent." Aubrey had for Lady Petty the greatest admiration. He portrays her as " a very beautiful and ingenuous lady, brown, with glorious eyes, and an extraordinary wit as well as a beauty." The Pettys, notwithstanding any differences about money, were a devoted couple. On one occasion Sir William writes: " I am almost weary of living, did not my wife, as she is at the moment doing, refresh me with the lute strings." Characteristically he goes on to complain of the price of the strings in question.

Sir William lived into the reign of James II, of whose Irish policy he strongly disapproved. James had, however, a high regard for both husband and wife, and almost his last act as a reigning monarch was to create Lady Petty, now a widow, Baroness Shelburne in her own right. William allowed the creation to stand, and as Baroness Shelburne she died, after withstanding with most singular success all the changes and chances of those eventful times. By Sir William Petty she had two sons, to whose education their father devoted the most anxious care; the directions he gave them should indeed have turned out Admirable Crichtons, prominent alike in intellectual, social and athletic qualities, but, as in the case a little later of Lord Chesterfield, paternal solicitude seems to have been of little avail, and neither son did anything in particular. The abilities of both parents, but not the mother's beauty, descended on the daughter, Anne Petty, of whom also the father was devotedly fond. He requested in his will that she should marry in Ireland, and with this she complied, choosing, however, a man to whom she was but little suited. Thomas Fitzmaurice, twenty-first Baron (29) of Kerry and Lixnaw and subsequently first Earl of Kerry, came of a sturdy but semi-barbarous stock, whose qualities he fully shared. His grandson, the famous Lord Shelburne, describes him as " a handsome man, no education and not much understanding, but strong nerves and great perseverance, the most severe character that can be imagined, obstinate and inflexible." Lord Kerry was, indeed, a typical autocrat of an autocratic period, not least autocratic in Western Ireland, and he ruled his family and his tenantry alike with a rod of iron, tempered, however, by a strict sense of justice, this being the best feature of his character. His wife did her best to introduce the graces and refinements of life into her somewhat wild surroundings. Sir William Petty had expressed a wish " that one day arithmetic and accountantship will adorn a young woman better than a suit of ribands, and will keep her warmer than a damnable dear *manteau*." Lady Kerry inherited in effect no small share of her father's mathematical gifts, and, like Lady Buchan a little later on, was able to combine those gifts with those of a notable housewife. Says Lord Shelburne : " By a conduct which was a perfect model of sense, prudence and spirit, she educated her children well, gained her family consideration at home and abroad, supported a style of living superior to any family whatever in Ireland, and with all this improved her husband's fortune." And as the same grandson remarks : " She brought into the Fitzmaurice family whatever degree of sense may have appeared in it or whatever wealth is likely to remain in it." The sense failed much to appear or the wealth much to remain with her eldest son, the second Earl of Kerry, and departed altogether with his son, the third Earl, a weak, extravagant man, who was forced to part with the estates in North Kerry, which had been held by his ancestors since the time of Strongbow.

In her own immediate family the abilities of Anne, Lady Kerry, descended most on her daughter, Lady Arabella Denny, of whom her nephew, Lord Shelburne, spoke in the highest terms. Anne Petty's younger son John, though not a man of any note, seems, however, to have retained some of his mother's sense, and, being fortunate enough to inherit the wealth of his Petty uncle, he was created Earl of Shelburne. With his son, the second Earl, whose autobiography has been quoted above, ability reappeared. This Lord Shelburne had a curious political career; for a brief time only he came clearly to the front, being Premier in 1783 at a very critical moment of history, but he never held office thereafter. He was quite extraordinarily unpopular, for reasons which it is now not very easy to see, but quite evidently he was without tact and unskilled in the management of men. He is, however, one of those statesmen who stand higher in the judgment of posterity than in that of their contemporaries. More of a political philosopher than a politician, his ideas were ahead of those of his age. He advocated Free Trade, Catholic Emancipation, Electoral Reform, and was the friend of Radicals like Priestly, Price, Bentham and Romilly. A munificent patron of literature and an excellent man of business, he had many points of resemblance to his great-grandfather, Sir William Petty, who would also probably not have been successful in purely political fields. Shelburne after his retirement was created Marquis of Lansdowne, a title which ultimately descended to his son by his second marriage with Louisa Fitzpatrick. This lady was a great-niece of Lady Mary Wortley Montagu, and sister of Richard Fitzpatrick, the bosom friend of Charles Fox, and very well known himself as a wit and a man of fashion. Qualities probably inherited from the maternal side rendered the third Marquis of Lansdowne as popular as his father had been the reverse, but his political career was also in many respects singular. Pushed forward in early life and at the same time possessed of obvious ability, he was Chancellor of the Exchequer at the age of twenty-five, and in that capacity pronounced a eulogy on Nelson after Trafalgar. Forty-seven years later, he, in the Lords, pronounced a similar eulogy on Wellington. Out of office during the long period of Whig exclusion, he lost all ambition, and though more than once he might have been Premier during the later period of Whig domination, he would never take that office, contenting himself with that of Lord President. He was, however, most influential in the councils of his party, and his moderation and good sense were held in the highest esteem. A typical *grand seigneur*, Lansdowne House and Bowood were, in his time, to a supreme degree the meeting-place of eminent men of every sort and kind. He married into the Fox family, and his son married the daughter of that most interesting character, the Comte de Flahault, a general under the First Empire and an ambassador under the Third, a most striking link between those two great periods. The career of the late Lord Lansdowne, grandson of the third Marquis and of the Comte de Flahault, was a worthy continuation of those of the best of his ancestors.

Lady Louisa, daughter of the third Marquis, married James Howard, of the Suffolk family, and her son married Lady Emily Bury, an Irish heiress who was descended from the famous beauty, Elizabeth Gunning, Duchess successively of Hamilton and of Argyll. Her son, Colonel Charles Kenneth Howard-Bury, has trodden—very literally trodden—fields of which his many distinguished forbears can never have dreamt. As leader of the first Mount Everest expedition, Colonel Howard-Bury performed his difficult task of reconnoitring with consummate skill. The leadership of the second and third expeditions fell to General Charles Granville Bruce, and both leaders can claim descent from Sir Hardress Waller, with whom this chapter opens. The line from which Colonel Howard-Bury derives has been shown to have achieved distinction in almost every generation. In the ancestry of General Bruce an equally interesting history is enfolded.

Bridget Waller, younger daughter of Sir Hardress, married, as has been mentioned, Henry Cadogan, the son of a Welshman who had settled in Ireland under Strafford. Henry Cadogan, a Dublin barrister, himself attained no distinction, but it was otherwise with his son William, who inherited to the full the martial instincts of his Waller connections. Entering the army in the reign of William III, William Cadogan was a major at the outbreak of the War of the Spanish Succession; his abilities were detected by Marlborough, who made him his quartermaster-general. In this capacity he served throughout the war, highly distinguishing himself in all Marlborough's great battles, and later was ambassador in Holland, where he took to himself a Dutch wife. (30) Ultimately created an Earl, he became Commander-in-Chief on Marlborough's death. Like his aunt, Anne Waller, Lady Petty, Cadogan was fond of magnificence and also, it appears, of gambling. In 1719 he won a considerable sum from the Duke of Richmond, Charles II's son by Louise de Quéraille. Richmond, being unable or unwilling to pay, it was agreed to liquidate the debt by the marriage of the Duke's elder son, Lord March, then quite a boy, to Cadogan's daughter Sarah, then only thirteen years old. This accordingly took place, and March was sent off on his travels, detesting the idea of the bride who had thus been forced upon him; she, for her part, went back to her parents. Four years later March returned to England, and, going to the theatre, was tremendously struck with the beauty of a young lady sitting in one of the boxes. On inquiring who she was, he was told: "That is the reigning toast, Lady March." He fell in love with his wife on the spot, and the marriage, thus strangely begun, proved successful to the highest degree; the second Duke and Duchess of Richmond were the most devoted of lovers throughout life, and in death they were divided by less than a year. The Duke, who, through his mother, belonged to the great Villiers connection, was hardly a man of parts, but was generally popular, and the usually spiteful Harvey describes him as "a friendly and generous man, noble in his way of acting, talking, thinking." A great patron of sport of all kinds, Richmond played cricket in the days of its infancy; an interesting challenge by his neighbour, Sir William Gage, to a match is still extant, but not so, alas, the score.

His and Sarah Cadogan's eldest son, the third Duke, was a man of far greater ability, but, like his relative, Shelburne, his political career was disappointing, partly from a lack of incentive to exert himself and partly on account of the advanced opinions which he also shared with Shelburne. Unlike the latter, however, his manners and bearing were perfect, and the contrast between them is satirically described by Wraxall on the occasion of the two noblemen, together with the Duke of Devonshire, receiving the Garter at the same time: "The Duke of Devonshire advanced up to the Sovereign with his cold phlegmatic air like a clown;

Lord Shelburne came forward bowing on every side, smiling and fawning like a courtier; the Duke of Richmond presented himself easy and unembarrassed like a gentleman."

It was not, however, with the third Duke of Richmond, so much as with his sisters, and still more with his sisters' sons, that the distinction of the line was primarily to be maintained. Lady Caroline Lennox became the mother of Charles James Fox, Lady Emilia Lennox of Lord Edward Fitzgerald (who added interest, if hardly distinction, to the connection), while Lady Sarah Lennox was mother of the Napiers. Lady Caroline eloped with Henry Fox, the son of a successful parvenu, Sir Stephen Fox, whose career bore many resemblances to that of Sir William Petty. Her parents highly disapproved of the match, and it was four years before they consented to see their rebellious daughter, who had, however, no reason in the end to regret her step, for Henry Fox, a brilliant but most unprincipled politician, proved a devoted husband, and Lady Caroline survived him for an even shorter time than her mother had survived her father. She lived only to see the opening of the career of her son Charles, that most versatile but in many respects disappointing man. Charles Fox is yet another instance where the central figure of a group of distinguished relatives fails largely by reason of his versatility.

The career of Lady Sarah Lennox, the youngest daughter of the second Duke of Richmond and Lady Sarah Cadogan, was one of singular vicissitudes. A most beautiful girl, she was but sixteen when George III came to the throne, and almost immediately she attracted the attention of the young monarch. During the summer of 1761 the probability of a Queen Sarah was eagerly discussed in Court circles, and it was generally thought that the marriage would take place. One lady, who was very proud of her figure, said to Lady Sarah at a Drawing Room: " Do let me go in before you this once as you will never have another opportunity of seeing my beautiful back." Lady Susan Strangways, Lady Sarah's greatest friend, wrote in her old age: " I almost thought myself Prime Minister." But it was not to be; the influence of the King's mother, who was determined on a German marriage, prevailed over her son's inclinations, and the beautiful Sarah was only a bridesmaid, completely outshining the very plain bride. It was observed that when the reference in the marriage service to Abraham and Sarah occurred, the King nearly broke down, and a terrible *contretemps* was only just avoided when a very short-sighted peer started to make obeisance to Lady Sarah. George III never forgot his first love. Many years afterwards, in 1813, her great-niece, another Lady Sarah Lennox, was presented. The blind old monarch asked to be allowed to pass his hands gently over her face, to which request she had, of course, to comply.

What manner of children would have sprung from a union of George III and Lady Sarah Lennox? One may be certain that they would not have equalled the Napiers, but one may be equally certain that they would have excelled George IV and his brothers.

The year after her frustrated hopes, when only seventeen, Lady Sarah married a sporting baronet, Sir Charles Bunbury, best known as the owner of the first winner of the Derby. The marriage was not a success; on the whole the fault seems to have lain chiefly with the wife, who eventually went off with her cousin, Lord William Gordon, but, soon leaving him, retired to a secluded existence in a small house in her brother the Duke of Richmond's park. Bunbury eventually obtained a divorce, and the career of one who was so nearly a queen was apparently finished in disgrace. But the end was not yet. At the age of thirty-five she won the affections of Colonel George Napier, a descendant of the famous inventor of logarithms, a man himself of many attainments and of a most noble character. Though she was never to enjoy "the pomp of panoply," for Napier's means were always exiguous, Lady Sarah had at last found a devoted husband, and the end of her long life was cheered by the affection and brightened by the achievements of her brilliant sons. When at the end of the eighteenth century Colonel Napier was quartered in Ireland during those troubled and rebellious times, his residence was known as "The Eagle's Nest," partly from the striking appearance and partly from the abounding vitality of his boys. Three, Charles, George and William, rose to general's rank in the army; all were highly distinguished in the Peninsula, where Lord Wellington himself wrote more than once to their mother in terms of the highest commendation. George, though the least notable of the three, lived to be Governor of the Cape, Charles to be conqueror of Scinde, on which occasion he sent his famous dispatch, the shortest on record, "*Peccavi.*" The personality of Sir Charles Napier was an outstanding one. A man of strong religious feelings and marked democratic leanings, he was devoted to his men, who, in their turn, adored him. A courageous tilter against injustice, but, like many other Radicals in politics, an autocrat by nature, with a strong vein of both cantankerousness and egotism, he was a man who made alike many friends and many enemies.

No actually stronger personality than Charles Napier could well exist, but his brother William was far more gifted. A notable athlete, a skilful soldier, a painter and a sculptor of no mean merit, Sir William Napier is, of course, best known for his famous history of the Peninsular War, probably the best military history ever written by an actual participator in the scenes depicted. Devoted, like his brother Charles, to the rank and file, William Napier did as ample justice to them in his history as did Charles in his dispatches from Scinde. William shared, in fact, the democratic views of his eldest brother, and, like him, his outspoken methods raised up many enemies against him, but, as has been well said, the faults of both brothers were those of noble and generous natures. On the death of the last survivor of the brotherhood, the *Daily News* paid a striking tribute to their memory: " We have many gallant men left, but there can never be any like the Napiers. They were a group raised from the mediæval dead and set in the midst of us, clothed in a temperament which admitted all the ameliorating influences of our period of civilization."

Sir William Napier married his second cousin, Caroline Fox, niece of Charles James and the inheritor of much of her uncle's intellectual powers, the collaboration with her husband in his litarary undertakings, and his survivor by only six weeks, the third occasion in this family history in which a devoted wife soon followed her husband to the grave. Twenty-seven years later their daughter presented new colours to her father's old regiment, the 43rd, on which occasion she delivered a speech, the eloquence of which stirred all who heard it. This daughter was Norah, Lady Aberdare, the wife of a statesman described by Gladstone, then his chief, as "a heaven-born Home Secretary," herself portrayed as a woman "of rare cultivation and fine mind, uniting in an uncommon degree sympathy, humour and good sense."

She was the mother of General Charles Granville Bruce, the leader of the Second and Third Mount Everest expeditions. Readers of Sir Francis Younghusband's brilliant book, *The Epic of Mount Everest*, will recall the fine tribute he paid to the qualities of leadership alike of General Bruce and of Colonel Howard-Bury. It is not difficult to see from whence these qualities of leadership are derived.

CHAPTER XIII

FOUR GREAT ARTISTS

IN the latter part of the seventeenth century Thomas Baker, vicar of Bishop's Nympton, in Devon, won some fame as a mathematician and obtained the commendation of the newly founded Royal Society by a work published in 1684 with the quaint title of *The Geometrical Key, or Gate of Equations Unlocked*. It is said, but this has not been substantiated, that the mathematical parson had at one time the misfortune to be imprisoned in Newgate for debt, in respect of which it was remarked that he had better have possessed the key of Newgate than that of equations. Be this as it may, Baker appears at his death to have been possessed of some means, as we learn that he totally disinherited his daughter Theophila for marrying one Thomas Potter, his curate, not, one would have thought, an unnatural alliance. The Potters, struggling on as best they could, were no doubt pleased to marry their daughter, also named Theophila, to a young schoolmaster, Samuel Reynolds by name. Samuel was likewise a man of Devon, son of John Reynolds, vicar of St. Thomas's, Exeter, by the daughter of a merchant of that city. The family showed much scholastic ability. John, elder brother of Samuel, was Fellow of Eton and of King's College, published Latin textbooks and was father of William, a Fellow of Exeter College, Oxford. Joshua, another brother of Samuel, was Fellow and Bursar of Corpus Christi College, Oxford.

Samuel himself was a Scholar of Corpus, later Fellow of Balliol, and passed the rest of his life as Head Master of Plympton School. He is described as a man totally without guile, ignorant of the world, but a most charming character, one who might well have sat for the portrait of Fielding's " Parson Adams."

Samuel and Theophila Reynolds had a large family, from whose heredity some ability might certainly have been predicted, most probably in either the classics or in mathematics. Ability did appear, but in quite other directions. One son was destined to take a supreme place in the world of art, one daughter showed some artistic talent, another daughter rather greater literary talent.

No origin is more difficult to trace, as a rule, than that of artistic gifts, and certainly the case of Sir Joshua Reynolds, the first really pre-eminent British-born artist, is no exception to this rule. We may surmise, however, that his talent was probably derived from the maternal side, mathematical tastes bearing, on the whole, a greater affinity to craftsmanship than do literary gifts. Perhaps the great portrait-painter took from the mother's side his manual dexterity, from the father's side the intellectual powers without which the dexterity would not have gone far. In any event, there is certainly no doubt that Sir Joshua throughout life preferred the society of literary men to that of his brother-artists; he was, as is well known, a prominent member of Johnson's famous Literary Club.

The artistic gifts, latent, as far as we know, in the ancestry, appeared to a certain extent in his sister Frances, a miniature-painter, with, however, a cantankerous strain which she shared neither with her father nor with her distinguished brother, and which was, perhaps, derived from Thomas Baker, the mathematician. Another sister, Mary, Mrs. Palmer, showed greater ability and a pleasanter disposition. Something also of a painter, her ability was best shown in her excellent *Devonshire Dialogues*, in which she broke what was virtually new ground. She was Sir Joshua's favourite sister, and he was even more attached to her daughters, to one of whom, subsequently Lady Thomond, he left the greater part of the large fortune which he, first of his family, had acquired. Both Lady Thomond and her sister, afterwards Mrs. Gwatkin, were exceedingly attractive; the latter was portrayed by her uncle as "The Strawberry Girl."

It is, however, to the descendants of another sister of Sir Joshua, Elizabeth Reynolds, to whom we must look for further distinction. She married William Johnson, also a Devonshire man, and with her great-grandson, another William Johnson, who took the additional surname of Cory, there appeared a revival of the classical tradition. After winning every possible scholastic distinction at school and at the university, William Johnson Cory became a master at Eton, where he was considered the best tutor of his times. Inheriting wealth and resigning this position, Cory subsequently failed to make full use of his great talents, but some of his poetry reached a high level; his *Ionica*, embodying the affection of a teacher for his pupils, is a model of its kind. His peculiar gifts were, however, best shown by his letters, paradoxical to the last degree, but invariably racy and amusing; also by the extremely entertaining *Modern History*, which he began but never brought to completion. He was in all respects a remarkable character, but lacked the power, or perhaps rather lacked the energy, to accomplish anything which would bring him lasting fame.

Cory's elder brother, Charles Wellington Furse, Archdeacon of Westminster, who took his mother's surname, married the daughter of John Monsell, vicar of Egham, a noted hymn-writer and the great-grand-nephew of Edmund Pery, an admirable Speaker of the old Irish House of Commons. From both sides the Furse family derive ability, and ability has been manifested in many different directions.

One son, Michael Furse, is the present Bishop of St. Albans; another, Sir William, who has attained general's rank in the army, was lately Master-General of the Ordnance. John Furse, the eldest brother, has attained some note as a sculptor, and his son Ralph has been Private Secretary to successive Secretaries of State for the Colonies. With Mr. John Furse we see a re-emergence of artistic ability, but this was most strikingly exemplified by another son of the Archdeacon of Westminster. This son, a second Charles Wellington Furse, had at the time of his early death from consumption in 1904 achieved a great position as a portrait-painter and an even greater one as a painter of scenes of animal life. Perhaps his two best-known pictures are " Diana of the Uplands " and " The Return from the Ride," both now in the Tate Gallery. The thorough zest with which he portrayed horses and dogs was doubtless due to his love of sport, as striking a feature of his nature as his love of art. A man of most attractive character, his early death called forth a bitter lament from a friend—a lament applicable to but few in 1904, applicable, alas! to many ten years later:

" A thousand thousand slimy things live on, and the being, in whom life was rich and ardent, filled with the prospect of vast labour and delight, is cut off." Charles Furse married Catherine Symonds. With a descent of equal interest to his own, the heredity of their two sons is altogether exceptional.

It seems most probable that we can trace the artistic gifts which have appeared in the Furse family to their Reynolds descent. The relationship is no doubt rather remote, but, as in the case of the connection of Dryden with Swift and Horace Walpole, this would seem to be a case of emergence of latent talent. In any event, there has been clearly a persistence of varied ability from Thomas Baker, the mathematician, to the present day.

WHEN, in 1755, Joshua Reynolds had already acquired fame in London, his somewhat younger Suffolk contemporary, Thomas Gainsborough, had still no more than a local reputation, but in the end the two stood practically on an equality. Of the ancestry of Gainsborough less is known than of that of Sir Joshua. His immediate forbears in the male line had been for some generations prominent tradesmen of Sudbury, of which borough the painter's grandfather was a Chief Constable. It is improbable that artistic gifts came from this source, and it is more likely that they were derived from Gainsborough's mother, who had herself some talent for painting in water-colours—a talent which we do not hear that Theophila Reynolds possessed. On this side the descent of the younger painter was similar in social position to that of the elder, Mrs. Gainsborough's brother, Humphrey Burroughs, being, like Samuel Reynolds, a parson and master of a grammar-school. Intellectual ability was, however, certainly less conspicuous in the Gainsborough than in the Reynolds family, but manual dexterity was undoubtedly greater. Two of Thomas's brothers showed great mechanical abilities. One, John, known as "Scheming Jack," was unfortunately never able to bring various inventive ideas to fruition; the other, Humphrey, passed his life as a dissenting minister, employing, however, all his spare time in mechanics. He is said to have thought of the steam engine before Watt, and it is quite possible that a very slight turn of Fortune's wheel would have made the name of the one brother as famous as an engineer as that of the other as a painter. As things turned out, it is curious to reflect that but for Thomas's success the very existence of Humphrey would by now be quite unknown.

As in the case of Reynolds, so in that of Gainsborough, distinction was carried on by the descendants of sisters; but while, as we have seen, talent lay for some time latent in the Reynolds connection, in that of Gainsborough it was soon to reappear. Gainsborough Dupont, son of Thomas's sister Sarah, worked in his uncle's studio, made engravings of several of his works, and after the great artist's death successfully completed his unfinished pictures. Dupont showed, indeed, much talent, and but for his early death in 1797, at the age of forty-three, might well have made a much greater name for himself.

The artistic gifts of the family were, however, not yet exhausted. Sophia Gardiner, daughter of another sister of Thomas Gainsborough, married Theophilus Lane, a Prebendary of Hereford. As a girl she spent much of her time in her uncle's studio, and she encouraged in every respect a love of art in her two sons, Richard and Edward. First as an engraver and then as a lithographer, Richard Lane made a great reputation. As a lithographer he reproduced the charm of his great-uncle's pictures with marvellous fidelity, and in his time executed over one thousand prints. His portrait of Princess Victoria as a child is well known. Elected early in life as Associate Engraver of the Royal Academy, he in his old age had the satisfaction of obtaining the privilege of full membership for engravers. Richard Lane was a very versatile man, something also of a sculptor, he possessed, in addition, a fine tenor voice, and his social gifts were very marked.

With his younger brother, Edward, a quite different form of ability was developed. He also started life as an engraver; his health proved unequal to the work, and, developing a taste for things Oriental, he in 1825 set sail for Egypt. This commenced a family connection with the East which in one way or another was to last for a full hundred years. Though he was destined to pass his life as a scholar, Edward Lane, on this his first voyage, showed qualities which might well have led him to success as a man of action. A considerable storm arising in the Mediterranean, the master of the ship, who seems to have been singularly incompetent, lost his head completely, and, no one else being able to take his place, Lane, who had studied mathematics to some purpose, took charge of the vessel and navigated her to safety. Arriving in Egypt, Lane adopted the Oriental style of living, acquired a perfect knowledge of Arabic, and as his cast of countenance was somewhat Eastern and his manner was solemn, the Arabs came to look upon him as almost one of themselves. He certainly acquired a wonderful knowledge of Eastern life and thought, the main fruits of which were, first a graphic and fortunately successful work entitled *The Modern Egyptians*; secondly, the standard translation of *The Arabian Nights*; and, finally, an English-Arabic lexicon, on which he spent all the last years of his life, being aided in the production of this last most financially unremunerative undertaking by the then Duke of Northumberland. Distinct resemblances are to be traced between Edward Lane and that well-known character of the present day, Colonel T. E. Lawrence, and it is more than probable that the careers of the two men would have been in all respects parallel had a great war involving the Near East taken place in Lane's as in Lawrence's time. As it is, Lane will live chiefly as the translator of *The Arabian Nights*, the delight of many generations of schoolboys.

During a second visit to Egypt, Lane was accompanied by his sister Sophia, who had married Edward Poole, a noted book-collector and bibliographer. Mrs. Poole obtained admission to the harems of many of the leading natives, and in her book, *The Englishwoman in Egypt*, she was able to supplement her brother's work, embodying most interesting information as to the life of Mohammedan women which it would have been impossible for him to have obtained. Mrs. Poole's two boys came out with her, and their uncle implanted in them a love for Oriental studies. Edward Lane-Poole, the elder, who died prematurely, edited a new edition of *The Arabian Nights*, and wrote much on

Near Eastern subjects. His younger brother, Reginald, retained throughout life an interest in Egypt, particularly in Egyptian archæology, but his energies were mainly absorbed by his work as head of the Coins and Medals Department of the British Museum. As a numismatist, he held in his time an unrivalled position.

With two sons of Edward Lane-Poole, Stanley and a younger Reginald, great-great-grandnephews of Thomas Gainsborough, this account closes. Mr. Stanley Lane-Poole has followed his father and great-uncle in a close study of the East. He is well known as a biographer of men who have won renown in Oriental fields; he is also, like his uncle before him, a numismatist of distinction. Mr. Reginald Lane-Poole has written mainly on mediæval history, and has filled many positions at Oxford, where he was, for a time, Curator of the Bodleian Library.

It will be noted that in the line of descent from Gainsborough through Lane to Poole ability has persisted, but that literary has gradually superseded artistic skill, though the latter has never quite died out. The succession may be illustrated as follows :

FIRST GENERATION.
    Gainsborough and his brothers, art and mechanics.
SECOND GENERATION.
    Gainsborough Dupont, art.
THIRD GENERATION.
    Richard Lane, art; Edward Lane, literature.
FOURTH GENERATION.
    Edward Lane-Poole, literature.
    Reginald Lane-Poole, art (numismatics) and literature.
FIFTH GENERATION.
    Stanley Lane-Poole, literature and art (numismatics).
    Reginald Lane-Poole, literature.

IN 1630 Henry Wolcott, a Somerset squire of strong puritanical leanings, emigrated to Massachusetts. He is stated to have descended from one John Wolcott, whose family bore the arms of three chess rooks, the origin of which is given as follows: " Playing at chess with King Henry V, John Wolcott gave him check with the rook, whereupon the King changed his coat of arms and gave him the rook for a remembrance."

A man in any case of position, Henry Wolcott soon took a leading place in the colony, and from his son Simon descended several men of note, among whom it is sufficient here to mention Oliver Wolcott, a signer of the Declaration of Independence and, like several of his relatives, a Governor of Connecticut. Anne, daughter of Henry Wolcott, the emigrant, married Matthew Griswold. Removing, like the Wolcotts, to Connecticut, the Griswolds played a prominent part in the affairs of that colony. John Griswold, grandson of Anne Wolcott, was a judge and a man greatly esteemed for his ability and integrity. His son, Matthew Griswold, was President of the Connecticut Convention which ratified the Constitution of the United States. He became successively Governor and Chief Justice of the State, being followed in both positions by his son Roger, whose mother was Ursula Wolcott, daughter of the signer of the Declaration of Independence. This Ursula Wolcott, who married her cousin, Matthew Griswold, was actually related to sixteen different Governors of States and to forty-three different judges. It is a record that is hardly likely to occur again in America, or indeed anywhere else.

Phœbe Griswold, daughter of John, the judge, and sister of Matthew, married Jonathan Parsons, a clergyman who in 1745 was dismissed from his charge for adopting the tenets of George Whitefield, the famous preacher and coadjutor of Wesley, under whose influence Parsons conducted revivalist meetings, a thing abhorrent to the conservative members of his congregation. He obtained, however, another charge, and twenty-five years later welcomed Whitefield to his house when on a preaching tour. The great evangelist was, however, at the time in very bad health, notwithstanding which he, in response to urgent calls, consented to preach late in the evening on the stairs of Parsons' house. Holding in his hand a lighted candle, he continued to speak until it flickered out, but the effort was too great, and he died that night in the arms of his host.

Jonathan Parsons survived this tragic episode five years, living to see the commencement of the Revolutionary War, in which his son Samuel, a lawyer by profession, highly distinguished himself, rising to be brigadier-general of the Connecticut contingent. After the war Samuel Parsons was appointed Chief Justice of the great North-West Territory, which is now the State of Ohio, but was drowned shortly after in a flooded stream. His brother, Thomas Parsons, married Anne Sawyer, whose mother was the daughter of the Rev. Jonathan Pierrepont. The latter was a cousin of that John Pierrepont, founder of Yale, whom we have met with in a former chapter. Their mutual ancestor, James Pierrepont, a trader between England and Ireland at the time of the Civil Wars, became bankrupt owing to the difficulties of the time and emigrated to America. The names of the distinguished descendants of the bankrupt trader would form a long list, but, having regard to his misfortunes, a particular piquancy attaches to the fact that one of these descendants was that most successful financier, the late John Pierpont Morgan.

To return to Thomas Parsons and Sarah Sawyer, his wife. Their daughter Anne came, as we have seen, of distinguished stock on both sides, and, in marrying Fitzwilliam Sargent, she became allied with a family which was to continue on the same high level of attainment. Fitzwilliam was the grandson of Epes Sargent, a successful merchant and shipowner in the middle of the eighteenth century. Apart from the line with which we are more immediately concerned, that of Fitzwilliam Sargent and Anna Parsons, the descendants of Epes Sargent have shown the most varied talents. Among them may be particularly noted Winthrop Sargent, who had the reputation of being the best-dressed man in the Revolutionary army, and achieved later the more solid distinction of being appointed the first Governor of the State of Mississippi. Another was Henry Sargent, an artist of no little note in his day, and a man also of inventive skill in mechanics, the father of Henry Winthrop Sargent, a noted horticulturist, whose garden was one of the show places of America. Finally, in a later generation, Charles Sprague Sargent, who died only recently, was recognized as the greatest authority in the United States on forestry, a position in which he has perhaps been succeeded by Theodore Dwight Woolsey. (31)

Fitzwilliam Sargent, the husband of Anna Parsons, was himself a successful merchant and shipowner, carrying on a large business with the East. To this business his son Winthrop succeeded, but proved lacking in practical affairs and failed. A man, however, of great culture, Winthrop Sargent handed on these characteristics to his sons, Winthrop and Fitzwilliam, both of whom became medical men. Winthrop, like his relative, Henry Sargent, was a painter of ability, particularly in marine subjects, a gift shared also by his brother Fitzwilliam. Shortly after his marriage to Mary Newbold Singer, Fitzwilliam Sargent left America for Europe, practising the medical profession and writing to his relatives at home letters the graphic skill of which show that he might have made a name for himself in literature. His wife, whose family was originally of Alsatian origin, and who, through her mother, is said to have derived descent from Sir Humphrey Gilbert, half-brother of Raleigh, was, however, the dominant force in the household. She is described as a woman of exceptional culture, " nervous, restless and never satisfied but with the best." Though more of a musician than an artist, she was quick to discern the genius of her son, whom she used to take out sketching when he was a little boy, always insisting that he should finish what he began. Such were the parents of John Singer Sargent, the greatest portrait-painter of modern times. As has been seen, artistic ability had already appeared on his father's side, but even more noticeable is the extremely varied general ability of his relatives, many of whom it has not been possible to notice in this sketch. For the special work accomplished by Sargent, a cultured heredity might be premised as essential, and that such an heredity existed has been abundantly shown.

SHORTLY after service on the British side in the American War of Independence, a young Ulsterman named John Whistler eloped with the daughter of a Sir Edward Bishop. (32) Fearing the wrath of that gentleman, no doubt his superior in social position, he went back to America and turned his previous experiences to account by joining the new United States Army, spending much time in frontier wars against the Indians. In 1803, when a captain at Detroit, John Whistler was ordered to lay out Fort Dearborn, at the south-west corner of Lake Michigan. This he did, and on its site now stands Chicago, of which city he may therefore be considered the founder. Curiously enough, thirty years later his eldest son, William Whistler, who followed him into the army, was in command at Fort Dearborn, when, owing to more settled conditions, it was decided to dismantle the fort, at which date, 1833, the real history of Chicago may be said to begin. That city the artist grandson of its founder never saw, and would, in any case, most certainly have disliked.

George, another son of John Whistler, also entered the army, and, showing great mathematical ability, he was much employed in topographical work. With him in the corps of military engineers served William Gibbs McNeill, the great-grandson of an emigrant from Skye after the '45, who had settled in North Carolina. Whistler married McNeill's sister at the period when the era of railway construction was just setting in. The brothers-in-law, perceiving that they could employ their talents to greater advantage in civil life, both gave up their commissions, and became perhaps the two greatest railway engineers in America. While McNeill stayed in that country, Whistler in 1840 went to Russia, where he was employed in constructing the railway from St. Petersburg to Moscow. When the Emperor Nicholas ordered the laying of this line he showed Whistler a ruler and directed that its course should be equally straight. Fortunately for the engineer, the level nature of the ground presented no obstacles to the accomplishment of this plan, but the autocrat cared little for the fact that important towns were left untouched. Following on this work, George Whistler was employed on harbour construction at St. Petersburg, but in 1849 the work and the climate together killed him. Though he had earned largely, George Whistler, whose genius was scientific but whose tastes and disposition were artistic, had also spent royally, and his widow returned with her two boys to America in comparatively poor circumstances. A son by a first marriage, another George Whistler, remained as an engineer in Russia, where he also achieved much success till he likewise, at an early age, fell a victim to the climate. Of his half-brothers, William, the elder, entered the medical profession, assisted the Confederates as a surgeon in the Civil War, and then, going to London, became a well-known physician. His younger brother, James McNeill Whistler, had preceded him to Europe. Placed at first at West Point to follow the military career of his relatives, he failed to qualify for a commission, and, allowed then to follow his natural bent, he resorted, as an art student, to Paris, from whence he gravitated to London, where after many vicissitudes he was at length to make his great reputation. Whistler's peculiar disposition and singularly cantankerous character is exceedingly well known; his pugnacity was evidently inherited from a pugnacious line, and, if he had no actual talent for military life, he had certainly inclination in that direction—in fact, at all times he expressed an admiration for militarism. Between him and Sargent there was some resemblance but more contrast. Both were born in America, and both spent but little of their lives in their native land, but here the resemblance ceases. It will be noted that Sargent was of purely Nordic origin, while in Whistler's descent there was a strong Celtic element. Intellectual power was, on the whole, dominant among Sargent's connections, manual dexterity among those of Whistler. And such also was the case as between Reynolds and Gainsborough. It is worthy of note that the men with the more scholarly connections excelled mainly in portraiture, while those with relatives of marked mechanic skill excelled more in other forms of art.

CHAPTER XIV

" GIANTS OF OLD "

*With Blayds and Merivale, Hope, Munro,
Ridley and Hawkins, years ago.*

THESE lines, occurring in one of the best known of the many Harrow School songs written by the late Edward Bowen, set out the names of six Harrovians of the mid-nineteenth century who, first at school and afterwards at the universities, won distinction in classical scholarship. This song, satirizing a well-known human weakness for belauding the past at the expense of the present, begins with a pretended lament over the puny race of the day, ending, however, on another note :

*But I think all this is a lie, you know ;
I think all this is a lie,
For the hero race may come and may go,
But it doesn't exactly die.*

A profoundly true observation. Bowen and his musical coadjuster, John Farmer, have been compared, on a smaller scale, with Gilbert and Sullivan; and Bowen, like Gilbert, had emphatically the power of embodying eternal verities in a humorous fashion.

In selecting his six scholars, Bowen was, no doubt, somewhat guided by the exegencies of metre ; for the rest he certainly thought only of the achievements of the men themselves and nothing at all of their ancestry. It is interesting, therefore, to see how far the individuals, thus selected, as it were, at random, furnish illustrations of the descent of hereditary ability. On examination, a most remarkable number of eminent relatives appear in the case of two of these scholars, Merivale and Hawkins, and a fairly considerable number in the case of two others, Monro and Ridley, but neither Blayds nor Hope would seem to have had relatives of any marked distinction. In other words, four out of six chance selections do clearly indicate the transmission of ability, and this proportion, or something like it, would in all probability prove to be true of the intellectual classes generally. Let us first turn to the most interesting examples, Merivale and Hawkins.

Herman Merivale was at Harrow from 1817 to 1823, and was very senior to the others of the six. Entering at the age of ten, he was head of the school at sixteen, and at Oxford subsequently carried off all possible scholastic honours. In his case intellectual distinction existed on both his father's and his mother's side, but most markedly on the latter, where its first beginnings are seen in two brothers, Benjamin and Thomas Heath, sons of one Benjamin Heath, a successful fuller and merchant in Exeter at the beginning of the eighteenth century. This business Thomas endeavoured to carry on, but he was more interested in publishing editions of the Book of Job and of the Psalms, and his mere mundane affairs suffered accordingly. The fortunes of this branch of the family were, however, retrieved by his son Thomas, who became a judge, while a grandson, Benjamin Heath Malkin, was Head Master of Bury St. Edmunds School during the palmy days 1809–23, when it ranked as one of the leading schools of the country.

Benjamin Heath, eldest son of the Exeter fuller, was

wise enough, from his own point of view, to make no attempt to carry on the family business; drawing out the capital, he lived comfortably on it at Exeter, became a great book-collector and dabbled in literature. On a tour abroad he met and fell in love with Rose Michelet, daughter of a Geneva merchant. Her maternal grandfather, Tessier by name, was a Huguenot who left France for Geneva after the Revocation of the Edict of Nantes. On account of his elegant manners he was known as "*le poli Tessier.*" Rose Michelet was only fourteen when she married Benjamin Heath, but she seems to have been remarkably precocious; she approved highly of the Englishman because he refused to play cards on Sunday—"a man of principle," she remarked. A woman of very strong will and of an intellect vigorous by nature, though but little cultivated, Rose Michelet proved an excellent helpmeet to her intellectual but somewhat unpractical husband. She lived to the age of ninety, dying in 1808, seventy-six years after her marriage, having seen one son Head Master of Eton, another of Harrow, a third an admiral and a fourth a successful merchant. For their success in life the Heath family probably owed, in almost equal proportions to their father and mother, the intellect of the former being supplemented by the energy of the latter.

John, the mercantile member of the family, lived for some years in Genoa, where, among other articles, he traded in the newly-invented umbrellas, the arrival of which in Exeter is described in a letter from his sister Elizabeth in 1766: "We find our umbrellas very useful. They are coming in fashion here; several people have got them; they do very well in a still shower, but we cannot manage them in windy weather." John Heath subsequently settled in London as a merchant and foreign banker; the connection with Italy was kept up; his son, John Benjamin Heath, was consul in London, first for Sardinia and then for the United Kingdom of Italy, for no less than sixty-two years, and was created an Italian baron. A man of varied attainments, Baron Heath was at once a Governor of the Bank of England and a Fellow of the Royal Society. He was the oldest Harrovian who attended the Tercentenary Celebrations in 1871.

George Heath, the Head Master of Eton, nicknamed by the school "Ascot Heath," was chiefly known to fame as a very severe disciplinarian, a trait probably derived from his mother. His note in this direction was, however, to be surpassed later by his successor, John Keate. The latter never, indeed, outvied Heath's performance of flogging seventy boys at the same time, as a result of which he was himself laid up with aches and pains for a week, no doubt to the great joy of his victims, who had been guilty of no worse offence than that of attending—of course, against orders—a cricket match between their school and Westminster. This match, which took place on Hounslow Heath on July 25, 1796, is interesting as being the first recorded between any two public schools, preceding by nine years the first known contest between Eton and Harrow.

George Heath was later a candidate for the Provostship of Eton, as was also his brother Benjamin, but neither was elected, George III at once vetoing Benjamin's candidature with the remark, "He will never do; he ran away from Eton." Benjamin Heath, like George, had been an Eton Colleger, but in 1769 he took a mastership at Harrow and two years later was elected Head Master. His appointment was by no means popular with a section, who resented the fact that Heath, like his two predecessors, (33) was an Etonian. "A school of such reputation," said the recalcitrants, "ought not to be considered an appendage to Eton." Their candidate was the famous scholar, Samuel Parr, who, on his failure, left the school and set up a rival establishment at Stanmore, to which he attracted a certain proportion of the boys. He also tried hard to induce Joseph Drury, the most brilliant of the assistant masters, to accompany him, but Drury, after hesitating for a time, refused. He had no reason to regret his choice, for the Stanmore school failed, and Drury, after marrying Heath's younger sister, Louisa, succeeded his brother-in-law in the Head Mastership of Harrow. Benjamin Heath proved an efficient and sensible head. Retiring in the prime of life, he devoted himself, like his father, to literary studies, and collected a fine library, which was ultimately sold for £9,000.

His brother-in-law and successor, Joseph Drury, proved an even more efficient Head Master, and during his regime the school attained what proved to be its high-water mark for many a long day. A man of remarkably fine appearance, he was a firm disciplinarian, but, unlike George Heath, had no belief in the value of excessive flogging. He was very generally popular, Byron, who went to the school not long before he left, always referred to him as "dear Drury." His wife, Louisa Heath, was an exceedingly able woman, but she suffered from bad health, as a result of which her husband left the school when at the height of his fame and retired to farm in Devonshire. It is a curious fact that Mrs. Drury's mother, the former Rose Michelet, lived to see the retirement as well as the successes of all her sons and her son-in-law. The family, energized at first by the ambition derived from the maternal side, developed in later life the philosophical attitude of their father, and gave up power for leisured ease.

Rose Michelet lived, moreover, to see two Drury grandsons masters at the schools over which their uncles had presided, Henry, the elder, at Harrow, Benjamin, the younger, at Eton. Both were remarkable characters. Benjamin, a man, like most of his family, of imposing appearance, was extremely popular at Eton; he was a candidate for the Head Mastership in 1809, when Keate was appointed, and would certainly have been the choice of the school. He was, however, a man of unstable character and an addiction to attending public boxing matches and even taking part therein—a proceeding singularly undignified having regard to the conditions under which these matches were carried on—led ultimately to an enforced resignation. His brother, Henry Drury, the Harrow master, universally known as " Harry," had no such disastrous ending to his career, which was, however, in some respects disappointing to himself. Though not a man of great learning, he was a born teacher, and in every respect the most influential of the masters of his time. Very popular, like his father and brother, big, stalwart, genial, but terrible when aroused, life was in some ways too easy for Harry Drury. His nephew, Charles Merivale, said of him: " Placed in a new country without a shilling in his pocket, he might have founded an empire." But his abilities rather ran to seed in work of a comparatively routine nature. Inheriting a propensity for the purchase of expensive books, he got himself in later life into serious financial difficulties, and though he stayed at Harrow till his death in 1841, his latter days were clouded not only by personal worries, but also by the fact that the school at the time had fallen to a position far below that which it had held in his father's days.

None of Harry Drury's sons achieved actual fame, but all were men above the average. Henry, the eldest, subsequently Archdeacon of Wilts, was a brilliant classical scholar; another son became an admiral, a third a general, a fourth was well known as a botanist, while the Harrow traditions were carried on by yet another, Benjamin Heath Drury, who succeeded to his father's house in the palmy days of Vaughan's Head Mastership. This house, still known as "Druries," perpetuates—and alone perpetuates—the name of this brilliant family, who had every gift except that of winning enduring fame in the greater world.

Louisa Drury, daughter of Joseph Drury and Louisa Heath, married John Herman Merivale and was the mother of the scholar, Herman Merivale, who derived his first name from a German great-grandfather, one Herman Katenkampf, son of a pastor at Bremen, who followed John Baring, a friend of his family, to England and settled in Exeter. His daughter Anna married John Merivale, son of a Presbyterian minister of some note in his day, and became the mother of Louisa Drury's husband, John Herman Merivale, a man of scholarly attainments, especially distinguished as a translator. From every side his children inherited intellect. Two promising sons, Reginald and Alexander, died comparatively young, but Herman and Charles lived to win great distinction. Herman, brilliantly clever but shy and retiring, was uninfluential at school; Charles, good all round, a cricketer as well as a scholar, was, on the other hand, a typical schoolboy hero, and, after having represented Harrow at Lord's, rowed at Cambridge in the first 'Varsity Boatrace of 1829. But in after years their rôles were, in some respects, curiously reversed. Herman, though never coming prominently before the world, took a great part in public affairs, first as Under-Secretary for the Colonies and then as Under-Secretary for India. In the former capacity he, more than any other man, was the author of the grant of responsible government to the present Dominions; in the latter he guided the new Government established in India after the Mutiny. The British Empire, as it stands to-day, owes much to that forgotten worthy, Herman Merivale. The impression he made on those who knew him best was profound. Bulwer Lytton spoke of his " intellectual massiveness—the massiveness of gold." Charles Merivale, on the other hand, who entered the Church and became ultimately Dean of Ely, devoted his life to scholarship, and in particular to *The History of Rome*, a work which secured him a place among the leading historians of the century.

Herman Charles Merivale, son of Herman, abandoned the scholastic traditions of his ancestors, winning distinction as a writer of every form of light literature, plays (particularly adaptations from the French), novels and fairy-tales for children, altogether a man of restless versatility. The end of his life was singularly tragic, his health breaking down from hardship incurred in a shipwreck off Brazil and his entire fortune being lost owing to the defalcation of a rascally solicitor.

He was the last to achieve distinction of the descendants of Benjamin Heath, the Exeter merchant.

There yet remain for mention certain other relatives of Herman Merivale, the scholar. His aunt, Frances, married John Louis Mallet, son of Mallet du Pan, the well-known journalist at the time of the French Revolution. Mallet du Pan, who himself belonged to a Geneva family, was forced to leave France, and settled in England, where his son, John Louis, made his career. His and Frances Merivale's son, Louis Mallet, entered the Board of Trade, and, indispensable alike for his knowledge of finance and his knowledge of France, he was Cobden's right-hand man in the negotiations for the famous commercial treaty concluded with Napoleon III in 1862, that treaty which, it was fondly hoped, was to herald universal Free Trade. Sir Louis Mallet later succeeded his cousin, Herman Merivale, at the India Office. It is noticeable that the cousins, who shared a German descent, had also alike a descent from Geneva families. To this the marked linguistic ability possessed by both was no doubt partially attributable. Mallet was distinguished for the breadth of his views and for his freedom from the intolerance of mere officialdom. Possessed of a remarkable grip on public affairs, he had, in addition, a great knowledge of both English and French literature. One of his sons, Sir Bernard Mallet, has been Registrar-General, while another, Sir Louis Mallet, was, it will be remembered, British ambassador in Constantinople just prior to the Great War.

FRANCIS VAUGHAN HAWKINS, the second of Bowen's six scholars to be considered, was at the school from 1845 to 1849. His scholastic distinctions, if anything, exceeded those of Merivale, and at Cambridge he was senior classic, the marks he obtained being among the highest ever recorded. Like Merivale, Hawkins inherited intellect from both his father and his mother's side; and again, like Merivale, the maternal side was, on the whole, predominant. Hester Vaughan, the mother of this senior classic, came of a family which can only be clearly traced back to one William Vaughan, a Fellow of the College of Physicians, practising at Colchester at the end of the seventeenth century. It has been, however, a tradition in the family that William was the son of Thomas Vaughan, poet and dabbler in alchemy, and nephew of Henry Vaughan, known as the "Silurist," a mystical poet whose works have of recent years received greater recognition than in his own day. This relationship, which would include one also with the gossiping writer, John Aubry, is inherently quite probable. Thomas Vaughan is known to have left a son named William, and dates agree; it has never, however, been clearly proved. More certain is the connection of the descendants of William Vaughan with a very different personage. William married Anne Newton, sister of Sir Henry Newton, ambassador to Florence and Genoa in the reign of Queen Anne, which Sir Henry was the maternal grandfather of the celebrated admiral, George, Lord Rodney.

Henry, son of William Vaughan and Anne Newton, was vicar of Leominster, in Herefordshire, a history of which town he wrote. A man of culture and agreeable manners, he was an intimate friend of Dean Swift. His daughter married one James Hodgson and was grandmother of Francis Hodgson, well known as Provost of Eton from 1840 to 1852. During his tenure of that office Hodgson abolished the ancient Eton custom of "Montem," which had given rise to great abuses. This he did though himself a rigid conservative by temperament, so conservative, indeed, that to the end of his life he never could be induced to enter a railway train.

In his younger days Francis Hodgson had been as great a friend of Byron as his great-grandfather had been of Swift, and throughout his life he was intimate with Harry Drury and with John Herman Merivale. The paths of the descendants of Benjamin Heath and of William Vaughan were indeed destined often to cross, and it is somewhat singular that no intermarriage ever took place between the two connections.

James Vaughan, grandson of the vicar of Leominster, was a prominent physician in Leicester for many years, but his reputation did not extend to any wider field. This, however, he was determined should, if possible, not be the case with his numerous sons; so inflexible, indeed, was he on this subject that he stated that he would rather follow them to their graves than see them fail to achieve distinction in their respective callings. His wishes, thus rather crudely expressed, were abundantly fulfilled. Henry, his eldest son, who took the surname of Holford, became the leading physician of his day, John attained a judgeship, Peter became a dean, and Charles rose high in the diplomatic service. Though the actual careers were different, there is much general resemblance between the successes of these four and of the four sons of Banjamin Heath and Rose Michelet. The Vaughan family seem, however, to have owed almost everything to the paternal and but little to the maternal side. They appear, on the whole, to have been men of great push and energy rather than of any profound intellect; this was to emerge in later generations. Sir Henry Holford, who rose to be President of the College of Physicians, owed much to his courtly manners, which rendered him a great favourite with George III. Without any very outstanding professional skill, he was possessed, however, of quick perception and sound judgment. Sir John Vaughan's legal career was very similar. Never regarded as a profound lawyer, he possessed a remarkable influence over juries, whom he addressed in a humorous and effective manner. As a judge he won great popularity from his exquisitely polished urbanity. Charles Vaughan did not at first seem likely to emulate his elder brothers. Something of a roving stone, he found himself in Spain at the time of the Peninsular War, brought himself into notice by an account of the siege of Saragossa, was appointed secretary to our representative at Madrid, and thus got a footing in the regular diplomatic service. He ended his career as Minister in Washington, where the family charm of manner enabled him to go down rather well with the Americans, who were apt to be somewhat touchy at this stage of their evolution.

Edward Vaughan, the youngest of the family, was the least successful from a worldly point of view, living and dying the vicar of a Leicester parish. Unlike his brothers, his temper was uncompromising, while his religious views were narrow and extreme. He was, however, destined by his wife, Agnes Pares, a descendant of the great Nonconformist, Philip Henry, to be the father of the most distinguished member of the entire family. This was his eldest son, Charles John Vaughan, who was sent to Rugby, following his father and all his uncles. He and Arthur Penrhyn Stanley, whose sister he ultimately married, were Arnold's favourite pupils. His numerous scholastic successes caused him to be known as "Half-Holiday" Vaughan, and in 1838 he was senior classic at Cambridge. Six years later, at the age of twenty-eight, he was appointed Head Master of Harrow. The numbers of that school at that time had actually fallen to seventy; when Vaughan left they were over five hundred. Never, probably, has any man had a more immediate effect on the fortunes of any school. When, in 1859, he, still in the prime of life, decided to resign the Head Mastership, Palmerston at once offered him a bishopric, and his ultimate translation to the Primacy seemed assured. For reasons which he always kept to himself, Vaughan refused this offer, as he also subsequently did more than one of a similar nature, and for a time was content to retire to an ordinary parish, though he did later accept the Mastership of the Temple and the Deanery of Landaff. A greater contrast in disposition to his pushing uncles could scarcely be afforded. As a preacher at the Temple, Vaughan's reputation reached the highest possible point, and perhaps he himself judged his own powers best, but at Harrow he undoubtedly showed leadership qualities of a high order, and one cannot but feel that a great Archbishop was lost to the country.

His retiring qualities were shared, or even exceeded,

by his brother David, who held, and never desired to leave, the Leicester vicarage previously held by his father. A scholarly man, David Vaughan became known for his translation of Plato, but his work has been largely superseded by that of Jowett.

A third brother, John Luther Vaughan, was a man of curiously different disposition. Entering the army and attaining general's rank in India, he in his autobiography bitterly laments his retirement at an age when he felt still capable of great things. Determined not to be left altogether on the shelf, John Vaughan did a very sporting thing and went out as *Times* correspondent during the Afghan campaign of 1879, a curious and difficult position for a retired general, but one in which he seems to have acquitted himself with great credit and a minimum of friction. He was an early example of the type now so common, the man of distinction in other fields turned journalist, but, unlike most of his successors at the present day, he had, at the time of his journalistic activities, at any rate relinquished his former calling.

The general absence of push and energy in this generation of the Vaughan family, to which John Luther Vaughan was such an exception, was strikingly exemplified in his first cousin, son of the judge, Sir John Vaughan. Henry Holford Vaughan, after making a great reputation as Professor of History at Oxford, suddenly gave it up, took up purely routine work as a Clerk of Assize in Wales and buried himself in scholastic seclusion. On his death a friend wrote : " It will seem no exaggeration to describe him as one of the great men of his generation, though his growing love of seclusion, due partly to delicate health and partly to an intense devotion to deep mental study, took him early out of the ranks of competitors for conspicuous success."

His son, Mr. William Wymar Vaughan, has taken up a more active line; after having been Head Master of Wellington, he is now Head Master of Rugby, that school with which so many of his family have been associated. (34)

Francis Vaughan Hawkins, the great scholar, was nephew of Henry Holford Vaughan, son of his sister Hester. His later career was not undistinguished, though utterly unknown to the world at large. Called to the Bar, he became a typical Chancery practitioner of the old school, and had an immense practice in complicated cases. As learned in the law as in the classics, he had no gifts of speech and never took silk, but was elected nevertheless a Bencher of his Inn and also a Governor of his old school, both positions usually reserved for men whose names are more widely known. To an inner circle, however, Francis Hawkins was a power.

The general resemblances between his maternal connections and the maternal connections of Herman Merivale are as marked as the general resemblances between the characters of the two men themselves, both fitted to be powers only behind the scenes. In both connections, while distinction was achieved in many fields, scholastic attainment on the whole took priority, centred in the one case mainly on Harrow, in the other mainly on Rugby.

THE Ridley of Bowen's song may refer to either of two brothers, Matthew White Ridley and Edward

Ridley, who were successively, in 1860 and 1861, heads of the school at Harrow, both subsequently taking firsts in "Greats" at Oxford. They were distant cousins of Francis Vaughan Hawkins, having likewise Hawkins descent, and this is therefore the place to give an account of that family.

A certain Colonel Cæsar Hawkins commanded a troop of horse for the King in the Civil Wars. Whence he derived his peculiar Christian name, continued to this day in his family, is not known, but it seems more than possible it was due to a connection with Sir Julius Cæsar, a man of Italian origin, a great scholar of Queen Elizabeth's time.

The Colonel's grandson, Cæsar Hawkins, was a county surgeon, and became father of two sons, Cæsar and Pennell, who both followed his profession and rose to great eminence therein, both filling the office of Sergeant-Surgeon to King George II, by whom the former was created a baronet, the first of his calling to receive that distinction. Sir Cæsar Hawkins had an immense practice, and is said to have made a thousand a year by phlebotomy alone. This practice, otherwise known as bleeding, was dear to the surgeons of that day, but now, fortunately, it has been quite abandoned. One of Sir Cæsar's sons, Charles, became likewise Sergeant-Surgeon to the King; another, Edward, went into the Church. Three sons of the latter attained distinction. Francis, the second, continued the medical traditions of the family, but as a physician, not as a surgeon. To good professional attainments Francis Hawkins added scholarly tastes and considerable administrative powers; he was for many years Registrar of the College of Physicians, and on the formation of the

General Medical Council in 1858 he became Registrar of that body. A courteous gentleman of the old school, Francis Hawkins filled his various offices with dignity and with efficiency. He it was who married Hester Vaughan and was father of Francis Vaughan Hawkins, the scholar. His youngest brother, Cæsar Hawkins, was as successful as a surgeon as his brother as a physician, twice President of the Royal College of Surgeons, a Fellow of the Royal Society, and Sergeant-Surgeon to the Queen, the fifth of his family to fill that office.

Edward, the eldest of the brothers, followed his father into the Church. Obtaining a double first-class at Oxford, he became Fellow and tutor of Oriel and eventually Provost of that college, an office he held for no less than forty-three years. Administration was, however, hardly his strong point; his great reputation was that of a preacher. Filling also the position of vicar of St. Mary's, he there introduced the "University Sermons," for which that church was to become so famous.

The Ridley brothers descended from Pennell Hawkins, younger brother of the first Sir Cæsar and himself, as has been said, Sergeant-Surgeon to the King, a position held also by his son George, whose daughter Laura married Sir Matthew Ridley, of an old Northumbrian family, and was grandmother of Matthew White Ridley and Edward Ridley. The mutual relatives of these scholars and Francis Vaughan Hawkins were, as has been seen, mainly surgeons, and it is probable that the brothers, like Francis Hawkins, derived their scholastic attainments chiefly from the maternal side. Their mother was daughter of James Parke, son of a Liverpool merchant, a highly intellectual man, senior classic and fifth wrangler at Cambridge, and subsequently, like Francis Hawkins, a most profound lawyer. Parke, unlike Hawkins, attained a judgeship, in which capacity he showed himself a master of lucid statement and cogent reasoning. He was ultimately raised to the peerage as Lord Wensleydale. Another of his daughters was mother of Lord Ullswater, so well remembered as Speaker Lowther.

Matthew and Edward Ridley both rose to prominence, the former being Home Secretary in the third Salisbury Administration, while the latter attained a High Court judgeship. It is interesting to note that the youngest daughter of the former is married to Lord Wolmer, who is grandson alike of a Lord Chancellor and a Prime Minister. Their children have an altogether exceptional hereditary.

LAST to be considered is the Monro of the song. The reference in this case may be either to Cecil James Monro or to Charles Henry Monro, both of whom were eighth classic at Cambridge. Their ancestry is mainly interesting in the direct male line. Alexander Monro, a cadet of the ancient Scottish family of Monro of Foulis adhered in the reign of James II to the Episcopalian Church in Scotland, obtained the position of Principal of Edinburgh University, and in 1688 was nominated Bishop of Argyll. Unluckily for him, the Revolution intervened, Presbyterianism won the day, the bishopric melted into thin air, and Alexander Monro, forced also to relinquish his post at the university, took refuge in Episcopalian England, in which country his descendants were henceforward to make their home. His son, James Monro, entered the medical profession, and in 1728 became physician to the Bethlehem Hospital for the insane, that institution so much better known as "Bedlam." For no fewer than five generations in succession Monros filled this position, James, John, Thomas, Edward and Henry. The last named died in 1891, closing a record of a hundred and sixty-three years. It was a most remarkable case of descent of specialised ability. Thomas, the middle one of the line, obtained the most eminence as a physician, being specially called on to attend George III in his periodical attacks of insanity. Other talents also manifested themselves in the line. A taste for art first evinced by John Munro was continued by Thomas, who, himself no mean artist, was a great patron of younger aspirants, encouraging, in particular, the early efforts of J. M. W. Turner. His younger son, Henry, adopted painting as a profession, and at the time of his early death at the age of twenty-four had already acquired a great reputation for his portraits.

The last of the physicians, the second Henry, had also artistic talent, and painted portraits of himself and his father for presentation to the College of Physicians, where they now are to be seen, together with those of the earlier medical members of the family. His brother, Edward Monro, first of the line since the unfortunate Alexander, entered the Church, winning a great reputation alike as a preacher and as a writer of religious allegories. A strong philanthropic bent led him to establish a college for poor boys at Harrow Weald; this ultimately brought him into great financial difficulties, and was the indirect cause of his breakdown and death in his prime.

The scholars Cecil and Charles Monro were first cousins of this Edward and grandsons of Thomas. Their attainments formed a new departure in this gifted family, but neither fulfilled his early promise. Cecil fell a victim to consumption, a sad fate which has befallen too many other men of ability. Charles, in many respects a most attractive character, suffered from oversensitiveness and a certain lack of sustained energy. Devoting himself entirely to the academic study of law, he did indeed leave behind him a great edition of Justinian's *Digest*, but even in the realm of pure scholarship he might well have made a greater reputation.

It will be observed that three of the six classical scholars—Hawkins, Ridley and Monro—were connected with a considerable number of eminent members of the medical profession. It is a striking illustration of the versatility of achievement characteristic of families of intellectual note.

Of the two remaining scholars of the song, Charles Stuart Blayds, under his later surname of Calverley, won a great reputation as a writer alike of scholarly and of humorous verse, but William John Hope died early without adding to his school and university record. Blayds's relatives belonged mainly to the professional, Hope's to the landed classes, and there is no doubt that behind them also lay a heredity of culture, even if this cannot be so strikingly demonstrated as in the cases of Merivale, Hawkins, Ridley and Monro.

CHAPTER XV

INTELLECT AND ATHLETICS

OF the players in the Sixth Form Game at Harrow in the year 1824, constituting the best twenty-two of the school at cricket, no fewer than six subsequently attained high ecclesiastical distinction. These six were Charles Wordsworth, Henry Edward Manning, Richard Chenevix Trench, Charles Merivale, Ashton Oxendon and Charles Perry. Three of these—Wordsworth, Manning and Merivale—played in the Eleven at Lords. The ecclesiastical distinctions attained were singularly varied as to locality: Manning, joining the Roman Catholic Church, became a Cardinal and Archbishop of Westminster; Trench, Archbishop of Dublin; Wordsworth, Oxendon and Perry, Bishops respectively of St. Andrews, Montreal and Melbourne; Merivale, Dean of Ely. Curiously enough, not one became a Bishop of the Church of England in the mother country. The connection of cricketers of the early and mid-nineteenth century with the Church was sufficiently frequent, but this particular set of contemporaries were probably the ones most distinguished in after-life.

As in the case of the scholars in the previous chapter, so in the case of these cricketers a division may be made. Three—Wordsworth, Trench and Merivale—had many relatives of note; the connections of the other three were comparatively undistinguished. The relatives of Merivale have already been considered. Trench, himself one of the most distinguished of the remarkably distinguished line of men who filled the Archbishopric of Dublin during the nineteenth century, came of notable stock on both the paternal and maternal side. His mother, Melasina Chenevix, herself an authoress of note, was grand-daughter of a Bishop of Waterford and cousin of Richard Chenevix, a distinguished chemist and mineralogist.

Of the six future dignitaries of the Church, Charles Wordsworth, who was captain of the Harrow Eleven in 1825, was by far the best cricketer. Later, at Oxford, he proved himself a most remarkable all-round athlete, not only playing in the first two 'Varsity cricket matches, those of 1827 and 1829, but also rowing in the first 'Varsity Boatrace in the latter year. A nephew of the poet, Wordsworth could, on the mother's side, claim descent from the famous apologist of the Quakers, Robert Barclay of Ury. From this Robert Barclay descended a quite exceptional number of able men, particularly represented in the Gurney, Buxton, Hoare, Galton, Wakefield and Wordsworth families. Of this connection, Charles Wordsworth was by no means the only great athlete. His brother Christopher, afterwards Bishop of Lincoln, was nearly as good as himself; several members of the Buxton and Hoare families have appeared on the score-sheets of the Eton and Harrow match at Lords, while in earlier days, before games were greatly played, Robert Barclay Allerdice, also a descendant of the great Quaker, became exceedingly well known for his exploits as a pedestrian. His physical endurance was astonishing. In 1808 he performed the following feat: First he walked thirty miles during the day, grouse-shooting, then sixty more during the night to his home; next afternoon, sixteen more to a ball, at which he danced all night, finally spending the third day partridge-shooting. On another occasion he walked one mile on each of one thousand successive hours.

There is little doubt that Charles Wordsworth inherited his athletic ability from his mother's, his intellectual mainly, though certainly not entirely, from his father's, side. He was, as has been stated, nephew of the poet, and the athletic distinction achieved by the nephews of William Wordsworth was paralleled by the athletic distinction achieved by the great-nephews of another of the "Lake Poets," Samuel Taylor Coleridge. The parallel in general between the Wordsworth and Coleridge families is, indeed, very close. In each case the poets left descendants of some mark, but in each case also the greatest note was attained by descendants of elder brothers. Christopher Wordsworth, brother of William, was father of two bishops and grandfather of a third. James Coleridge, brother of Samuel, was father, grandfather and great-grandfather of judges, of whom the grandson, the first Lord Coleridge, was Chief Justice. James Coleridge was likewise, however, grandfather of an eminent cleric, John Coleridge Patteson, Missionary Bishop of Melanesia, who, after a career of singular romance, was murdered by the natives of those islands. Patteson had played in the Eton Elevens of 1843 and 1844, sharing that distinction with no fewer than five of his Coleridge cousins, two of whom, Frederick and Charles, afterwards obtained their Blues at Oxford. The last of this generation of Coleridges played for Eton in 1854; then the name disappears from the record of the Lord's match. In 1927 the tradition was all but revived, but F. J. R. Coleridge, grandson of Frederick, after playing against Winchester, was unluckily only twelfth man at Lord's.

The athletic ability of the Coleridges was probably derived from the side of their grandmother, the wife of James Coleridge. She was descended from an old Devon family, the Dukes, and from this family also descended the Yonges, some of whom made their mark at cricket about the same period as their relatives, the Coleridges. Charles Yonge appeared for Oxford in 1836; his younger brother George was one of the greatest bowlers of the day. After captaining the Eton Eleven, he represented Oxford for five years and took no less than forty-one wickets in the matches against Cambridge. (35) He subsequently played several times for the Gentlemen.

Charles and George Yonge were first cousins of the well-known authoress, Charlotte Yonge, who was thus related to a remarkable number of cricketers, especially remarkable as the Coleridges and Yonges by no means exhaust the list. Charlotte Yonge's grandmother was a Crawley, from whose brother descended that brilliant family of whom nine members belonging to three generations have played for Harrow at Lords, besides winning much distinction at other games, particularly rackets. From first to last no fewer than sixteen relatives of Charlotte Yonge have played in the Eton and Harrow match at Lord's. It may be mentioned that while the Yonges were related to both the Coleridges and the Crawleys, the two latter families were not themselves inter-related.

While no other authoress of any note can boast of such an array of cricketing relatives as Charlotte Yonge, she is by no means the only woman writer thus connected with the noble game. A greater than she, Jane Austen to wit, had her full share of cricketing relatives also. Her nephew, James Austen, vicar of Bray, who took the additional surname of Leigh, was father of four sons, of whom the two elder, Charles and Spencer Austen-Leigh, were in the Harrow, and the two younger, Edward and Augustus, in the Eton Eleven. Three attained also considerable intellectual distinction: Charles was Craven Scholar at Oxford, Edward was for many years a master at Eton, and Augustus became Provost at King's. Spencer, the least intellectual of the brothers, was the greatest cricketer. In 1862 he took part in a match, Kent *v.* Sussex, historical directly from the peculiar interest of the cricket and indirectly from its curious connection with literature. Playing for Kent was a certain professional, Joseph Wells, who secured four wickets in four successive balls, the first occasion on which this feat had been performed in a match of any importance. The second of his four victims was Spencer Austen-Leigh. While the batsman was the great-nephew of Jane Austen, the bowler was destined to be the father of Mr. H. G. Wells. The Wells case is a striking and almost isolated example of athletic skill in an earlier, intellectual in a later, generation. In almost all other instances intellect precedes athletics.

To Charlotte Yonge and Jane Austen we can, in this connection, add the name of George Eliot, whose nephew, Frederick Evans, was successively in the Rugby and Oxford Elevens, in the latter playing on the great side of 1865, probably the finest that the Dark Blues have ever put into the field. Frederick Evans, who entered the Church, died only the other day. Finally, Mrs. Humphrey Ward's son, Arnold Ward, played for Eton in 1895.

It is clear that these great women writers of the nineteenth century came of families enjoying to the full the *mens sana in corpore sano*, but it is not with women writers solely that the remarkable links between literature and athletics in general, and cricket in particular, can be exemplified. We have already noted the athletic connections of the poets Wordsworth and Coleridge. Three of the supreme writers of the mid-nineteenth century—Macaulay, Thackeray and Tennyson—had each, at least, one really brilliant athletic relative. In Macaulay's case we at last leave cricket for athletics in the narrower sense of the word. Reginald Heber Macaulay, first cousin once removed of the historian, and uncle of Miss Rose Macaulay, the novelist, was, in addition to being a great football player at Eton, one of the finest quarter-mile runners that have ever appeared in the Inter-'Varsity Sports, winning, as he did, that event three years in succession, and in each case with consummate ease.

With Thackeray and Tennyson we return to cricket. The novelist's second cousins, Frederick and Charles Thackeray, were both in the Eton Eleven, the former also playing for Cambridge, while the latter, a very fine bowler, captained his school in 1851. The poet's grandson, Major Lionel Tennyson, has, as is well known, captained England against Australia. He had played for Eton at Lord's, though in those days he was by no means the great batsman that he afterwards became, and at one time or another the famous literary names of Coleridge, Yonge, Thackeray, Austen, Ward, and Tennyson have appeared in the Eton Eleven.

The great Harrow family of Butler, though not associated with any special literary note, has, as is well known, shown a remarkable combination of intellectual and athletic gifts. This is well exemplified in the direct male line for four generations. George Butler, Head Master of Harrow from 1804 to 1829, seems to have been purely a scholar. His son, Henry Montagu, later himself Head Master and also a fine scholar, was, in addition, a good cricketer. His son, Edward Montagu, universally known as Teddy, was more of an athlete than a scholar, a triple Blue at Cambridge for cricket, rackets, and " royal " tennis and winner of the first Amateur Racket Championship. His son, Guy Montagu Butler, is the great quarter-mile runner of the present day. Athletic ability can be traced through Henry Montagu Butler's mother, who was related to that great cricketing family, the Walkers of Southgate. His wife was an Eliott of Minto, the well-known " leadership " family more than once previously referred to in these pages.

It is, indeed, in connection with leadership rather than in connection with purely intellectual families that we might expect athletic ability to arise, and in the main this is no doubt the case, albeit, as has been indicated, there are many striking instances of athletic ability in most obviously intellectual families.

In the case of two famous Eton athletic brotherhoods, the Lyttletons and the Lubbocks, leadership qualities undoubtedly predominated among their ancestry, but the Lyttletons were, all the same, the sons of a senior classic and the Lubbocks were the sons of an eminent mathematician. Of the former family, seven out of eight brothers played for Eton and four for Cambridge at cricket, while of the Lubbocks, also eight in number, three played in the Eton cricket Eleven, two rowed in the Eight and one played in the football Eleven. Each family produced one supremely great cricketer, the two Alfreds, Alfred Lubbock and Alfred Lyttelton, and the eldest of the Lubbocks was the eminent naturalist, Lord Avebury. On the mother's side this family descended from the Hothams, a leadership family *per excellence*, of whom three members were notable in the Civil Wars, and which produced in later times no fewer than five well-known admirals.

The Lytteltons belonged, on the side of their paternal grandmother, to the great Spencer connection, to which reference has been made in the second chapter. This connection, notable for the charm of its women, was certainly not less notable for the athletic brilliance of its men. In addition to the Lytteltons, from the first Earl Spencer descended also the present Lord Desborough, perhaps the most versatile athlete of his time, who, after playing cricket for Harrow, represented Oxford at both rowing and running. To this family group belonged also the Ponsonbys and the Gores, both names famous in the cricket history of the mid-nineteenth century. Spencer Ponsonby was a founder of the I Zingari, while Spencer Gore, in addition to captaining the Harrow Eleven, won the first lawn-tennis championship ever held. He was brother of Charles Gore, lately Bishop of Oxford, and at school the one brother was as distinguished as a scholar as the other as a cricketer.

In the Eton Eleven of 1868 three players—Thornton, Longman and Walter—were members of families which had previously made names for themselves in fields far removed from those of cricket. C. I. Thornton belonged to the Clapham family, which earlier in the century had been eminent alike in finance and in philanthropy. They were related to William Wilberforce, the best-known member of the " Clapham Sect." G. H. Longman was a member of the famous publishing family, whose record of distinction dates back to the early years of the eighteenth century, while H. M. Walter, whose father and elder brother had both previously played for Eton, was great-grandson of the founder of *The Times*. In this connection it is interesting to note that Major John Astor, (36) now closely connected with *The Times*, represented Eton at both cricket and rackets. Thornton and Longman got their Blues at Cambridge. Both brilliant batsmen, they likewise played for the Gentlemen. Thornton won special renown as the greatest hitter of his time; in his schooldays he drove a ball clean over the old pavilion at Lord's.

Before finally leaving cricket, mention may be made of one or two other interesting links. Edward Bray, who played for Cambridge in 1871 and 1872, was great-nephew of Thomas Malthus, whose views on the population question are still so much to the fore. Edward Hugh Bray, son of Edward, was in the Cambridge Elevens of 1896 and 1897. The Brays had been seated at Shere, near Guildford, since the reign of Henry VII, when Sir Reginald Bray was architect to the King and designer of that monarch's chapel at Westminster.

In the 'Varsity match of 1836 one of the opening batsmen for Oxford was George Rawlinson. He himself was destined to become the historian of the

Ancient Empires of the East, much of whose history was unfolded by the work on the spot of his brother, Sir Henry Rawlinson, the great Assyriologist. The latter's son was the late Lord Rawlinson, commander of the First Army in the Great War.

Two great cricketers of very different dates belonged to families which showed singularly varied ability. About 1820 the leading batsman in the country was William Ward. In that year he performed the astounding feat for those days of scoring 278 for M.C.C. *v.* Norfolk at Lords, which actually remained the record score on that ground for over a hundred years. It was singularly appropriate that Ward's should so long remain the record at Lord's, for it was he who advanced the money which saved that historic spot from the builders at a crisis in the affairs of the M.C.C. Ward was a man of wealth, as eminent a financier as a cricketer; his financial abilities were no doubt derived from the side of a Jewish grandmother, Rebecca Raphael, but his athletic skill probably emanated from other sources. His uncle, Robert Plumer Ward, was a novelist, one of whose books, *Tremayne*, made a considerable sensation at the time, while a cousin, Sir Henry Ward, was a diplomatist of distinction. William Ward's eldest son, William George Ward, became exceedingly well known as a leader of the " Oxford Movement," and was designated " Ideal Ward " from his book, *The Ideal of a Christian Church*. The association between the Church and cricket was, in any case, sufficiently marked at this period, but the very versatile Ward family were certainly exceptional in producing at once so great a cricketer and so active a theologian; they were, however, followed later in this connection by the Gores,

INTELLECT AND ATHLETICS

already mentioned. Arthur Ward, a younger son of William, was captain of the Cambridge Eleven, and entered the Church, but, unlike his brother, took no leading part in theological controversy. (37)

The versatility of the Wards was equalled by that of the Bosanquets, perhaps the most distinguished of Huguenot families. Its earlier members were chiefly known as successful merchants, but there appeared later Sir John, a judge; Charles, a writer on economics; James and Samuel, both writers on chronology; Bernard, author of philosophical works; Sir Day, an admiral; and finally, the cricketer of the family, Mr. B. J. T. Bosanquet, the originator of " googlie " bowling, whose great performances for England against Australia in 1904 and 1905 will be well remembered by cricket lovers.

There remain certain instances of members of distinguished families who signalized themselves in athletic pursuits other than cricket. Of 'Varsity oarsmen, Charles Wordsworth, Charles Merivale, Lord Desborough and (in Chapter VIII) Francis Penrose, have already been mentioned. In the first Cambridge Eight, that of 1829, rowed George Augustus Selwyn, to be followed by his son John in 1864 and 1866. Both father and son became bishops, the former the first Bishop of New Zealand and afterwards of Lichfield, while the latter succeeded the cricketer, J. C. Patteson, as Missionary Bishop of Melanesia. John Selwyn escaped Patteson's tragic fate, but his health was ruined by the climate. Another of the Selwyn family was a judge, and they were related to a singularly different personage, the George Selwyn of the eighteenth century, wit, gossip and man of the world.

In the forties, Charles Wordsworth's feat of playing in the 'Varsity Cricket Eleven and also rowing in the 'Varsity Boat was repeated by Joseph Chitty, afterwards a Lord Justice of Appeal, the most distinguished legal member of a distinguished legal family. Coming to later years, Lord Ampthill, who rowed in the Oxford Boat from 1890 to 1892, was son of our ambassador at Berlin, grandson on the mother's side of Lord Clarendon, the Foreign Secretary, and great-nephew on the father's side of Lord John Russell, the Prime Minister.

At the singular Wall Game at Eton one of the greatest heroes was J. K. Stephen, who played for the Collegers for four years, 1874–77. Alike for his intellectual brilliance and his prowess at the game, Stephen acquired a quite exceptional reputation at Eton. Every St. Andrew's Day the " Keeper " of College Wall, and after him each member of his team, stands up in Hall in front of the big fireplace and drinks " *In piam memoriam J. K. S.*" So unique a tribute testifies to the impression made by one whose brilliant promise was cut short by an early death. Son of a famous judge, nephew of the first editor of the *Dictionary of National Biography*, grandson of a great civil servant, great-grandson of a leading member of the " Clapham Sect," few have been more fortunate in their heredity than J. K. S.

Turning to those two closely allied games, rackets and " royal " tennis, Cecil Clay, who represented Oxford at the former for four years, 1867–70, and who himself became later well known as a dramatist and in especial as the author of *The Pantomime Rehearsal*, was brother of the song-writer, Frederick Clay, best remembered for that universal favourite, " I'll tell thee

INTELLECT AND ATHLETICS

Songs of Araby." Their father, James Clay, was considered the finest whist-player of his time.

Alfred Lyttelton, to whom reference has already been made, was for many years champion of "royal" tennis, and among later champions of that game are to be numbered Sir Edward Grey and Mr. Neville Lytton, whose ancestries have been set out in other chapters. Mr. Clarence Bruce, so well known at the present time for his skill alike at cricket, rackets and "royal" tennis, is a nephew of General Bruce, of Mount Everest fame, though he does not share the Napier descent. On his mother's side Mr. Bruce is, however, a great-grandson of Lord Lyndhurst, the Lord Chancellor, who was himself son of a distinguished artist, John Singleton Copley. The connections between art and athletics have been singularly few; another instance is, however, furnished by J. W. Dolignon, a great-grand-nephew of Sir Joshua Reynolds, who played cricket for Eton in 1832, making the highest score then recorded in the Harrow match, fifty-two to wit. (38)

"Royal" tennis furnishes also an American instance. Mr. Jay Gould, the greatest amateur exponent in recent years of that game, being a grandson of the well-known financier. The Gould family, moreover, were related to Aaron Burr, that politician whose singular career has been detailed in the fourth chapter.

Two examples may be taken from golf. Mr. Leslie Balfour-Melville, amateur champion in 1895, was second cousin of Robert Louis Stevenson, and from this joint descent, through the Balfours of Pilrig, both novelist and golfer were connected with a remarkable number of eminent Scotsmen. Mr. Bernard Darwin, well known as a player but even better known as a writer on the game, is, of course, grandson of the great naturalist, can also claim descent from the great potter, Josiah Wedgwood, and is related as well to many other men of note, including Francis Galton. The founder of the science of eugenics had, indeed, many links with athletics, belonging, as he did himself, to the Barclay connection, the athletic prowess of so many members of which has been already noted, while his wife was one of the Harrow Butlers.

Finally, skill with gun, rifle, and revolver may be noted. The last Marquis of Ripon, better known as Lord De Grey, was by general consent the best game-shot of his day. The son of a Viceroy of India and grandson of a Prime Minister, Lord Ripon sprang from a long line of politicians, but their achievements must be admitted to have been somewhat commonplace, and, in his own special direction, the last of the line was the one to attain the greatest absolute distinction.

At rifle-shooting, for many years after the establishment of the international contests in the sixties, there was no greater exponent than Sir Henry Halford. His father and mother were first cousins, the former a son of Sir Henry Halford, the physician, the latter a daughter of Sir John Vaughan, the judge. The remarkable intellectual relationships of these two have been detailed in the previous chapter. The last Sir Henry Halford shot altogether no less than twenty times for England, first appearing in 1863 and finally as late as 1893.

As a revolver-shot, the American, Walter Winans, stood supreme in the days just before the Great War. His grandfather, Ross Winans, had shown great inventive genius, particularly in connection with the construction of locomotives in the early days of railways, while his father, Thomas Winans, also a mechanical genius, held the contract for the first railroad construction in Russia, on which he employed George Whistler, the father of the artist. There was a connection by marriage between the Winans and Whistler families, but no actual relationship between the former and the artist himself. (39)

It has already been noted that authors and men of affairs have had, on the whole, far more relatives of distinction than have scientists or artists. What applies to distinction as a whole certainly applies also to athletics in particular, for here again we more often find athletes related to politicians and to writers than to scientists or to artists. The association between literature and cricket is especially remarkable. It has been observed that a heredity of culture would seem to be more particularly requisite for success in literature ; it would certainly be going too far to say that a similar heredity was essential for success in cricket, but there can be no manner of doubt that cricketers, taken as a whole, have sprung from more distinguished families than have the great exponents of other games and sports. Data is only available to any extent for amateurs ; it is almost wholly lacking for professionals ; the Wells case is practically the one notable exception. It would seem, however, to be at least highly probable that the families from which professional cricketers have sprung have been in their more restricted sphere of higher mental calibre than the families from which have arisen notable professionals in other branches of athletes. Be this as it may, the evidence as regards amateurs is almost conclusive ; the contrast in this respect between cricket and football is especially marked. Those who consider cricket to be the finest of games may rely not only on its own intrinsic merits, but also on the fact that its indirect connection with varied forms of intellectual distinction altogether exceeds that of any other game or form of sport.

CHAPTER XVI

THE ANTECEDENTS OF A CRIMINAL

AMONG the zealous Puritans who arose in the latter part of Queen Elizabeth's reign none showed greater zeal than a certain Hugh Clarke. Born, as his son tells us, " of honest parents," at Burton-on-Trent in 1563, Clarke matriculated both at Cambridge and at Oxford. Entering the Church and taking up a living at Oundle, in Northants, he early set his face against profanation of the Sabbath, and in particular against dancing on that day. Some of his flock refused to obey his exhortations in this respect, " but the judgment of God found them out in their wickedness. For, shortly after, on a Lord's Day, the Leader of the Dance, a lusty young man, fell down and died. Yet these obdurate persons, though a little affected for the present, soon shook off their fears and returned to their vomit again." Thus far the son, who most clearly exulted in the " judgment," as no doubt did the father, who, we may be sure, referred to the matter in no uncertain terms in his sermon on the following Sabbath.

Hugh Clarke was altogether a fiery spirit; naturally he fell out with his bishop, who for a time had him lodged in gaol, and one of his parishioners was sufficiently incensed with his proceedings to waylay him with murderous intent. Clarke, however, discoursed with such eloquence " of his disordered life " to his would-be assailant that he repented and went. The worthy cleric seems indeed to have been possessed at all times of eloquence and also of " an excellent pair of lungs."

His son, Samuel Clarke, from whose biography of his father these quotations have been taken, was, as is sufficiently obvious, a man of like character and leanings to his parent. The father died just before the triumph of Puritanism after the Civil Wars, which triumph the son, who occupied an important City living, survived to share. To his credit be it said, he was one of fifty-seven ministers who signed a protest against the execution of the King. After the Restoration, however, Samuel Clarke was ejected for refusing to comply with the Act of Uniformity, and occupied the remainder of his life in writing, chiefly biographies of persons of religious note. Included in these biographies, besides that of his father, was also one of his wife, Katherine. To the latter he was devoted, but with the devotion of the Puritan of those days for whom all women held a position subservient to his own, above which even the most favoured was never allowed to aspire. That Samuel highly approved of Katherine's conduct is shown by the following : " She never rose from the table even when they were alone, but she made curtsey to him. She never drank to him without bowing. His word was a law unto her. . . . In care of his sickness she was a tender, diligent and painful nurse about him, skilful and careful in making him broths and what else was needful for him." She was apt at dealing with her maids and " she was careful, so far as she could, to bring such as were religious, at least seemingly, into her family." " At least seemingly " is good; the reverend gentleman, it appears, was

THE ANTECEDENTS OF A CRIMINAL

very doubtful whether the extreme piety demanded of his retainers was altogether genuine.

The son of this worthy couple, a second Samuel Clarke, had taken Holy Orders before the Act of 1662, on which occasion he, like his father, was ejected from his living. The elder Samuel, however, never definitely left the Church of England, whereas the younger drifted into open Nonconformity and became minister of an Independent congregation. Inheriting his father's love of writing, he published an annotated edition of the Bible, which proved very popular, but unfortunately he did not imitate the parental example and leave behind him an account of his own wife. His daughter Elizabeth married a relative, Benjamin Clarke, a great-grandson of Hugh; their son was a third Samuel Clarke, also an Independent minister and also a religious writer, whose chief work, *The Christian's Inheritance*, went through numerous editions, the last over a hundred years after its first publication. One of his daughters married Hugh Rose, who carried on a very successful school at Chiswick till his death in 1786. Rose was a great friend of Samuel Johnson, who, however, by no means approved of the fact that he was apt to spare the rod: "What they (the boys) gain at one end they lose at the other," remarked the pundit of Fleet Street.

Samuel Rose, son of Hugh Rose and Sarah Clarke, was a great friend of Cowper, the poet, and his sister married Charles Burney, brother of Fanny. Charles had started life as an usher in his father-in-law's school, but afterwards himself conducted a very well-known establishment at Greenwich and also made a name for himself as a classical critic. His son, Charles Parr

Burney, obtained the prize for the English Essay at Oxford in 1809, and he, with two cousins, Cowper and George Rose, were the last of the descendants of Hugh Clarke to obtain any note of a respectable kind. Cowper Rose, an officer in the Royal Engineers, published a work on South Africa, while his brother George was from 1821 to 1824 professor of English at a college in Poland. From this position he was forced to retire by the Russian authorities, owing to his sympathy with the Poles. He died shortly after, while in course of preparing an account of his experiences.

To Charles Burney's school at Greenwich went also another cousin of his wife's, Thomas Griffiths Wainwright by name, a clever boy who distinguished himself especially by his talent for drawing. His maternal grandmother was Elizabeth, daughter of the third Samuel Clarke, and second wife of a somewhat remarkable man, Ralph Griffiths, who had in 1749 established a periodical, *The Monthly Review*, which he continued to edit for no less than fifty-four years. At the time of its inception there was no review in the country specially devoted to literature, and this want Griffiths set himself to remedy, eventually meeting with considerable success. Carrying on also the business of a publisher, Griffiths early in his career made much money by a work entitled *The Memoirs of a Lady of Pleasure*, written by one John Cleland. This extremely licentious book attracted the unfavourable notice of the authorities, and Griffiths narrowly escaped penal proceedings; another publisher, who had apparently pirated the book and even altered it for the worse, was condemned to the pillory, a form of punishment for which, as befitting the crime, there was much to be said, and its revival may yet be taken into consideration by future generations !

Griffiths, warned by his escape, passed the rest of his life in the odour of respectability. He had later to face the competition of the *Critical Review*, a comparison of which with *The Monthly* was made by Samuel Johnson to George III. "*The Monthly*," said Johnson, "was done with most care, the *Critical* upon the best principles; the authors of the *Monthly* are enemies to the Church." The sin was, however, it later appeared, merely hostility to the Establishment, Griffiths being apparently a strong supporter of the Nonconformity to which his wife's ancestors were so deeply attached. By this wife he had two children, a son George and a daughter Ann. George succeeded to the conduct of *The Monthly*, which he ultimately sold. Ann married Thomas Wainwright, son of a respectable solicitor. Both she and her husband died young, leaving their son to the care of his grandfather, Ralph Griffiths, who, by his will, left him £5,000 in trust.

Thomas Griffiths Wainwright, as we have seen, went to his relative's school at Greenwich, after leaving which he was for a short time in the Yeomanry, subsequently deciding to take up art journalism. For this he appeared to be well qualified, combining, as he did, an easy fluency in writing with a practical knowledge of art, and his future success in life seemed assured. Wildly extravagant, however, gratifying all his æsthetic tastes without thought of the future, his earnings and the interest on his £5,000 were together far too little for his expenditure. Becoming hopelessly involved in debt, Wainwright in 1826 forged an order on the Bank of England for the payment to himself of the capital sum of £5,000 held for him in trust, and this, curiously enough, was not discovered for some years, the trustees presumably thinking that the interest was still being paid. The money was soon spent, and Wainwright and his wife went to live with his uncle, George Griffiths, who not long after conveniently died, having made a will in his nephew's favour. This money, in its turn, also disappeared, and Wainwright proceeded to heavily insure the life of his sister-in-law, Helen Abercrombie. Within a year the girl died, but though her death was certified as due to natural causes, the insurance offices were suspicious and refused to pay. Wainwright thereupon fled to the Continent, but the claim against the companies was allowed to proceed, and, after two trials, a verdict was found in their favour, there being strong indirect evidence that Helen Abercrombie had been poisoned. Wainwright, who unwisely returned to England, was arrested, was not, as might have been expected, charged with murder, but merely with the bank forgery, which had at last been discovered. For this he was sentenced to transportation for life, a harsh sentence for the offence itself, but he was, of course, extremely lucky to escape the capital charge.

In Tasmania, as a convict, he passed the remainder of his life, dying there in 1852, but being allowed to spend part of his time in painting portraits. His only child, Griffiths Wainwright, described as an excellent young man, went to America in early life and changed his name. Of his further career nothing seems to be known.

There can be little doubt that Wainwright poisoned

THE ANTECEDENTS OF A CRIMINAL 281

Helen Abercrombie and probably George Griffiths as well. From first to last his conduct showed a total absence of the least semblance of moral feeling. From whence did he derive his evil qualities? From his Clarke descent all was excellent, and though Ralph Griffiths may have had a somewhat unscrupulous side, there was nothing in his general character to account for such a grandson. Much less is known of the Wainwright descent, but what little is known seems to have been quite creditable.

It remains an enigma, and in any case Thomas Griffiths Wainwright is peculiar among the murderers of the nineteenth century. In earlier days poisoners and suchlike sometimes had distinguished relatives, but in later times such criminals have almost invariably sprung from thoroughly degenerate stocks, without a spark of real distinction in any direction. So far as the writer is aware, no other murderer of later days in this country possessed a single ancestor who appears in the *Dictionary of National Biography*, while Wainwright had no less than four direct ancestors in that work, three of whom were men of exceptional piety.

In this latter connection it has no doubt often been remarked that parsons' sons, by a process of reaction, are apt to become rakes, a remark which has, however, extremely little basis in actual fact. In any event there could be no such reaction in Wainwright's case, as his Puritan ancestors were some way back, and he was not, as a matter of fact, brought up under specially puritanical conditions.

His case is, in fact, unique.

NOTES

1 (p. 19).   Here lies our Sovereign Lord the King,
Whose word no man relies on,
Who never said a foolish thing,
Nor ever did a wise one.

2 (p. 29). His father is very generally thought to have been Carr, Lord Hervey, elder half-brother of John, Lord Hervey.

3 (p. 32). The Bishop of Derry certainly achieved prominence, but not as a Churchman!

4 (p. 40). The father of this Gervase Clifton married no less than seven times, thus beating the record of Henry VIII.

5 (p. 43). While the portrait is probably that of Penelope Rich, its actual identity cannot be said to be fully proved.

6 (p. 58). Lady Caroline Lamb is now remembered chiefly for her eccentricities, but at any rate in early life she must have possessed much charm.

7 (p. 62). From this Sir William Sidney a remarkable number of men of eminence have descended, including the Montagu and North families, who were dealt with at some length by Galton.

8 (p. 63).   Underneath this sable hearse
Lies the subject of all verse,
Sidney's sister, Pembroke's mother.
Death! ere thou hast slain another,
Learn'd and fair and good as she,
Time shall throw a dart at thee.

9 (p. 67). The character of the late President Wilson bore a strong resemblance to that of Algernon Sidney.

10 (p. 71). In allusion to the redness of his face, though the poor man was quite temperate. An early use of the word "tight" in this connection.

11 (p. 92). His uncle, Peyton Randolph, had headed a delegation from Virginia at the beginning of the troubles.

NOTES

12 (p. 97). Page derived his descent from the Randolphs through the Grymes and Nelson families, both themselves well known in the annals of Virginia.

13 (p. 103). He held the Speakership, curiously enough, in conjunction with a judgeship.

14 (p. 119). It was from Hull that he derived his title. The full name of that town is still Kingston-upon-Hull.

15 (p. 123). There was only a very distant relationship between this Edward Raleigh and Sir Walter.

16 (p. 140). The historian owed his second name of Babington to the " fairy godfather " of the family.

17 (p. 147). He derived his second name owing to a descent through his mother from a brother of Archbishop Cranmer.

18 (p. 150). Mrs. Humphrey Ward's daughter is the wife of Mr. George Trevelyan, the historian; the heredity of their children is singularly brilliant.

19 (p. 158). Horatio, son of Frederick, also entered the medical profession, the sixth in direct succession in the family.

20 (p. 160). Sir Francis Aglen's name became well known in 1927 during the Chinese disturbances, when he was forced to retire from his post. The British Government expressed the strongest disapproval of the action taken by the Chinese in this matter.

21 (p. 165). Though then located in Holland, this family were of Scottish descent, deriving from Henry Hope, *temp*. James I (see Chapter XI).

22 (p. 165). Similar all-round activity was shown by the late Lord Curzon.

23 (p. 170). To this family belongs Miss Katharine Mayo, whose recent book, *Mother India*, has attracted so much attention.

24 (p. 184). The recent Marlborough case is reminiscent of this incident.

25 (p. 190). The present Archbishop of Canterbury.

26 (p. 191). Sir Dunbar Barton's interest in the Gascon Bernadotte may have been occasioned by his own descent from a line of Bordeaux wine-merchants (see Chapter XI).

27 (p. 191). Miss Somerville's cousin and collaborator, Miss Violet Martin, who wrote as "Martin Ross," was also descended from Charles Doyle.

28 (p. 206). Sandwich, like Erskine, belonged to a connection of great ability (see Chapter I).

29 (p. 212). Twenty-first baron is the usual reckoning, but the early history of the Barons of Kerry is very obscure.

30 (p. 216). The descendants of the Anglo-Dutch marriages of this period were remarkably distinguished. Besides the instance in the text and that of the descendants of Lord Kincardine mentioned in Chapter VIII, the Bentincks and the Keppels both came from Holland at this time.

31 (p. 234). The last of the distinguished line set out in Chapter IV.

32 (p. 236). The writer has been unable to identify this Sir Edward Bishop. If he belonged to the family of baronets of that name, he would have been descended from Marlborough's sister, Arabella Churchill.

33 (p. 243). The two predecessors were Thomas Thackeray and Robert Sumner, both ancestors of highly distinguished families.

34 (p. 253). His wife was Margaret Symonds (see Chapter VIII).

35 (p. 262). This is the greatest number of wickets ever taken in the 'Varsity matches, but Yonge played five times. Shortly after this it was ruled that no one should represent his university on more than four occasions.

36 (p. 267). Major Astor's elder brother, the present Lord Astor, rowed in the Eton Eight. Their ancestors, as is well known, were very prominent American merchants.

37 (p. 269). This family was not related to Mr. Humphrey Ward, the husband of the novelist.

38 (p. 271). Spencer Austen-Leigh, already referred to, made eighty-five in 1852, the highest score then recorded for Harrow.

39 (p. 273). The *Encyclopædia Britannica* appears to be in error in stating that the mother of the artist belonged to the Winans family.

INDEX

Abercromby family, 105
Abercromby, Sir Ralph, 105
Adam family, 175
Adam, Robert, 175
Aglon, Sir Francis, 160
Ampthill, 2nd Baron, 270
Apsley, Sir Allan, 17
Arnold family, 149
Arnold, Matthew, 148
Arnold, Thomas, 148
Astor family, 284
Auckland, Earl of, 193
Austen, Jane, 263
Austen-Leigh family, 263

Babington family, 140
Balfour, Earl, 104
Balfour-Melville, L., 271
Barham family, 143, 144
Baring family, 164 et seq.
Baring, Maurice, 168
Baring-Gould, S., 164
Barton family, 207
Bateman family, 162
Beaumont, Francis, 118
Bentinck family, 137, 138
Berwick, Duke of, 24, 27
"Bess of Hardwick," 118
Bessborough, Henrietta, Countess of, 58
Boleyn, Anne, 34
Bolingbroke, 1st Viscount, 23
Bosanquet family, 269
Boswell family, 131, 132
Boswell, James, 131
Bray family, 267
Breckinridge family, 181
Brougham, 1st Baron, 172
Browne, Sir Thomas, 204
Bruce, Charles G., 222
Bruce, Clarence N., 271
Bruces of Kinloss, 128, 129
Buchan, Agnes, Countess of, 204
Buchan, David, Earl of, 205
Burnet, Gilbert, 104

Burr, Aaron, 83, 271
Bushe, Charles K., 189
Buxton family, 260

Cadogan, William, Earl, 216
Calderwood, Mrs., 204
Carlisle, Lucy, Countess of, 48
Carnock, 1st Baron, 177
Castlereagh, Viscount, 25
Cecil family, 109
Chamberlain family, 198
Chamberlain, Houston S., 199
Chesterfield, 4th Earl of, 120, 125
Childers, Erskine, 208
Chitty family, 270
Chudleigh family, 145
Chudleigh, Elizabeth, 146
Churchill, Arabella, 27, 284
Clarke family, 275
Clay family, 270
Cleveland, Barbara, Duchess of, 25
Cockerell family, 114, 115
Coleridge family, 261
Coleridge, Samuel Taylor, 261
Compton, Fay, 163
Compton, Henry, 160
Conway family, 134
Conybeare family, 141
Coolidge family, 97
Cope family, 122
Cornwallis, 1st Marquis, 72
Cory, William Johnson, 225
Coutts, Thomas, 193, 201
Cowell family, 162
Crawley family, 262
Cromer, 1st Earl of, 168

Dallas family, 170
Darwin family, 272
Davidson, Archbishop, 193, 203
Denny, Lady Arabella, 213
Derry, Bishop of, 29
Desborough, 1st Baron, 266
Devonshire, Elizabeth, Duchess of, 29
Devonshire, Georgiana, Duchess of, 58

Digby, Sir Kenelm, 123
Downing, Sir George, 78
Doyle family, 182 et seq.
Drury family, 243 et seq.
Dryden, John, 123
Dudley, Edmund, 59
Dundonald, 10th Earl of, 131
Dupont, Gainsborough, 228
Dwight family, 86
Dwight, Timothy, 85

Edwardes family, 82
Edwardes, Jonathan, 81
Eldon, 1st Earl of, 107
Elgin, Earls of, 130
"Eliot, George," 263
Elizabeth, Queen, 33
Elliot family, 173, 265
Empson, Richard, 117
Erskine, 1st Baron, 193, 206
Erskine, Henry, 205
Essex, 2nd Earl of, 39
Evelyn, John, 120

Fielding, Henry, 25, 121
Fox, Charles James, 25, 218
Furse family, 226
Furse, Charles W., 226
Furse, Dame Katharine, 158, 227

Gainsborough, Thomas, 227
Galton family, 260
Galton, Sir Francis, 272
Gardiner, Samuel Rawson, 164
Gascoigne, Sir Crisp, 102
Goodenough family, 115
Gore family 266
Gould, Jay, 271
Grafton, 3rd Duke of, 26
Grant, Sir John Peter, 155
Granville, Harriet, Countess, 58
Greene, Sir Conyngham, 191
Greene, Plunket, 191
Greville, Charles, 138
Greville, Fulke, 134, 138
Grey, Charles, 2nd Earl, 73, 168
Grey, Earls, 73
Grey, Sir George, 72
Grey of Fallodon, Viscount, 74
Guildford family, 61
Gunning, Elizabeth, 215
Gurney family, 260

Haldane family, 106, 109
Haldane, Viscount, 109
Halford, Sir Henry, 1st Baronet, 249
Halford, Sir Henry, 3rd Baronet, 272
Hall, Basil, 197
Hall, Sir James, 196
Hamilton, Sir William, 193
Harcourt family, 209
Harley family, 135, 136
Harley, Brilliana, Lady, 134
Harley, Robert, Earl of Oxford, 135
Hawkins family, 254
Hawkins, Francis Vaughan, 253
Heath family, 241
Henry, Patrick, 177
Hertford, 3rd Marquis of, 27
Hervey family, 25, 29
Hervey, John, Lord, 29, 121
Hill family, 157
Hill, Sir Rowland, 157
Hoare family, 260
Holland, Elizabeth, Lady, 143
Hope family, 193 et seq.
Hotham family, 266
Howard-Bury, C. K., 215
Howard of Effingham, 2nd Baron, 64
Hungerford family, 16
Hunsdon, 1st Baron, 35
Hutchinson, Mrs., 16
Huxley, Aldous, 150
Huxley, Julian, 150
Huxley, T. H., 150

Iddesleigh, 1st Earl of, 164

Jefferson, Thomas, 91
Jeffreys, John, Lord, 103
Johnstone, Joseph, 180

Kerry, Anne, Countess of, 213
Kincardine, 1st Earl of, 129
Kirkpatrick family, 153

Labouchere, Henry, 166
Lamb, Lady Caroline, 58
Lane, Edward, 229
Lane, Richard, 229
Lane-Poole family, 230, 231
Lansdowne, 3rd Marquis of, 214
Lansdowne, 5th Marquis of, 215
Lauderdale, 8th Earl of, 101

INDEX

Lee family, 96
Lee, Harry, 91
Lee, Robert E., 95, 170
Leicester, Earls of (Sidney family), 64 *et seq.*
Leicester, Lettice, Countess of, 36
Leicester, Robert Dudley, Earl of, 61
Livingston family, 170
Loch family, 176
Lombe, Sir Thomas, 99
Longman family, 267
Lubbock family, 266
Lyttelton family, 266
Lyttelton, Lucy, Lady, 58
Lytton family, 188
Lytton, 1st Earl of, 187
Lytton, Rosina, Lady, 187

Macaulay family, 139 *et seq.*
Macaulay, Rose, 142, 264
Macaulay, Thomas Babington, 140, 264
Mackenzie family, 159
Mackenzie, Compton, 163
Mackenzie, Sir Morell, 159
Maitland, Sir Thomas, 100
Mallet family, 247
Malthus, Thomas R., 267
" Markham, Mrs.," 147
Marlborough, 1st Duke of, 24, 26
Marshall, John, 92
" Martin, Ross," 283
Mayo family, 170
Mayo, Katharine, 283
Merivale family, 245
Merivale, Charles, 246, 259
Merivale, Herman, 246
Monro family, 256 *et seq.*
Montagu family, 282
Montagu, Lady Mary Wortley, 25, 111, 121
Morgan, J. Pierpont, 234
Mures of Caldwell, 202

Napier, Sir Charles, 25, 220
Napier, Lady Sarah, 218
Napier, Sir William, 25, 220
Nevill, Lady Dorothy, 145
Newcastle, Thomas, Duke of, 69
North family, 282

Northumberland, Dorothy, Countess of, 44
Northumberland, John Dudley, Duke of, 55, 60

Orkney, Bishop of, 127, 170

Page, Thomas Nelson, 97
Pelham, Henry, 69
Pembroke, Earls of, 63
Pembroke, Mary, Countess of, 62
Penrose family, 146 *et seq.*
Pepys, Samuel, 112
Petty, Anne, Lady, 211
Petty, Sir William, 211
Pierrepont family (English), 119 *et seq.*
Pierrepont family (American), 81, 233
Pitt, William, Earl of Chatham, 31
Pitt, William, 31
Plowden family, 155
Plunket family, 190
Plunket, Archbishop, 190
Pollen family, 116
Ponsonby family, 266
Portal, Sir Gerald, 174
Preston family, 179
Pringle family, 195

Raleigh, Sir Walter, 64
Randolph family, 90 *et seq.*
Randolph, Edmund, 92
Randolph, John, 94
Randolph, Thomas, 88
Rawlinson family, 267
Reynolds family, 223 *et seq.*
Reynolds, Sir Joshua, 224, 271
Rich, Penelope, Lady, 40
Richmond, Dukes of, 217
Ridley, 1st Viscount, 255
Ridley, Sir Edward, 255
Ripon, 2nd Marquis of, 272
Robertson, William, 171
Rochester, John, Earl of, 19
Rodney, 1st Baron, 248
Romney, Henry Sidney, Earl of, 68
Rosebery, 5th Earl of, 193
Russell, Bertrand, 174
Russell, Lady John, 174

Salisbury, 3rd Marquis of, 104, 109
Sandwich, 1st Earl of, 111
Sandwich, 4th Earl of, 21

Sargent family, 234
Sargent, John S., 235
Selkirk, 4th Earl of, 197
Selwyn family, 269
Seymour, Jane, 34
Shelburne, 2nd Earl of, 214
Sidney, Algernon, 55, 67
Sidney, Sir Henry, 61
Sidney, Sir Philip, 62
Somerville, Edith, 191
Spottiswoode family, 170
Stanhope, Lady Hester, 31
Stephen family, 270
Stevenson, R. L., 193, 271
Stewarts of Coltness, 200
Stoddard family, 79, 80
Stoddard, Lothrop, 80
Stowell, 1st Baron, 107
Strachey family, 152 et seq.
Strachey, Lytton, 155
Strachey, Sir Richard, 154
Strachey, St. Loe, 153, 158
Sumner family, 284
Sunderland, Dorothy, Countess of, 52
Sunderland, Earls of, 54, 58
Sutherland, Harriet, Duchess of, 58
Swift, Jonathan, 124
Symonds family, 156
Symonds, John Addington, 158

Tennyson, 1st Baron, 264
Thackeray family, 264, 284
Thackeray, William Makepeace, 264
Thornton family, 267
Townshend family, 70
Townshend, Charles, 25, 30, 71
Trench, Archbishop, 259
Trevelyan, Sir George, 140
Trevelyan, George M., 140, 283
Trevor, Sir John, 103
Tucker family, 98, 132
Tucker, Beverley, 95
Tucker, Charlotte ("A.L.O.E."), 132

Ullswater, Viscount, 256

Vaughan family, 248 et seq.
Vaughan, Charles John, 251
Verney family, 133
Villiers connection, 24, 121, 146
Villiers, Elizabeth, 27

Wainwright, Thomas G., 279
Wakefield family, 260
Walkers of Southgate, 265
Waller, Edmund, 209
Waller, Sir Hardress, 209
Waller, Sir William, 209
Walpole, Horace, 126
Walpole, Hugh, 144
Walpole, Sir Robert, 126, 145
Ward family, 268
Ward, Mrs. Humphrey, 150, 265, 283
Wedgwood, Josiah, 272
Wellesley family, 104
Wellington, 1st Duke of, 104
Wells, H. G., 263
Wensleydale, 1st Baron, 256
Whistler family, 236, 273
Whistler, John MacNeill, 237
Wilberforce, William, 267
Winans family, 273
Windham family, 167
Windham, William, 167
Windle, Sir Bertram, 191
Winthrop family, 76, 77
Winthrop, John, 77
Wolcott family, 232
Womersley family, 96
Woolsey family, 86
Wordsworth, Charles, 260
Wordsworth, Christopher, 260
Wordsworth, William, 261

Yonge, Charlotte, 262
Young, Sir Hilton, 164

Milton Keynes UK
Ingram Content Group UK Ltd.
UKHW051457030124
435149UK00037B/168